# The 10 Actions® To Transform Your Life

## Bernard Genge

Pen Press Publishers Ltd

First published in Great Britain by
Pen Press Publishers Ltd
25 Eastern Place
Brighton
BN2 1GJ


ISBN 978-1-906206-24-6

Printed and bound in the UK

A catalogue record of this book is available from
the British Library

Cover design by Jacqueline Abromeit

This book is dedicated to my parents Ron and Beryl and
my daughters Karla and Stephanie
for their enormous support.

# Acknowledgements

I would like to acknowledge the support and dedication of the following people in helping me develop this book, the accompanying training programme and our company ethos. My eldest daughter Karla Genge who spent her one day off each week working with me on any task that needed doing; my running colleague and friend Amanda  Mooney who did much proof reading, word-processing, scripting and other work behind the scenes; Sallyann Sheridan for her copywriting and for being such an inspiration to me; Marcus Tuke for all his web and technology based work and support, and my business partner Mark Ogden who helped develop the ethos of our business, its not-for-profit set up and for doing much off the work I am not good at.

# About the Author

 Bernard Genge's business, which provides the workshops and training for the *10 Action®* life-changing training programme, is a *not-for-profit* Community Interest Company Limited by Guarantee. All trading surpluses from this company will be diverted to the creation of thriving and sustainable communities. Further details of the company ethos, philosophy, vision and mission is on the website www.10actions.com together with details of how you can become a licensee of the *10 Action®* life-changing training programme

Bernard spent the first twelve years of his career in the medical branch of the Royal Navy, followed by eleven years in commerce and business before setting up his own training and consultancy business in 2001. His work is based primarily around the development and success of individuals. He enjoys combining a mix of personal, business and organisational success with learning in the great outdoors.

He coaches individuals to achieve previously unimaginable highs in their careers and business. In the business sector he works with organisations as a facilitator and consultant ensuring clients attain new heights of achievement by providing carefully designed training programmes. When training he engages audiences so they can truly enjoy the learning experience also ensuring an environment where people learn from each other.

As well as successfully providing training in areas such as management development, motivating teams and individuals, improving performance and sales, Bernard is a respected international motivational speaker.

Bernard is involved in much charity work and fundraising. In 2003 he completed a charity desert trek in Namibia, Africa. In November 2006 Bernard cycled across Vietnam and in 2007 he completed the London marathon. He is involved in many other fundraising community events and in 2008 plans to cycle from Lands End to

John O'Groats. He is also committed to progressing his personal and spiritual development.

# Introduction

by
Bernard Genge

*'Life is not measured by the number of breaths we take,
but by the moments that take our breath away.'*

Welcome to **The 10 Actions® To Transform Your Life**. This inspiring book sets out the core principles behind **The 10 Actions®** course and workbook. With it, you can achieve the success you previously only dreamed about. So, get ready as the rest of your life is about to change.

## Who is The 10 Actions® for?

It's not for those who are perfect! It's for *real* people with *real* issues, who are ready to make *real* changes to ensure lasting results.

You'll discover practical insights and tried and tested principles that apply universally whether you are a judge or a student, a business executive or unemployed. Perhaps you've never really succeeded, or maybe you want more success. Or you've previously made it, lost it and want it back again. Whatever your situation, **The 10 Actions®** is for you!

I find it extraordinary that people buy insurance to safeguard themselves against sickness, death, accidents, and natural disasters, yet never think about insuring themselves against personal failure. Would you invest in an insurance policy that guaranteed your success? Would it be worth investing 2% of your annual income, for example? I think so. And when you enrol on **The 10 Actions®** that's exactly what you're doing – investing in your success.

If a business fails to invest in itself, its products and services soon become obsolete and the business fails. You're no different. Don't leave your success to anyone else. Take responsibility for your success and invest in you. Improve some aspect of yourself *every* month. Be more understanding, more creative, more affluent or put yourself in a better position to give more back in some way.

Your life will change significantly when you implement the principles of **The 10 Actions®**. It is not a quick fix however – you need commitment to make the changes necessary to achieve your goals.

*'We are not what we know, but what we are willing to learn.'*
Mary Catherine Bateson

**The 10 Actions**® offers you tools and a discipline, and it is up to you how much you use and to what end. Some people, and I hope you are one of them, will overcome all sorts of life's obstacles as a result of the insights I share here with you. Insights that I know will be the catalyst for you to make groundbreaking change.

Maybe you feel like a bee trapped in a jar, buzzing around, crashing, yet remaining trapped until the lid is removed. Or maybe you are stuck at a crossroads in your life not knowing which way to go. Bewilderment and indecision can overpower you at times like these. You become so fearful of taking a wrong turn that you can't move forward at all. You doubt yourself and your ability to discern if you're taking the right path. And you can't conquer those fears by simply reading a book any more than you can taste a good meal by reading the menu. But you can learn to face fear and doubt head-on by recognising that it is only a state of mind.

**The 10 Actions**® is not about the survival of the fittest, more survival of the wisest. In it you learn the philosophies of co-operation rather than competition, and gain an understanding of what contributes to life fulfilment and *true* happiness.

Your happiness is the natural by-product of living a purposeful and worthwhile life. A life in which you earn self-respect and the respect of others. You can't drink, inhale, buy, wear, drive, inject or swallow happiness. Ultimately, success is a journey, not a destination.

In the 2004 Olympics I listened to the language used by the winners. They talked of: *'dreams..., positive effort..., vision..., a total belief in all of us as a team..., never giving up..., I just fought through the pain..., I had so much confidence in myself and the team..., you have to start positively..., I have the highest respect for my opponents but just had to win...'*

After Kelly Holmes' success in the 1,500 metres, the British 4 X 100 metres team came out to the tune of the national anthem, looked at each other and said, 'We want some of that.' They went on to win the final although the USA were the firm favourites. Holmes said of her success, 'I've worked hard for 20 years for this. I hope my performance can inspire other people.' Of course these winners are in peak physical condition, but how much of their success comes down to inner attitude?

This course mimics the process of a seed's growth. Planted in the dark soil, the seed expresses the exact picture held within its life cell and, in obedience to natural law, sends up a shoot seeking light. At the same time, it sends down roots for nourishment. If, on the way up, that shoot encounters obstacles, it does not attempt to force them out of the way, it simply travels around them. And if the roots fail to find the required nourishment, the plant withers away.

Yet if all goes well, the plant blossoms and, having reached its goal, a seed is again dropped and the process repeated. This process happens in darkness and beneath the surface. It is the same with us. Beneath our surface is where our dreams, attitudes and important ideas are developed.

If you plant your own seed for the future, and nourish it and nurture it by practising and internalising the concepts of **The 10 Actions**® you *will* achieve success. Will you encounter resistance? Absolutely, because action requires reaction to support it. If there were no resistance, action would be impossible.

It is resistance that keeps a plane in the air; without it, the plane couldn't fly. Birds couldn't fly and fish wouldn't swim without resistance. With a plane, the greater the momentum, the greater the altitude, and so it is with us – to reach the heights of achievement and our true potential, momentum must be first attained and then maintained. Once the apparent difficulty of the first steps have passed, the work you put in will become enjoyable, for there is nothing more satisfying than achieving something worthwhile.

**The 10 Actions**® offers you valuable life lessons – something I'll bet you were never taught in school. You may have learned about the direction migrating birds fly, yet were never taught how to find your own direction. You probably analysed chemical formulae, but never explored the dynamics of human relationships. You know who Einstein is, but are not sure who you are. Our educational system is not designed to teach us the secrets for living a successful life. We learn everything in school except how to live!

By embracing the material in **The 10 Actions**®, you will find that the material and your learning will be *evolutionary*, and the results *revolutionary.* You will benefit from a significant increase in self-confidence, self-esteem, self-awareness, self-control and self-achievement. You get to know yourself in a much deeper, more meaningful way. You connect to your deepest values, chose your direction in life and enjoy the fruits of your success. Your new self-image will give you inner strength, and external influences will become less important as you gain the confidence to follow your own convictions.

Some of the learning will take place as you work through **The 10 Actions**®, but most occurs by using and trying the concepts shared here. And I make no apology for including so many quotations – there's often more wisdom in ten great quotations than in ten books.

A lot can be learned through adversity, yet most of the same lessons can be learned through laughter and joy. If what we do is not enjoyable, should we be doing it? You can be *sincere* about life without being *serious* about it. **The 10 Actions**® is not about serious and heavy instruction. You'll find it packed with creative suggestions – take from it whatever works for you.

## Good Learning Principles

*'Learning is not attained by chance,*
*it must be sought for with ardour and attended to with diligence.'*
Abigail Adams 1780

To learn better and get the best out **The 10 Actions**® I suggest you consider yourself not the Learner but the Teacher. By sharing (teaching) what you learn with someone else, you are more committed to learn. You remember better, your understanding is deepened and your motivation stronger as you seek to share the concepts with others. As you do so you reinforce the process of growth and change within yourself.

The well-known research of William Glasser summarises why this concept of changing our perception from learner to teacher is so powerful.

We retain:

> 10 % of what we READ
>
> 20 % of what we HEAR
>
> 30 % of what we SEE
>
> 50 % of what we SEE & HEAR
>
> 70 % of what we DISCUSS
>
> 80 % of what we EXPERIENCE
>
> 95 % of what we TEACH

*'Aim for success, not perfection. Never give up your right to be wrong, because then you will lose the ability to learn new things and move forward with your life. Remember that fear always lurks behind perfectionism. Confronting your fears and allowing yourself the right to be human can, paradoxically, make you a far happier and more productive person.'*
Dr. David M. Burns

Don't cling to what you know and close off other viewpoints and possibilities. Instead of asking, 'Who is right?' it is better to ask, 'What can I learn?'

*'We don't receive wisdom; we must discover it for ourselves after a journey that no one can take for us or spare us.'*

Marcel Proust

# Action 1

## Lay Your Foundation

*'What the future could hold and what each of us could become is limited mainly by what we believe.'*
Louise Hay

### The Success Attitude

You would never build a house on shaky foundations if you expected it to last, so why should your life be any different? Laying a good foundation is often the action people skip and it never pays. That's because sooner or later the cracks begin to show and what was perceived as success simply cannot last on such shaky ground.

Whatever you do – don't skip this action. Because once you lay your foundation in the ways suggested here, whatever happens, you will be on firm ground. And this is one of the things that mark a truly successful person. Being on firm ground means becoming more self-aware. It means you get to understand your strengths and weaknesses and how best to use them. It means discovering the true meaning of success and developing habits that are necessary to achieve it. It means you get to realise the enormous power of positive belief.

In laying these all important foundations to your success you get to empower yourself to deal with negative perceptions and assumptions. You establish principles and create that all important life balance you so often hear talked about. Above all, you get to realise what *your* deepest held values are. And once connected to those values your life will take off in ways you might now only dream of.

Have you ever spoken to anyone who has pulled through against remarkable odds or achieved something extraordinary? When you ask them what made the difference, invariably they will say it was all down to their *attitude*. They had a purpose and a reason to carry on regardless of the circumstances.

Professor Suzanne Skevington heads the World Health Organisation's Field Centre for the Study of Quality of Life at the

University of Bath. She says, 'Surgeons tell us they can carry out exactly the same procedure on two similar people and whilst one is back at work within a week, the other can become depressed and disabled by their situation. It is the patients' perception of how the operation affects them that is the greatest influence on the outcome.'

Our attitude affects everything else in life and it is only you who decides your attitude. It can attract people to you or distance them from you. It affects your health. Doctors now acknowledge there is a connection between mental and physical health, and most admit that our attitude is as important to curing illness as many other factors.

How you respond to a situation, and whether the situation claims you as its victim or *you* claim it as an opportunity for learning and personal growth is all a matter of your attitude. And you get to choose your attitude. In fact with the right attitude you can achieve almost anything. In selling, for example, research shows that a salesperson with a positive attitude can be ten times more successful. Attitude **is** more important than aptitude.

*'Attitude is a little thing that makes a BIG difference.'*

Our attitude is a priceless asset because it controls the choices we make, the path we take, our plans and the results we get. The Poet Henley once wrote: 'I am the master of my fate, I am the captain of my soul.' Take control and possession of your mind as our attitude patterns our thoughts and determines the ideas we use to create the experiences in our life.

*'How can you get the best out of your employees? Expect the best.'*
Sterling Livingston

Your attitude towards your potential is either the key or the lock to your fulfilment. Many from modest beginnings have achieved greatness through their attitude. The desert peasant boy, falsely imprisoned in Egypt who suffered several years of confinement went on to become Egypt's President. This was Anwar Sadat.

Our attitude is our way of looking at something. Our point of view, our perspective, our outlook, and our frame of mind. It is like the window of a house – large or small, high or low, facing beautiful scenery or a rubbish tip.

*'Your attitude, almost always determines your altitude in life.'*

*How high are you going to soar?*

So can we choose our attitude? I hear many people spending a great deal of energy arguing for their own limitations, 'I can't do that,'

'I've always been like this,' 'I've never been successful,' and many other self-defeating negative statements. When you decide something is impossible it becomes difficult to pierce through this self-created hurdle to make it possible, when the fact is that it almost certainly is possible.

The trouble is that when you argue for your limiting position, you look for examples to support your thoughts. You fill your head with limitations that prevent you trying. The key is to silence your greatest critic – you. You need to learn to stop expecting things to go wrong, and start expecting things to go right.

Your attitude is creative, because it structures your reality through its influence on the patterns of your thoughts. Like the theories a scientist uses in research, your attitude shapes how you experiment with situations. How you approach a situation influences the situation's response. Life mirrors your attitudes making your attitude an active ingredient in the creation of your reality.

Your attitude determines the emotions you feel. A pessimistic attitude is a hazard both to your health and your life. Even though optimism *may be* unrealistic, from an objective point of view it creates such a positive physical effect that it gives a person an edge in overcoming difficulties and in life itself. Optimism is not only healthy, it's great for coping.

Ralph Waldo Emerson talked about an attitude called self-reliance – a frame of mind that says, 'I can make a difference.' I believe this is a very powerful attitude for us to adopt. The contrary: the feeling of helplessness, of victimisation by circumstances, is a destructive attitude.

*'A bright attitude is the right attitude. It is a source of empowerment that can move everyone in the right direction.'*

Once you realise that no matter what happens to you, you get to choose your response, it's liberating. Because you are now in a position to turn a situation that seems defeatist into an opportunity – the difference between defeat and survival.

Winners, because of their positive attitude, love to be told things are impossible or unrealistic. They know they are behind the wheel of their life, not the government, their peers or the economy. Think in terms of success and you will get success.

Before Roger Bannister broke the 4-minute mile, commentators suggested it was impossible. But Roger Bannister had a vision of being successful, a positive attitude and an action plan to get to the fitness level to achieve it. He knew he could run a quarter of a mile in one minute, and therefore *knew* it was possible to run a whole mile in

4 minutes. Within a short period of time after he broke this 'impossible' feat, 32 other people did the same. Why? Because it had suddenly become possible.

Not only will changing to a positive attitude change your life, it will change your world as well. Take a moment to answer the following:

What do you want most from life?

What is success to you?

Can you visualise what you want most from life and what success would look like for you?

There are three basic components to achieving success:

- having the knowledge (what to do),
- having some skill (how to do it),
- having the right attitude/desire (the *will* to do it).

As you can see from the following diagram, we need all three components to be successful. Yet would it surprise you that research shows that while knowledge and skills make up just 15%, the other 85% of success is based on having the right attitude?

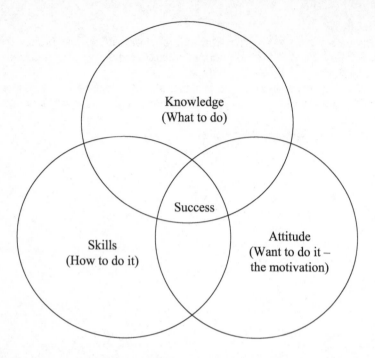

There are many opinions on the ingredients of success, such as this one drawn up by a group of delegates when I was delivering a *Management Success* programme.

**S**pirit
**U**nited
**C**ommunication
**C**onfidence
**E**mpathy
**S**kills & knowledge
**S**trength

If you have all of this in place you will have a positive attitude and be capable of creating success.

*'We should always choose the path that moves us in the direction of our dreams. Though our journey may be filled with many winding roads, when we are inspired to follow our dreams we eventually find success, and discover, it is perhaps less about the destination and more about the manner in which you travelled.'*

---

Imagine and see yourself as creative. It's a talent you can cultivate and the more you use it, the more it delivers.

In the 1930s, a group of young nuns were asked to write short autobiographies. The papers were analysed in 2004 in terms of the amount of positive emotions expressed in the writing. A strong relationship was found to exist between the amount of positive emotion expressed and the longevity of the nuns (who all had very similar lifestyles). Ninety per cent of the quarter who expressed the most positive emotion in their autobiographies were still alive at the age of 85 compared to just 34% of the quarter who expressed less positive emotions. There is ongoing discussion about how the relationship between happiness and age actually operates. Are happy people less stressed or do they look after their bodies better? However, what is clear is that there is a strong relationship between a positive attitude and longevity.

Fear is something that holds us back and stops us seeing what is possible. Decide now to dispel the following fears:

- Poverty
- Criticism
- Ill health
- Loss of love, liberty or freedom
- Old age
- Death

Your behaviour and habits are made by your thinking and thinking as you have discovered is the one thing that is under our control – so control it! As Mark Twain once said when asked about negative thoughts, *'Some of the worst things in my life never happened.'*

The laws of successful human achievement are as available to the poor and humble as they are to the rich and proud. The following people did the unimaginable and saw things differently to how they were initially conditioned.

- A farmer invented the typewriter
  (predecessor to the modern day computer)
- A poet invented the sewing machine
- The telephone was invented by a teacher of the deaf
- A doctor invented the first car tyre

Consider:

What would happen if you always expected the best of yourself?
What would happen if you converted problems into opportunities?
What would happen if you never accepted the status quo?

What would happen if you focussed on where you are going rather than where you came from?

What would happen if you decided to be happy?

Successful people say, 'Stop thinking why something won't work and start thinking of ways in which we can make it work.' So, are you a possibility thinker or an impossibility thinker? It is a habit of attitude.

Don't be put off by another's perception of us: Over the fireplace in the late Fred Astaire's house in Beverly Hills was an enlightening memo written by the casting director who first auditioned Astaire. The memo reads:

*Name*: Fred Astaire. *Comment*: Can't act, slightly bald, can dance a little.

Now consider the following questions:

**Question 1:**

If you knew a woman who was pregnant, had syphilis, already had eight children, three of whom were deaf, two who were blind, and one mentally retarded, would you recommend an abortion?

**Read the next question before looking at the answer for this one.**

**Question 2:**

It is time to elect a new world leader, and you have the deciding vote. Here are the facts about the three leading candidates:

Candidate A – Associates with crooked politicians, and consults astrologists. He's had two mistresses, chain smokes, and drinks 8 to 10 martinis a day.

Candidate B – He was kicked out of office twice, sleeps until noon, used opium in college, and drinks a quart of whisky every evening.

Candidate C – He is a decorated war hero; a vegetarian who doesn't smoke, drinks an occasional beer and never cheated on his wife.

Which of the three candidates would be your choice? Decide first, before looking below at the answers.

If you said yes to Question 1, you have just killed Beethoven.

The answer to Question 2 is:

> Candidate A is Franklin D. Roosevelt.
> Candidate B is Winston Churchill
> Candidate C is Adolph Hitler.

Are you pleased with your choice?

Imagine working for a company that has over 500 employees and the following statistics:

- 29 have been accused of spousal abuse
- 7 have been arrested for fraud
- 19 have been accused of writing bad cheques
- 117 have directly or indirectly bankrupted at least 2 businesses
- 3 have done time for assault
- 71 cannot get a credit card due to bad credit
- 14 have been arrested on drug-related charges
- 8 have been arrested for shoplifting
- 21 are currently defendants in lawsuits (2004)
- 84 have been arrested for drunk driving in the last year (2004)

Can you guess which organisation this is?

It's the United States Congress. The same 535 members that send out hundreds of new laws each year designed to keep the rest of the USA in line!

A positive attitude pays dividends in the workplace too. Successful leaders and managers will deliberately increase the flow of positive emotions within their organisations. They choose to do so not simply because it is a nice thing to do or as a means of improving morale, but because it increases productivity and performance. It also gives enhanced job satisfaction for all, greater engagement, and a more positive mood generally within the organisation.

So, where does our attitude come from? It comes from our mindset; how we see ourselves, others and the world at large – in other words, our perceptions.

## Perceptions

Perceptions form the basis of all our beliefs and actions. Our decisions, the way we make judgments, our attitudes and emotions, and all the choices made by individuals, organisations, and communities are based on the perceptions of the people involved. Understanding the concept of perception is necessary to make correct decisions, choices and fundamental changes in our lives. Every invention began as a single thought. The motor car is now here because someone once said: 'Let's build transport with a motor.'

Some years ago I read the following story, which explains different perceptions. Two sales people working for a shoe manufacturer were sent to Africa to explore the market opportunities. At the end of the first day one of the people phoned into the office and said, 'You had better bring me back. They don't seem to wear shoes over here.' However, an hour or so later, his colleague phoned, and was very excited. He said, 'Send 30,000 pairs of shoes immediately... the opportunity is absolutely vast – I am going to stay for a month.'

Perceptions are based on assumptions and/or opinions that are often subconscious. Indeed sometimes these assumptions are buried so deeply in the subconscious that the person is not even aware of their source. Becoming aware of the source of your assumptions is one key to making correct and effective decisions.

The thoughts you entertain shape your experiences, and your life circumstances reflect the history of your thought patterns. Your expectations, your beliefs, and even the thoughts you use to understand the world will ultimately determine what you experience.

Imagine seeing a car for the first time. If you see it as a sculpture you see its shape and lines. If you see it as some kind of storage you see the space inside and how many items you could store in it. If you see it as some kind of technological advancement you might examine the dials, levers and buttons. Whatever you see it as would depend on your conception of what the car is. Being objective requires that we know both what to look at and how to process it in our mind. Knowing what to look for assumes that we have in our mind some concept, model or frame of reference that applies to what we are looking at.

The key to becoming aware of your own perceptions is in the question why? Why do you feel uncomfortable in the presence of a person different to yourself? Why do you think that money or technology is evil or good? Why are you in favour of, or against a political position? Why are you afraid of a country, person or thing? Why do you need to influence? Why do you need approval from other people? You must answer these questions honestly.

The next step is to look at situations again and try to be objective or see it from a different point of view.

Now ask yourself why you answered your first question the way you did? Why do you feel uncomfortable in the presence of a person different to yourself?

If you originally saw that person you thought of as a threat, try to see if the person is perhaps feeling threatened by you, or are they in an unfamiliar situation and acting defensively. Try to understand why you think as you do. You must learn to keep your eyes and mind open to possibilities and recognise the difference between speculation and fact.

> *'When we change the way we look at things,*
> *the things we look at change.'*
>
> Wayne Dyer

Most people spend far more time reacting than thinking. They often react, using their speculations as facts to make decisions. There is an element of laziness in this. Researching and/or honestly and resolutely trying to recognise the truth is much more difficult than speculating. It is easier and quicker to react than to think. It takes a desire for improvement to overcome this habit.

The only person that you even have a chance of really knowing is yourself. Every time you decide that you know someone else's mind, you are basing that judgment on the way *you* think. Your own mind is the only one that you can possibly know, and you'll be lucky if you fully understand that!

Accurate perception can only be achieved by observing without opinion. You must look only at what happened, and recognise when you are merely guessing or speculating. In response to the first question therefore, you must see that the person only *appears* uncomfortable, and that you *suspect* them to be hostile. You can only *suspect* it will rain when you see clouds in the sky. Always keep in mind the difference between what happens and how you actually interpret it.

Sometimes it is necessary to speculate and extrapolate in order to plan. But you must be aware that your plans are based on guesswork, however educated the guess, and that your speculation could be incorrect, and adjust your plans accordingly. You will find that your actions and plans become more appropriate as your perceptions become more objective and accurate. Accurate perception will introduce you to the joy of discovery and the fun of finding out what happens next.

> *'Unless you try to do something beyond what you have already*
> *mastered, you will never grow.'*

However, the paradox is that thoughts, on their own, have little power. Try this. Without touching it, or letting anyone else touch it, fold over the corner of the page you are reading now. Think really hard and give it all your concentration, attention, mental strength, focus and power. Can you see the page folding over?

At this point you may be inventing interesting ways of getting the page to fold over within the limitations I gave you, but unless something is *actually done* the corner of the page is never going to fold over. Thoughts alone will not make it happen. Now simply, without any restrictions fold over the corner of the page and you can do it without having to think about it.

Note the power of thought without action. Note how in contrast the physical action of folding the page was easy. However, without the power of thought to guide it, human physical energy is like letting a set of monkeys loose in NASA or a mindless chimp in 10 Downing Street!

When thought and action are combined, the results are powerful. The combination of successful communication (sharing of thoughts) and determined, committed action can literally move mountains.

*'I have found power in the mysteries of thought.'*
Euripides 438 BC

As Stephen Covey quotes in his best selling book, *The 7 Habits of Highly Effective People,* 'If you want to make small changes, work on your behaviour; if you want to make quantum-leap changes, work on your paradigms.' The word paradigm comes from Greece and today it means model, theory, perception, assumption, view or a frame of reference. It basically means *the way we see the world*, not visually, but in terms of perceiving, understanding and interpreting it. In some respects it is our map of the world.

*'Assumption is the mother of screw up.'*
Angelo Donghia

The danger is that we assume the way *we* see things is the way they really are, or the way they should be. Because everyone else also thinks this way, is this where misunderstanding, conflict, frustration and negative living come from?

## The Blind Men and the Elephant

There is an old parable from ancient India that shows how our perspective limits our perception. Once there were four blind men who came upon an elephant. The first blind man went to investigate and felt a tusk of the elephant. He concluded that an elephant is smooth, narrow and long and pointed at the end like a spear. The second blind man felt the trunk of the elephant. He concluded that the elephant was like a giant python. The third blind man felt the leg of the elephant. His conclusion was that the elephant was like a large tree trunk with hair. The fourth blind man felt the elephant's tail. He concluded that the elephant was like a thin hairy snake with a brush on the end.

Now each of these blind men concluded that the elephant was a different and even contradictory object, yet each of them were partially correct in their assumptions. This is because each of them perceived only a partial aspect of the entire object. This parable gives us an idea of how limited our perceptions can be in forming our reality. In our assumption of the material world we possess a very limited view of the complete reality. Each person perceives himself as the centre of his universe, so his perceptions of reality are limited to his own personal perspective, which may be very different from someone else's.

In the past you have probably been encouraged to change your behaviour or actions, which can bring short-term changes. But if you want to make fundamental change, then change your perceptions. This will then change your actions which will in turn change your results, which will then change the way you see things next time.

As a stool requires a minimum of three legs for stability, ongoing accomplishment needs:

1.   thought (perception),
2.   feelings and action (to keep the thought alive, to generate more thoughts and to move us into doing) *and*
3.   acknowledgement of our results (so we can rejoice, build, and learn from them).

Without all three, the stool collapses. If you have a dream, or are working on a project, which doesn't seem to be working, consider which legs of the stool are not in place.

So where does our mindset or perceptions evolve? They come from our values, those things which are worthy or important to us. And our beliefs, which are the things we tell ourselves to be true or right.

## Beliefs

Is belief everything? Do beliefs make a difference? Can our beliefs create the sort of world we live in? Can our beliefs create the kind of day and week we have, and the life we lead? Certainly what we believe has important consequences for us. I am sure you have heard of self-fulfilling prophecies. In other words, what you believe and predict you create.

*Build what you can, with what you have, from where you are.*
*While some are waiting for the perfect situation,*
*others are building their own destiny.*

Research shows that when teachers expect good work from students, the students do well. Whereas if the same teachers do not expect other students to do well, the students usually don't.

Have you ever experienced the power of someone *really* believing in you? It can be a wonderful source of inspiration, encouragement and support. On the contrary, it is easy to be deflated around people who only focus on our weaknesses. It makes us feel insecure, and can lead to low self-esteem and a lack of confidence. The poor expectation has been confirmed. So, does it make a difference what we believe? I'll leave you to consider this and write your own answers to the following questions.

How much belief do you have in yourself?




What are the five most disempowering beliefs you hold to be true?




Closely examine these beliefs and find reasons that they are not true.




What are the five most empowering beliefs you hold to be true?




Expect the best and always do the best you can and see what happens. One of the most limiting beliefs we can hold is that there is power or powers outside of us greater than the power within us. Self-belief is the key to self-confidence and a calm mind.

> *'Some people dream of worthy accomplishments,*
> *others stay awake and do them.'*

We have looked at developing a positive attitude, how our perceptions and the way we see things affects our beliefs and how what we do affects our results. But we also need to know what motivates us – what really gives our lives a spark.

In 2004 a workplace based survey asked 2,000 people what motivated them. The results were:

| | | |
|---|---|---|
| 1. | To be treated fairly and valued | 78% |
| 2. | To have good workplace relationships | 69% |
| 3. | Pay/salary | 56% |
| 4. | Job security | 54% |
| 5. | Effective leadership within the organisation | 50% |
| 6. | Good benefits | 47% |
| 7. | Feeling important & involved | 45% |
| 8. | To have a good relationship with their boss | 45% |
| 9. | Training | 43% |
| 10. | Good location & environment | 38% |

It is interesting that fairness and being valued as a member of staff is the highest, followed by workplace relationships. If you either employ staff or have people reporting to you, it would be worth noting the above statistics. But to really get the best out of other people we must find out what motivates them as an individual.

What motivates you? What is it that gets you up in the morning and makes you want to really achieve something?

### So how can you change negative beliefs?

First you need to be aware of how you currently see things (including yourself), how you think, and how your beliefs affect the things you do.

Because you identify with your emotions it is easy to move from 'I'm angry' to 'I am an angry person', and allow this to become a long-lived self-image. You can free yourself from this trap by acknowledging that emotions arise out of conditions, and can vanish equally quickly.

Be mindful of how emotions are triggered by unnoticed thoughts and images, stirring up memories of a past event or anticipation of a future one. This can often flood your mind with strong emotions very quickly. However, the more you notice emotions arising out of conditions, the less you will personalise them which is an important step to master as strong emotions can pull you down. This ability to separate emotions from self and instead experience them as part of the flowing current of life releases you to a greater sense of freedom.

Jot down notes from times when you felt strong emotions in the following areas and make some notes next to them:

**MAD** (annoyed, bitter, angry, hostile or very frustrated).

**SAD** (feeling down, a sense of loss, helpless, depressed, very unhappy or extremely disappointed.)

**GLAD** (on top of the world, proud, full of excitement, joyful, extremely satisfied or euphoric).

Now think about the ways emotions, both positive and negative can have an impact on you. Try to describe situations, for example 'I was overly angry when…'

**POSITIVE**

**NEGATIVE**

There are many ways you can use your emotions in a negative way, including:

- **Abusing your position of power:** Usually due to feelings associated with fear – creates a need to 'get even'.
- **Being overly critical:** Criticism without explanation, reason or any suggestions for improvement – creates resentment and anxiety.
- **Being insensitive:** Particularly in delivering bad news without dignity and respect – results in depression and demotivation.
- **Creating a culture of mistrust, blame or discrimination –** people feel de-valued and only do what they have to rather than their best.
- **Being negative:** affects morale.

**Some Facts...**

- By 2020 it is predicted depression and mental illness will be responsible for more lost workdays than heart disease.
- Over two-thirds of stress related problems result from abuse or problems in relationships.
- Over 8% of employees have suffered bullying at work, and this figure is increasing.

Examples of how we use our emotions in a positive way:

- **Listen with empathy:** Trying to understand deeply another's thoughts and feelings builds trust and improves communication.
- **Give effective and honest feedback:** Well-structured, honest feedback given with respect can motivate others.
- **Deal with conflict positively:** Facing, rather than avoiding, conflict and finding mutually beneficial outcomes overcomes problems and builds trust.
- **Building culture based on trust:** Building trust to eliminate any blame-culture nurtures a learning and improving environment.
- **Be open:** Creates an open rather than a closed mind, while responsible expression of feelings and views generates trust with others and develops personal integrity.
- **Be positive:** Those who are fun to be around and have an optimistic attitude find this rubs-off on others.

If you are unaware of what makes you tick, you will simply play out all the habits of your conditioning. Without knowing what your motivations are, you have little chance of letting go of unskilled and unhelpful motivations, or of developing genuine wisdom. We can all suffer from unwelcome states of mind such as pride, jealousy, selfishness or ill will. The secret is to observe these unskilled patterns so we can unhook them and let go of the burden they bring to our lives.

One teaching says that if we had the choice of coming down to breakfast one morning and finding a very large sum of money or someone who could accurately point out all our faults, the latter would be of much greater long-term value to us. Such is the benefit of self-knowledge and self-awareness. And yet how many of us would make that choice?

*'The greatest thing in the world is to know how to be oneself.'*
Montaigne (Michel Egguem de Montaigne) 1622–73

## Values

What is important to you – and why? Your values are what are important to you, whereas your beliefs are things you tell yourself are true. Your values and beliefs dictate your mindset. They are responsible for how you see yourself, how you see others, and how you see the world. Your mindset dictates your attitude – which is simply the outward expression of all this. If you are not getting the results you aspire to, you need to evaluate your attitude, perception, beliefs and values.

Your values should be carefully thought through, otherwise they can blur your perception of what is right and wrong and become meaningless. People who carry out house robberies share the same values, but they have chosen to violate the basic principles of right and wrong. So when we decide the values that are important to us we need to bring our conscience into play and ask ourselves 'Is this value important to me, and is my conscience happy if I follow it?'

We are not a passive target of life's misfortunes, but an active creator of our life. Our life and everything we experience in it is a creation and reflection of the ideas and values we accept. We can choose to take this fact and blame ourselves for our misfortunes, or we can use it to take charge and create an ideal life. We will come back to this in the next chapter, but let's begin by looking at any problem as an opportunity to learn or develop new skills or levels of knowledge.

Having carefully thought through values can help you develop greater personal emotional strength and wisdom for your future.

So, what values are important to you? Below is a list of values, look through the list and tick the five that are the most important to you at this stage:

| | | | | | |
|---|---|---|---|---|---|
| Appreciation | ☐ | Compassion | ☐ | Co-operation | ☐ |
| Environmental Awareness | ☐ | Fairness | ☐ | Faith | ☐ |
| Family | ☐ | Forgiveness | ☐ | Freedom | ☐ |
| Friendship | ☐ | Generosity | ☐ | Hard work | ☐ |
| Harmony | ☐ | Health | ☐ | Honesty | ☐ |
| Humour | ☐ | Integrity | ☐ | Kindness | ☐ |
| Helping others | ☐ | Politeness | ☐ | Reliability | ☐ |
| Love | ☐ | Loyalty | ☐ | Perseverance | ☐ |
| Being Respectful | ☐ | Responsibility | ☐ | Self-Discipline | ☐ |
| Sharing | ☐ | Tolerance | ☐ | Trustworthiness | ☐ |
| Truth | ☐ | Unity | ☐ | Wisdom | ☐ |
| Courage | ☐ | Restraint | ☐ | Calmness | ☐ |
| Hope | ☐ | Patience | ☐ | Understanding | ☐ |
| Optimism | ☐ | Enthusiasm | ☐ | Modesty | ☐ |
| Sincerity | ☐ | Self-Esteem/respect | ☐ | Inner peace | ☐ |
| Life Balance | ☐ | Perfection | ☐ | Determination | ☐ |
| Having a Purpose | ☐ | Contentment | ☐ | Creativity | ☐ |

Now list each of the values you have identified, and write next to it why it is important to you. Take time on your own to do this, and think deeply about each value. Remember, your values can act as your life-long guide and source of inspiration and hope in times of perceived hopelessness. They are your connecting force for emotional strength, courage and willpower.

**VALUE          REASON THIS VALUE IS IMPORTANT TO ME**

1.

2.

3.

4.

5.

# Conclusion

In this chapter you've been shown that there is a foundation to success. One that you ignore at your peril. You've also had an opportunity to define what success means to you. And you know that having the right attitude accounts for 85% of all success, and no amount of skill or knowledge will make up for this.

The way you perceive yourself, and all around you, has an enormous impact on your success too, which is why it was important to look at your own perceptions and how they help or detract from your life.

Your beliefs, often formed for no better reason other than those around us held them, are a matter of habit. Change negative beliefs for life-affirming ones and you immediately give yourself a stronger, more powerful foundation. Your values too are such an intrinsic part of who you are that your life will always be happier when you live and act in accordance with them.

Now that you are about to build on a firm, solid foundation, you have a much greater chance of succeeding. So, here's to you!

# Action 2

## Make Powerful Decisions

*'There is no more miserable human being
than one for whom nothing is habitual but indecision.'*
William James

Welcome to **Action 2**. With this action you learn how to truly take charge of your life, your future and, ultimately, your destiny.

You must make decisions for anything to happen in your life. Yet in order to make changes you have to generate positive reasons to want things to change in your life. In doing so you improve your self-worth as you begin to understand the different characteristics of a *proactive responsible* person compared to a *reactive irresponsible* person.

By knowing how to choose your responses to everyday events, especially highly charged ones, you'll gain greater control. You will see the difference in how a *proactive* person focuses their time and effort and how a *reactive* person focuses their time and effort. And you discover the benefits of using proactive language. Best of all you truly appreciate what real commitment is and how to make it. And in doing so you will understand how you too can become an influential figure.

### Making Life-Changing Decisions

Many of us have read self-help books, attended motivational seminars, and put ourselves through Personal Development workshops. No matter how good or interesting the work was however, most of us never really **decided** to make the actual change needed.

The trouble with most of us is that we sidestep and backtrack, and seldom make up our mind to do what we really want. Nor do we clearly determine the road our future should travel. Often the only decision we make is the worst of all – we make excuses for our own inactivity.

When you make a decision you exercise power. All your dreams, wishes and ideals could become reality if you kept them constantly before you and let go of fear. In common with others you might think you know what you want, yet when being honest most admit they don't. It sounds paradoxical, but if you knew what you wanted, you would get it, provided you made the decision, and developed the stamina and the fight to go after it.

*'Normal is not something to aspire to,*
*it is something to get away from.'*
Jodie Foster

Some people suggest the world is split between two groups of people: the *I will-ers* and the *Should-I-or-shouldn't-I-ers*? The great majority of people are in the latter group. 'I can't make up my mind,' is one of the most disempowering statements you can make as it is the death of hope, ambition, self-esteem, initiative and achievement. The longer you are unable to make up your mind, the longer you will be helpless, insecure, and unable to move in any direction.

Unless you change your thinking, you will stay where you are now, or sink down further — nothing stands still in life. You need to get out of the rut and start doing what you know you want to be doing! After all, the difference between a rut and a grave is just a few feet!

Do you want to remain where you are now? It is an interesting question to ask. What is your answer?

Now think of something in your life that you know you should make a decision about, but haven't. What's holding you back? Think about how you can make the decision, write it down, and commit to seeing it through.

You have only two choices – to go higher or lower. You can wander through the rest of your life, moaning about what might have been if you had lived your life differently. Well, it's never too late, and **you** can make the decision to change that 'might have been' to 'I'm glad I made the decision to change'.

Even happiness begins with a decision. If you're tired of being miserable, **you** must decide to be happy. It really is that simple! You are responsible for your own personal happiness, so don't lay it at other people's doors. And don't make the mistake of putting it off until the circumstances are 'perfect'.

*'Can you come to the frightening conclusion that you are the* ***decisive*** *element? It is your personal approach that creates the climate. It is your daily mood that makes the weather. You possess tremendous power to make your life miserable or joyous. You can be a tool of torture or an instrument of inspiration, you can humiliate or*

*humour, hurt or heal. In all situations, it is your response that decides whether a crisis is escalated or de-escalated, a person humanised or de-humanised. If you treat people as they are you make them worse. If you treat people as they ought to be, you help them become what they are capable of becoming.'*

Hiam Ginott

Decision is born of courage, and courage springs from self-belief. Decide to do away with the problems and conditions that hold you back from achieving your true potential, and get rid of them NOW! Visualise a different life, free from constraints and full of decisive results, and a future full of promise and accomplishment. Can you see this for yourself?

*'It is not your conditions that determine your life destiny, it's your decisions.'*

Anthony Robbins

Now think of a decision you could make (maybe go back to the one you identified earlier), and go through this 7-step process for making a committed decision.

1. Remember the power of decisions can shape the destiny of your life. The decision releases the creativity and energy necessary to see it through. Make the decision before the plans!
2. Commit to it quickly and do not procrastinate. Attach pleasure to the pictured outcome. Attach pain, frustration and annoyance to not making a decision or being indecisive. Write it down and take concrete action. Develop a plan and do it! Deciding instantly and correctly is an acquired habit, one we can all acquire.
3. Make decisions often. You now have the knowledge, skill and attitude to make decision making a positive life forming habit for yourself.
4. Always be prepared to be flexible with your decisions as you may want to change course. We all make mistakes from time to time. It's not the mistake that is important but what we do with it! Only when we are free to make mistakes are we empowered to grow, explore and progress.
5. Stay committed to the decision, keep your flexibility, and really see it through.

6. This decision-making acronym may help: STAR – Stop, Think, Act and Review.
7. Enjoy being decisive. Evaluate the success of your decision, celebrate your success, and use it as a springboard for further decisions.

DECIDE is another acronym you can use for making decisions:

D – DEFINE the decision
E – EXAMINE and gather information
C – COMMUNICATE to all involved
 I – INCLUDE all alternatives
D – DETERMINE the best alternative
E – EDUCATE and implement

D – DEFINE the decision, criteria, and results you want. It is easy to make the wrong choice by not properly defining the exact decision that needs to be made. The criteria are the measurable characteristics that the decision MUST meet such as cost, time, and expected quality. In this first step it is important to know the end result that the decision will achieve.

E – EXAMINE the defined decision by gathering and interpreting information. This is a step where it is useful to ascertain whether data confirms or negates the decision created in the DEFINE step.

C – COMMUNICATE with everyone involved. Don't leave anyone out who may give much needed insight. From an organisation's perspective, this can help you get resources and support as well as getting specialised knowledge OR different points of view.

Once you have completed the DEC portion of the process you have the data to proceed.

I – INCLUDE all alternatives you gathered from the EXAMINE and COMMUNICATION steps. Alternatives are more necessary as the risk of the decision is increased. To INCLUDE all alternatives requires an open mind, mind storming, and not discounting unusual ideas. An unusual idea can generate a really good alternative that was never originally considered.

D – DETERMINE the best alternative. This is the evaluating and choosing step. Some alternatives may become obviously unworkable, while others pose a high to medium risk. Narrow down the alternatives and… JUST DO IT. Make a move! In this step the key is to make sure that the chosen decision is in alignment with the desired results and chosen criteria established in the first step, DEFINE.

E – EDUCATE everyone affected by the decision by communicating the implementation of the decision made. Many great decisions have been derailed because everyone affected by the decision was not EDUCATED on the implementation. This step includes making sure the implementation happens at the right time, in the right place, with the right people and ensuring that everyone understands the implementation procedures.

But sometimes we should JUST DO IT!

In making decisions there are times when you have to JUST DO IT. Now when you JUST DO IT that does not mean that you jump in without thinking. In order to make a JUST DO IT decision, here are a few things to remember:

J – JUSTIFY why the decision is important to you.

U – UNDERSTAND the results and outcomes.

S – STOP and consider all the possibilities and pitfalls of your decision.

T – TRUST YOURSELF and have the courage to move forward.

D – DON'T DECIDE it is OK to NOT make a decision.

O – ORDERLY. If you do move forward, make sure you plan.

I – INVOLVE OTHERS who your decision will have an impact on.

T – TITANIC. Remember the *Titanic*... even with the best plans and decisions there can be icebergs along the way.

Changes take place one hour, one day, and one week at a time as you come face-to-face with your challenges. Throughout this book you are asked to make a personal commitment to follow through on the actions. In doing so you gain a strength and power you never thought possible. It will impact positively on your work, your personal life, your mental and physical health, your relationships and your overall attitude and outlook on life.

Where does it all begin? *When you make the decision to change*? When you make decisions about your thoughts, vision, goals, attitude, habits and the way you interact with others. But making these decisions will be futile if you fail to make the most important decision of all – deciding to be open to change.

Sir Edmund Hilary who climbed Everest said;

> *'It's not the mountain we conquer, but ourselves.'*

During World War Two, a chaplain visited a soldier who was badly wounded about the face and had lost a limb.

Sympathetically, the chaplain said, 'My dear fellow, you realise this is going to change the colour of your life?'

'Yes, Padre,' came the brave reply, 'but I shall choose the colour.'

## Do We Need To Change?

Nothing is permanent – in fact change is the only constant. Our personality, emotions, perception, assumptions, and even our behaviour are all in constant flux. I have taken many Personality Tests over time and even within the same year results were different even when using the same test.

The worrying thing, however, is that most change happens to us without thought, direction, personal control, or by us taking responsibility for it. The result is often that we get disappointed, and become reactive to outside circumstances, so we change our jobs, dump our partner or change friends. We think that if we had the perfect boss, job, partner or house then everything would be OK. But how often do we recognise and accept the responsibility to change ourselves instead?

> *'Sometimes in the wave of change we find our true direction.'*

In this respect, there are two groups of people – those who embrace change, and those who resist change by putting up defences and blaming others. Successful people are changing all the time, and are prepared to do what others are afraid to do.

How would you feel if you were told that in five years' time your life would be exactly as it is now? That is why it is important you make the decision to change and transform your life. To change your perception and therefore your attitude and beliefs to experience phenomenal personal growth. Do not delay. Start immediately.

> *'We learn to make decisions by making decisions.'*
>
> Old Proverb

Before you go any further, write down now how committed you are to making change. Are you totally committed or are you allowing things to get in your way?

*'Embrace change. What seems like only a ripple today… can become the wave of the future. If you're not riding this wave of change, you'll find yourself beneath it.'*

Your next question when looking at your map of your life is to ask 'Where am I now?' When you see things as they really are and are honest with yourself, you create more desire to change. If you have a *10 Actions*® Workbook take a look at the self-awareness exercise in Action One, and assess where you are at the moment.

*'Change is life-giving.*
*It helps us grow into someone greater than we already are.'*

Whatever happens to us is the result of the choices we make. If we do not like what happens to us we can make new choices. So often we complain: 'If something different had happened to me, I would be different!' We are good at blaming others and external circumstances for our problems. The longer we see ourselves as victims, the longer we remain the victim, powerless to make change.

*'The best years of your life are the ones in which you decide*
*your problems are your own. You do not blame them on your*
*mother, the economy, or the Government. You realise that you*
*control your own destiny.'*

Albert Ellis

External circumstances can only *influence* our decisions and lives. The final responsibility lies with each of us as individuals. It is how we see things and how we process information that moulds our beliefs, and our attitude that determines our action. Say out loud now, 'Yes, I am willing to change.' Do you feel ready for this transformational growth? The decision is yours.

## What Are You Worth?

If you had to write a price tag for what you are worth, what would it be?

Most people underestimate what they are worth, because they focus on their weaknesses rather than on what they are good at, and what is working well in their lives. When I ask people to tell me what they want from life, they often start to tell me what they *don't* want. The other thing that holds us back is comparing ourselves to others. Poor self-perception is a source of emotional and psychological pain. Is your self-esteem in the valley, or at the bottom, middle or top of the mountain?

Remember the work we did in **Action 1** about our perception of ourselves? Now ask, 'Do I really know myself?' Have you ever asked a friend, 'Please be honest with me about how you see me? What am I good at, and what frustrates you about me?' Most of us don't, because we are afraid of the answer.

Think now what it would be like to be at peace with yourself. Reflect and imagine what it would be like. Now describe yourself in the most positive, optimistic way that you can.

How does it feel?


Accept your weaknesses. Have you ever met anyone who is perfect? Start focussing on your strengths, because whatever you focus on is what you will get. Let me explain – in a few seconds I want you to close your eyes and think about anything *except* a bright pink elephant.

What happened? Did you get the picture of the bright pink elephant out of your mind? No. So, even if you say to yourself, 'I won't think about my failures,' that thought is what your mind will focus on. Instead choose to focus on your strengths, what you want to do, and the kind of person you want to be.

Let's go back to the question at the beginning of this session. If you had to write a price tag for what you are worth, what would it be? If you were a car it might depend on the model, or if you were a house it might depend on the number of bedrooms. The true value, however, is not the metal in the car or the bricks in the house – it is the perceived value. The house of greatest value to me was a small terraced Victorian house that I used as my sanctuary – the monetary value was little, but the value perceived by me was vast.

Now answer the question again, what are you worth?


## Responsible or Irresponsible – the *Choice* is Yours!

The problem here is in deciding what we are and what we are not responsible for. Everything in your life is a result of a *decision* you make. You don't *have* to go to work, you don't *have* to get up in the morning, you don't *have* to treat people fairly and with respect, you don't *have* to pay your mortgage. If you decide to do some or all of these things, it's because you consider them to be the best choice for you to make.

Truly responsible people are *opportunity miners* rather than *opportunity whiners*. The whiners are the ones who whine about not enough opportunity, while the opportunity miners say, 'No one is going to do it for me, so I will unearth my own success.'

When trying new things, ask yourself: 'Would I hurt myself *physically* (not emotionally) doing this? If the answer is no, then do it. It may not be comfortable, and for sure you will make mistakes, but you will learn far more than sitting at home wondering, 'What if.'

Most of us live within what is called our *comfort zone*. If you imagine your comfort zone as a circle, inside the circle are all those things you are comfortable doing, on the outside is everything else. The wall of the circle is not a protective wall, but a wall of limitation and fear. When you do something new, different, creative, or innovative you push against the wall and make it bigger – this is something we call experience and growth. But by not doing it, by backing off, your comfort zone shrinks – this is inexperience and backward development.

> *'When we contend with challenges that test our strength,*
> *we move more surely to the top.'*

Once you start to expand one area of your life, you start to expand other areas too. Once you taste success you increase in confidence and take this with you into every area of your life.

Staying in your comfort zone is actually far more dangerous. As the zone contracts, it generates the belief that you can't do something. This thought then stops you even trying to stretch yourself so you become increasingly frustrated. Feel the fear and do it anyway. If anything, be afraid of living within your comfort zone.

> *'What we have to do is to be forever curiously testing new opinions*
> *and courting new impressions.'*
> Walter Pater (1873)

No one denies that our past and past conditioning can prove restrictive. Peer pressure, genetic conditioning, parental influence, environmental conditioning, the way our colleagues and friends treat us, yes they can all restrict us – but only *if* we let it.

As we mature we often make decisions that narrow our opportunity to achieve what we truly want. We keep the same friends, which doesn't open us to the fresh ideas that new, maybe more inspirational friends, could give us. We limit our educational choices which limit our career choices. We limit our exercise regime which holds back our physical development. And all too often we seek the path of least resistance in the name of playing it safe.

Another restriction is destructive emotion. For some, the mere thought of a particular person evokes negative reactions. What we must ask ourselves is, 'Who is really the source of the problem?' Some philosophers and psychologists suggest that if we hate a person, we actually hate something in that person that is a part of our own make-up. Whether we like it or not, what others say or do to us can only affect us if we allow it to. It is also true that we will find it difficult to be released from these hate emotions until we really *understand* that other people are not responsible for our happiness or unhappiness – we are.

Whether we blame others or us, it is us who hurts. Guilt is anger directed at ourselves, and resentment is anger directed at others. Who is it that feels the hate we have for another person? Those of us who have a tendency toward regular anger need to exercise our emotions less. When we *don't* exercise something, it grows weaker. Rather than exercising your emotions, try exercising your body, and see what happens; go for a run, do some dancing, go for a brisk walk.

*'If you do not wish to be prone to anger, do not feed the habit; give it nothing which may tend to its increase. At first, keep quiet and count the days when you were not angry: 'I used to be angry every day, then every other day: next, every two, then every three days!' And if you succeed in passing thirty days, sacrifice to the gods in thanksgiving.'*

Epictetus

For many people releasing destructive emotions can be a liberating experience, although to do this you may need to examine and revisit painful experiences. This involves a 3-step process:

1. *Revisit* the incident that caused the emotion
2. *Relive* the memory in the present
3. *Review* the buried memory with the conscious mind using your new awareness to defuse its negative power.

Carl Jung said, 'A man who has not passed through the inferno of his passions has never overcome them.' So decide now not to suppress your emotions, but to control them.

The mind and emotions are a powerful combination. Learning to direct them only toward good – your own and others – is a challenge of epic proportions, of epic achievement and of epic reward.

*As keepers of our own attitudes, we must constantly choose
to be the light we wish to see in others.*

Abraham Maslow, a noted psychologist, identified five basic needs for human beings. He ranged them from lower to higher, and added that we cannot be free to satisfy our higher needs until our lower ones are met. They are:

1. *Physiological needs* – Food, water and air to breathe.
2. *Safety needs* – Freedom from threat of danger, security, and familiar surroundings.
3. *Belongingness and love needs* – To be accepted and united with associates.
4. *Esteem needs* – Achievement, reputation, status, and prestige.
5. *Need for self-actualisation* – Self-fulfilment, the realisation of your potential.

Most people rise above steps 1 and 2, but never reach fulfilment in step 5. That's because we become bogged down in dealing with the emotional issues of steps 3 and 4. Many people continue to measure their self-worth by comparing material wealth, or by building a work related status, and by developing a superficial prestige that provides only external security.

People who take personal responsibility for their lives and believe they exert some control over life's situations find events much less stressful than those who do not feel they have any control. The former group don't stop when obstacles are encountered, are less stressed by negative events, less fearful, get sick less often, and recover from illness much faster.

People who have no sense of personal control become a hostage to circumstances. But if you control even a minor aspect of a situation, your self-confidence improves, and gradually you gain more control over the situation. There is a lot of value in taking one small step at a time – even a knotted ball of string has a starting point.

Sometimes problems can seem so overwhelming that anxiety and depression further deplete your ability to cope. This can intensify feelings of helplessness to the point of panic. Relaxing, however, calms you down, and allows you to begin the process of recovery; to clear your mind and become re-energised. Often just a few minutes of relaxation helps you to regain your self-confidence and develop a solution or strategy for solving your problem.

It is important that you learn to turn stumbling blocks into stepping-stones. Asking what you can learn from a bad situation changes your attitude from being the victim to being in control.

## So What Choices Can You Make?

You can make choices in every area of your life. Who decides whether you are happy or not? You do. When you get up in the morning you have two choices – to be happy or unhappy.

You don't always have the choice of what you have to face, but you can choose how you face it. Sometimes it's the only choice you have. Even if there is no other choice, you can still choose your attitude.

As Abraham Lincoln once said:

*'People are just about as happy as they make up their minds to be.'*

Self-pity and self-punishment can end up consuming you. If you are thinking unhappy thoughts, STOP, and replace them with happy thoughts. Make happy thoughts a habit. And being happy is a habit.

List some of the things that make you happy:

Start the day with happiness psychology by saying, 'I feel good mentally, physically and emotionally. I am grateful to be alive.'

10 steps to happiness:

1. Keep your heart free from hate and your mind free from worry.
2. Live simply.
3. Expect little.
4. Give much.
5. Fill your life with love.
6. Scatter sunshine.
7. Remember yourself, and think of others.
8. Do as you would be done by.
9. Get your spirit from the inside, not from a bottle.
10. Do this for two weeks.

Who decides whether you worry or not? You've guessed it, you do. Worrying is behind many diseases: causes stress, high blood pressure, ulcers, heart disease, stroke, and even cancer. The word worry comes from the Anglo Saxon word *to choke*. If someone puts their hands around your neck to strangle you, they will *choke* off your power and vitality, and that's exactly what worrying does to you.

Many surveys indicate that a person who worries a lot does not live as long as someone who doesn't worry. Worrying is a mental habit you've acquired. You were not born a worrier, so you can change this habit.

Three simple steps to stop worrying:

- Empty your mind daily, especially at night. Picture your current worrying thoughts leaving you.
- Refill your mind with positive thoughts of hope, courage, happiness, belief in yourself and other positive thoughts.
- Don't fall prey to worrying again. If you are a worrier, set yourself the challenge of not worrying about anything for two weeks – simply deal with things as they arise!

What about when something happens that you really have no control over, such as when someone dies? You can still choose what attitude you will take, and this will affect the impact on you and your life. Understanding the process of recovering from an emotional wound such as bereavement may also help. There are three phases that people go through:

- **Numbness, shock and denial.** Our body and emotions become numb. We deny the loss. We say things such as, 'No, this can't be.' At this stage we may turn to cigarettes, alcohol or other prop.
- **Fear, depression and anger.** We become angry at whomever, or whatever, caused the loss, closely followed by guilt about what we did or did not do. We are also depressed and sad at the loss.
- **We accept, understand and move on.** We realise that life goes on, and loss is an unfortunate part of life.

Even people who go through life *going with the flow* are making choices – it is that maybe they are not conscious of making life-changing choices. So, whether you are conscious of them or not, your choices lead you down one road or another. Which road do you want?

One paradox we need to be aware of, as shown by psychologist Barry Schwartz, is the danger of too much choice. We live in times where the choices we face are numerous and can overwhelm us. We have a multitude of choices – whether to continue our education, get married, focus on our career, have children, decide on friendship groups, where we live, what to do in our leisure time, and ultimately what we want out of life. Yet, many people, rather than taking the initiative in these or any other area of life, put off decisions altogether, and instead focus on the problems of our society – how unfair the world is, and the hardships our generation faces.

The words of Stephen Covey in his book *The 7 Habits of Highly Effective People* have stayed with me for years: *'It's not what happens to us, but our response to what happens to us that hurts us.'*

This is not always easy as we live in a reactive world where we are conditioned to react to things. I came across the idea of *choosing our own way and choosing our own response to things* some years ago, and it has made an enormously positive impact on my life, yet there are days I still struggle with it.

So, how do responsible and irresponsible people respond to situations? Irresponsible people react impulsively as soon as someone says or does something to them. A responsible person puts a gap (such as counting to 30) between what another person says or does before giving *their chosen response.*

The word Proactive means that as human beings we are responsible for our own lives. Our basic nature is to act – not to be acted upon. It's interesting to break the word responsibility into two parts: response-ability, the ability to choose your response.

## Irresponsible – Reacting to Situations

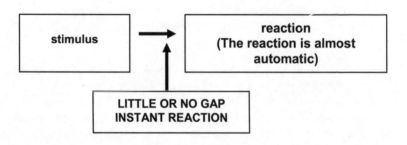

## Responsible – Choosing a Response

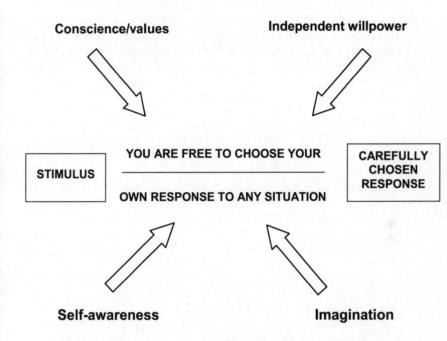

The above diagram shows that responsible, proactive people still experience the 'stimulus', but they put a gap between this 'stimulus' and their chosen response by for example counting to 30 as we've suggested. During this time through their conscience and values ask themselves "what is the best response to this" then using their willpower exercise their chosen response.

They also use their self-awareness to become aware of how they have responded/reacted to events in the past and their imagination to visualise and imagine themselves choosing appropriate responses to similar events in the future.

Highly proactive people recognise the responsibility in choosing their response. They do not blame circumstances, or conditioning for their behaviour. Their behaviour is a product of their own conscious choices based on their values.

The opposite of proactive is reactive. The spirit of reactive people is the transfer of responsibility. Their language absolves them of responsibility. 'That's just the way I am.' 'There's nothing I can do about it.' 'He makes me so mad!' 'My emotional life is governed by something outside my control.' Words are a reflection of what is happening inside, so listen closely to what you say. Rather than say, 'I don't want to get fat,' say, 'I will keep to a healthy and nutritious diet.' Not only is it a great affirmation, but your subconscious mind will start to believe it.

Regarding the style of language we use, I often hear people say things *cannot be done* and I think the following poem says more than any further explanation:

## It CAN be Done!

*Somebody said that it couldn't be done, but with a chuckle he replied*
*That maybe it couldn't, but he would be one who wouldn't say so till he tried,*
*So he buckled right in, with the trace of a grin on his face, if he worried he hid it,*
*He started to sing, as he tackled the thing that couldn't be done as he did it,*
*Somebody scoffed 'Oh you'll never do that, at least nobody has ever done it'*
*But he took off his coat and he took off his hat, and the first thing he knew he had begun it.*
*There are thousands to tell you it cannot be done,*
*There are thousands to prophesise failure,*
*There are thousands to point out, one by one the dangers that await you,*
*But buckle right in, with a bit of a grin,*
*Throw off your coat and go to it,*
*Just start to sing, as you tackle the thing that cannot be done and you'll do it.*

Many behavioural scientists have built reactive, deterministic, stimulus-response models of human behaviour. The basic idea is that we are conditioned to respond in a particular way to a particular stimulus. In contrast, the proactive model shows that between stimulus and response we have the freedom to choose our response.

I remember leading a session in a school on the subject of responsibility and how we respond to things. Afterwards a 16 year old told me of his strict upbringing and how his father physically abused him. Previously he'd worried that he might pass on this behaviour if he had children. But after doing the work on responsibility, he said he now realised that, regardless of what had happened to him, he could *choose* not to pass it on. He said he felt released from shackles. He felt free. He could focus on being a good father when he had children of his own.

The key word is *focus.* Responsible people *focus* on taking the initiative, on creating solutions rather than problems, and ultimately *focus* on things they can do something about within their sphere of control and influence. On the other hand, irresponsible people wait for circumstances to happen to them, and focus on the problems – it is never their fault!

In the last company I worked for I knew a middle manager who through his own influence changed the direction of the company because he focussed on solutions rather than problems – things he and the company could do something about. His ideas were backed up with data and analysis that made simple sense, and he gradually gained the trust and respect of the senior managers and directors who would seek his opinion. As a result, major changes were made because of his ideas and his responsible approach to sharing these ideas.

Responsible people choose to control the only thing they can control – themselves. They focus on being a great partner, husband, wife, friend, colleague, a better listener, to be more cooperative with others and, above all, to inspire others.

Now the choice is yours. Do you want to be responsible or irresponsible? Write down some areas where you are going to increase your level of responsibility.

Winners *make* it happen, losers *let* it happen. Winners are people who take the initiative. If you want to be a winner, *decide,* and make that decision big, make it a real commitment.

You have within you an enormous number of hidden talents. They are hidden because their potential is seldom used. Your power lays dormant, waiting to be unleashed and used to full capacity.

### Are you Drawn Towards your Goals or do you Avoid Them?

Are you proactive and pro risk or reactive and averse to risk? We all either move toward or away from something in our lives.

The *toward* person is focused on their goals and achieving them. They tend to be visionary, see the big picture over the detail, and prefer to leave the doing to others. They can be impatient with others who do not think like them, and can be chronic breakers of tradition and rules which may irritate and upset people who like formal structure and tradition. They do not like to look at the past and can therefore miss the lessons that the past holds.

The **away from** person is often motivated by the need to avoid danger and failure. They tend to like the detail of things and are very good at planning. They often look at past situations to see how well they handled it, what they can learn from it, and what they can take into the future. They consult with other people, but can find it hard to forgive which sometimes makes them hard to work with.

Which are you? Can you take the best from both?

## Now Make the Commitment

*'Nothing can withstand the power of the human will if it is willing to stake its very existence to the extent of its purpose.'*

Steve Redgrave, the Olympian rower, achieved results on a long-term basis way beyond what his age should have allowed! How did he keep going?

The answer is **commitment.** Commitment is **deciding** to do whatever it takes to take you to where you want to go. Looking at the work we have done so far, you can now make a commitment to change your perceptions, your attitude, to be driven by your values, make life-changing decisions, and take responsibility for your future. Make a commitment and see how empowering it feels.

*'There is a difference between interest and commitment. When you are interested in doing something, you do it only when it's convenient. When you're committed to something, you accept no excuses, only results.'*
Ken Blanchard.

So, what do you need to be committed? Well the first thing is resistance. Any worthwhile accomplishment will need you to resist things that pull you in the wrong direction.

*'Nearly everyone develops an idea and works at it to the point where it looks impossible, and then gets discouraged. That's not the place to become discouraged.'*
Thomas Edison.

This can include resistance against pressure from family, friends, peers, advisors, self-doubt, lack of resources, thinking inside (rather than outside) the box, or red-tape. Overcoming such resistance is an experience encountered by all achievers in shaping their destiny and going beyond their current reality.

Albert Einstein stated:

*'Great spirits have always encountered violent opposition
from mediocre minds.'*

**The key element for all successful people is not talent,
but drive, thirst for success, and determination!**

Commitment is the mental resolve to never give up. Determined action is the evidence of that resolve, and success requires first mental and then physical effort.

*'I could not wait for success – so I went ahead without it.'*
Jonathan Winters

Do remember that Rome was not built in a day, so make commitments in bite-size chunks, one day at a time. However, one commitment you can make right now is the decision to be a *possibility thinker* who looks for the opportunity no one else has thought about. If you can find something that inspires you, the way ahead will be easier. Examine the possibilities in detail, define them as thoroughly as possible, and write them down. Once written down, rate the opportunities in order of importance as this will help tap into your subconscious and right brain creative side.

As individuals, worthwhile goals are often only achieved through struggle, yet this can be a positive thing. Struggle clarifies our purpose, develops our willpower and fires our imagination. It also stops us becoming lazy, and forces us onwards and upwards towards our mission. *Strength, both physical and spiritual, is the product of struggle!*

Are you a self-starter model, one that does not have to be coaxed into action? Will you automatically get up, decide to take the initiative and accomplish your mission, goals and purpose? A self-starter will wake each morning excited with their day's goals firmly in mind. Plus they have the motivation and positive attitude to strengthen the determination and commitment to meet every challenge. Live a dream with muscle power in the understanding that life is an opportunity not to be wasted.

*'The motivated man or woman must have that personal quality of initiative, that inner urge that prods him or her from a position of inertia to movement, change and action.'*

Self-starting means giving it all you've got. If we expend only half the energy or go forward half-heartedly, the best you can expect is half of what you set out for.

> *'It's not the hours you put into your work that count – it's the work you put into the hours.'*
> Sam Ewing

Once you have generated this dedication to what you do, it will ignite a positive energy from within you. Your times of feeling negative and frustrated will diminish by 95%!

> *Do a little more than you are paid to do,*
> *Give a little more that you have to,*
> *Try a little harder that you want to,*
> *Aim a little higher than you think possible,*
> *And give a lot of thanks for your peace of mind,*
> *health, family and friends.*

Don't sit back and wait for some sort of external conclusive proof, because nothing will happen. Be bold, make that commitment and then act. Rather than just telling your friends that you are off to Spain for a year or so to do the sabbatical work you have always dreamed of, tell them whilst heading for the door, suitcase and ticket in hand – they will want to drive you to the airport to find out where this inner determination came from!

Commitment is not measurable. With a goal, there is a specific point in time where you have either accomplished it or not. For example: You have either increased your income by 30% by the end of this year or you have not. In contrast, commitments are ongoing quality of life shifts – the state or kind of being you want to create in your life. For example: I am committed to having joy and self-expression in my work.

## Becoming an Inspirational Figure

Changes begin on the inside and work their way to the surface. After all, your character shines through in everything you do, especially when you are under pressure. What you wear and say, what your expression and body language say are all a reflection of who you are. We could learn from the eagle – at the first sign of a storm it spreads its wings and climbs above the storm. Adversity, in fact, allows the eagle to use less effort, rather than more. It glides into the wind and the stronger the storm, the higher it soars. Influential figures, like eagles, let difficulties work for them.

An influential figure is someone who transmits positive energy, helpfulness, encouragement, enlightenment and hope to other people. A person with values, principles and character traits that you respect and admire. Consider:

1. Who has been an inspirational figure in your life? (It does not need to be someone famous.)
2. What impact and influence has this person had on you? How?
3. What have you learnt from this person? What else can you learn from them?
4. Where in your life (at work, at home, within your community, country or the world at large), could you become an inspirational person?

*'Be more concerned with your character than your reputation, because your character is what you really are, while your reputation is merely what others think you are.'*
John Wood (1910) American Basketball Coach

## The Four Week Challenge

*'Our greatest glory is not in never falling, but in rising every time we fall.'*
Confucius (551–479 BC)

It is the ordinary events of everyday life which test our decisiveness, sense of responsibility, and levels of commitment to handle the extraordinary pressures of modern life. This 4-week challenge will test your level of decisiveness in taking responsibility and committing to that responsibility.

---

**For 4 weeks:**
- **work only on the things you can influence and do something about**
- **remove negative feelings from your life**
- **make small and regular decisions and commitments and keep them.**

---

Try to do this across your whole life – with your family, at work, socially, with your friends, but most of all with yourself. Take responsibility. Don't defend your shortcomings, but forgive yourself if you make a mistake, and then do something about it to learn and grow from it – and do this immediately. Just work on yourself in this way for four weeks and notice the difference.

If you find yourself failing, start the four-week period again from scratch; by doing this you will find being a responsible, positive achiever will become a habit.

Finally, once you have completed the 4-week challenge, celebrate your success. That's because this is not an easy challenge, but it is the foundation for real success, happiness and contentment in your life. And if you can't commit to trying something different for just four weeks, well…

## Summary

In this chapter, you discovered the importance of decision making and the need to generate positive reasons to change. You can now recognise the characteristics of a *proactive responsible person* and a *reactive irresponsible* person. You also know that you get to choose how you respond to everyday events, even highly charged ones. And you can see where a *proactive person* focuses their time and effort compared to a *reactive person*.

Proactive language plays its part in all this too and you recognise this. You understand what real commitments are, how to make them and, most importantly, how to stick to them. In the process your self-worth rises to a new level and you realise that you too can be an inspirational person.

Now let's enjoy the next part of our journey together. Ready?

# Action 3

## Determine Your Future

*'Though no one can go back and make a new start,
anyone can start from now and make a brand new end.'*
Carl Bard

Have you heard people talk of *having a purpose?* But what is a purpose and how do you find yours? This chapter helps you discover the answers to these questions and helps you understand the difference between self-leadership and self-management. You get to know what it takes to be the leader of your life, your future and what characteristics leaders enjoy. In the last chapter I showed you the importance of using positive self-talk and here I expand on this by revealing the power of affirmations and visualisation. Here too is where you get to detail what you *want* in your life, what you want to *do* and what kind of person you want to *be*. And by writing your own vision and mission statement you move one step nearer to determining your future.

Firstly, answer the following questions as if under exam conditions.

1. What makes a leader?


2. What's the difference between leadership and management?


3. What would you include in your own vision/mission statement?


4. Comment on the following quotation: *'Success is the continuous journey towards the achievement of a predetermined, worthwhile vision.'*

5. Can I have purpose, growth and all-out massive action without having a vision/mission statement to guide me?

6. Think of someone who fulfilled an inspirational leadership role in your life. Write down the three main qualities you admire in that person.

7. Robert Kennedy once stated; '*It doesn't matter whether or not as individuals we rank among the famous. What does matter is that each of us has a purpose in life, to somehow make a positive contribution to the world in which we live.*' What are your thoughts on this?

8. I believe I will bring the following *special something* to humanity that no one else can offer:

9. My life matters because:

10. To pass this exam, do not answer any of the above questions.

How did you get on? Did you pass the exam by reading question 10 and not completing the previous questions? Life is a bit like climbing a mountain. You must not think you have arrived because you can see the summit. The last step depends on the first, so watch your footing and be sure of the next step, but never let it distract you from your vision.

It's incredibly easy to get caught up in an activity trap. You work harder and harder at climbing the ladder of success only to discover upon reaching the top that it's against the wrong wall. It is possible to be extremely busy without being effective. People often find themselves achieving victories that are empty – success that has come at the expense of things they suddenly realise were far more valuable to them. At the end of the day it is better to be at the bottom of the right ladder than climbing the wrong one!

In today's world most people place their self-worth and value purely on the material possessions they have, but if you think about great leaders such as Gandhi and Nelson Mandela you realise that they are remembered not for what they had, but for what they did and the kind of person they were. You don't need to be in the league of these great people to be effective leaders however. Joseph Badaracco in his book, *Leading Quietly – An Unorthodox Guide to Doing the Right Thing,* writes '...the most effective leaders are ordinary, unassuming men and women who possess three quiet virtues – modesty, restraint and tenacity. These quiet virtues are not reserved for special people or extraordinary events...' I mention this so that if you are the quiet, unassuming type you will know that you can also be a leader.

> *Whether it is in our own life, at work, or an individual project we are working on we need leadership before we get into the managing and doing.*
> *Leadership is about taking a step back, thinking about the end result, thinking about the direction to go in, looking at the 'big picture' and being focussed on the whole.*
>
> Joseph Addison

Find somewhere quiet and do the following: Visualise your perfect life – a life in complete balance, full of joy, fulfilment, and achievement. What does it look like to you?

This picture of your perfect future will help you when you come to do your plans as you will have a clear picture of the end result you are striving towards. This equally applies to everything else in your life – every project, every day, every week, every month and every year. If you know what result you want, you can put in the correct plans and take the correct action to get there.

Never underestimate the power of imagination and visualisation, especially when coupled with a positive attitude and life-affirming beliefs. Just think of how many inventions came from this special combination, which is sometimes referred to as *visionary determination* – aeroplanes, electricity, radio communications to name a few.

You need to identify what is most important to you and how, by creating a direction in accordance with this, you can achieve worthy goals, create balance, and leave some kind of legacy. Most people's major weakness lies not in the riches they lack, but in their *failure to make use of that which they already have!*

Defining an ideal is not a once only proposition. You can decide on one today, and change it later. In fact, re-evaluating and re-forming your ideal is normal. The important thing is to start developing an awareness of your ideal. One way of doing this is to keep a journal of your daily experiences to help you make an honest evaluation of your life in terms of an ideal. You can even use it to write a first outline of your ideal life.

In your journal or diary each evening, or morning if this suits you better, make notes about your experiences including your thoughts, actions, emotional responses and any inner experiences. Write about how you overcame problems you encountered, and your frustrations and satisfactions. Allow these notes to accumulate and review them at the end of each month. Ask yourself what your best and worst moments were. You will be able to pinpoint aspects that moved you closer to your ideal, and see others that led you further from it. Analyse the positive aspects to find out what it is about them that you particularly like.

Your best moments are celebrations and expressions of positive values. Look at those values. There you will find clues to the ideals you hold. It is also important to analyse the negative aspects to find out what it was about them you disliked. In summary, ideals can be used to both chart the course of your ideal life and to reach your goals. You will then have a solid foundation to bring your ideal life into reality.

The first (leadership perspective) principle for a successful life is the written goal (mission/vision statement), which creates the clear picture in your mind of your perfect life. This will act as a rudder for your *life–ship* and gives you the energy and commitment to follow through with the second principle: the action that produces the results.

Look at the room you are in now and notice the décor and layout. What you are looking at is a *visual perception* – thoughts that have come into materialisation through someone's creativity. You will use this same visualisation capacity to transfer your thoughts into a written statement – only instead of designing a room you design your life.

## Purpose

*'Few will have the greatness to bend history itself, but each of us can work to change a small portion of events… it is from numberless acts of courage and belief that human history is shaped.'*

Robert F. Kennedy

What's it all about? What's the point? Is there any point? Should we bother? Are we here for a reason – if so what is it? Who am I? Why? I'm confident you've asked yourself one, or some of these questions at one time or another.

Consider the following people – what do they have in common? Mother Teresa, Martin Luther-King, Nelson Mandela, Gandhi, Mikhail Gorbachev, Winston Churchill, Isambard Kingdom Brunel and Bill Gates. Although they all had significantly different beliefs, careers and trod different paths, their commonality lies in the power of *purpose* they had in their lives. Other relatively unknown people can also possess a deep sense of *purpose*. I have met ordinary people driven by their own purpose to help make the world a better place – for example, a farmer who is driven to change the way we see food production and a school teacher who works to change children's perspectives about racism. We all have a choice of either designing a life around a purpose, or one that is just about survival. For what purpose were you created? This is a question only you can answer.

No one else can give you a sense of purpose; if they did could you commit to it fully? Your purpose will be instinctive, intuitive, something that requires you to search your mind, heart and soul. Before considering your purpose, look at some of the characteristics of a purpose: It focuses on *contributing,* it uses your *gifts and talents,* it is *meaningful,* it is *enjoyable and fun* for you, it *inspires* you and it is *continuous.*

Unlike a goal, which is something that can be reached, a purpose is a direction. When you are *on course* you are *on purpose.*

> *'Know what you want. Great minds have purposes;*
> *others have wishes.'*
> Washington Irving

Having a purpose in our lives is not a formula for happiness and success – we need action as well for that – but it is the fundamental answer to what makes living worthwhile. If you have a *why* you will certainly find the *how,* regardless of the challenges ahead. A purpose can bring fame and fortune, but the real reward is in how it enriches our lives.

In studies of successful men and women one of the most impressive discoveries is that they moved with purpose. They succeeded because they knew what they wanted, and committed themselves to plans to achieve their goal. Thomas Edison had 10,000 failures but his persistence and commitment finally had him discover the secret of the electric lamp.

> *'If one advances confidently in the direction of his dreams, and*
> *endeavours to live the life which he has imagined, he will meet with a*
> *success unexpected in common hours.'*
> Henry David Thoreau.

Our purpose and dream gives us a *future* focus, and prevents us from wasting our life. I've lost count of the number of people in their 30s, 40s or 50s who have suddenly realised they are not who they want to be. Their life has nothing to show for the years they have been here, so they panic, live in regret, or endure a crisis wishing they had chosen differently. One person I spoke to expressed deep regret, saying, 'I never learned to dream dreams. They were there at one time and I let them disappear. I have no purpose to keep me going.' If you have a purpose and believe you will achieve your dreams, you will wake up in your 60s, 70s and 80s and realise not only how much you have accomplished, but also how much you still want to accomplish.

As children we are full of excitement and enthusiasm, but when we experience setbacks in life we begin to question whether we should dream and have a purpose. It is then that we become *given ups* rather than *grown ups*. Having a purpose and dream gives us a fulfilled life that is meaningful, exciting, and deeply rewarding.

Some of the *purposes* I have come across include: 'I am a devoted father.' 'I serve the planet in which we live.' 'I am an exuberant explorer.' 'I give more than I take.' 'I love life.'

> *'The problem with many people in the west is not that they aren't where they should be, but that they aren't what they should be where they are!'*
> Os Guinness

However the discovery of a purpose can take time. Here are a few suggestions to help you find your purpose.

1. Use visioning (see below) to tap into your creative mind and visualise yourself fulfilling your purpose.
2. Make a list of all your positive qualities – ask true friends and family members for help if necessary. Narrow down each good quality to one or two words – giving, caring, loving, for example. Choose a few of the words you feel comfortable with and arrange them in sentences starting with: 'I…' or 'I am …' When you discover your purpose, it will *click* and you will know it.
3. Before going to sleep, give yourself the following instruction: *When I wake up in the morning, I will know my purpose*. And write down whatever comes to you as soon as you wake up.
4. Go to a peaceful place, and ask yourself the question: *What is my purpose*? See what thoughts come to you, and make a note of them.

Once you discover your purpose, I suggest you don't tell anyone. This will make it powerful and keep it powerful.

Once you know your purpose it becomes easier to choose and achieve goals. The real test of any action is to ask yourself: 'Does this help fulfil my purpose?'

As Robert Byrne once said,

*'The purpose of life is a life of purpose.'*

The use of powerful words will help you discover your purpose, acting upon our conscious and sub-conscious mind just as the nutrients in food act upon your body. Below is a list of powerful words to help you create your purpose. Think of your own words to add to the list.

Achievement, activity, alertness, abundance, concentration, charity, consideration, confidence, capable, compassion, creative, courtesy, decisive, energy, faith, freedom, goodwill, guidance, grace, gentleness, generosity, humility, health, happiness, harmony, honesty, inspiration, intelligence, justice, kindness, law, life, love, memory, merit, mastery, non-resistance, peace, poise, persistence, purpose, power, resourcefulness, sympathy, spirit, strength, sincerity, success, serenity, tolerance, unity, vitality, youth.

Look at the words that seem most appropriate to you, and examine and interpret their meaning, noticing the effect they have on you. Now write down your own purpose – remember to start with 'I...' or 'I am...'

## Do you Have a Pipe Dream... or a Pipeline Vision?

**The Parable of the Pipeline** (1801, valley in central Italy)

*Two ambitious young cousins named Pablo and Bruno were best friends and big dreamers waiting for an opportunity. One day that opportunity arrived when Pablo and Bruno were hired to carry water from the river to a cistern in the village square, earning one penny for each bucket of water.*

*'This is our dream come true!' shouted Bruno. 'I can't believe our good fortune.'*

*But Pablo was sure there was a better way of transporting water. 'Bruno, I have a plan,' Pablo said the next morning as they headed* for the river. 'Instead of lugging buckets, let's build a pipeline from the river to the village.'

Bruno stopped dead in his tracks. 'A Pipeline! Whoever heard of such a thing? We have the best job in town. Don't go on to me about your pipeline.'

But Pablo was not easily discouraged. He knew it would take a year or two, but eventually his pipeline would pay big dividends. Pablo believed in his dream, and went to work while Bruno and the rest of the villagers mocked him.

## Small Actions Equal Big Results

The work was hard, but Pablo kept reminding himself that tomorrow's dreams are built on today's sacrifices. One day after months of toil Pablo realised his pipeline was halfway finished. Now he only had to walk half as far to fill up his buckets! Finally, Pablo's big day arrived – the pipeline was complete! The villagers crowded around as water gushed from the pipeline into the village cistern! The pipeline brought prosperity to the village, and Pablo the Pipeline Man was now known as Pablo the Miracle Maker. But for Pablo this was merely the first stage of a big, big dream. You see, Pablo had plans that reached far beyond his village. Pablo planned to build pipelines all over the world!

## Recruiting His Friend to Help

The pipeline had driven Bruno the Bucket Man out of business, and it pained Pablo to see his old friend begging for free drinks in the tavern. So, Pablo arranged a meeting. 'Bruno, I've come here to ask you for your help.'

Bruno straightened his stooped shoulders and his dark eyes narrowed to a squint. 'Don't mock me,' Bruno hissed.

'I haven't come to gloat,' said Pablo. 'I've come here to offer you a great business opportunity. I could build a pipeline a year by myself, but that would not be the best use of my time. I plan to teach you and others how to build a pipeline until there is a pipeline to every village in the region… then a pipeline to every village in the country… and eventually, a pipeline to every village in the world!

Bruno finally saw the Big Picture. They shook hands…. and then hugged like long lost friends.

## Pipeline Dreams in a Bucket – Carrying World

Years passed. Pablo and Bruno had long since retired from their worldwide pipeline business. Sometimes on their trips through the countryside, Pablo and Bruno would pass young men carrying water *buckets. The childhood friends would stop and offer to help them build their own pipeline, but while a few would listen and relish the opportunity to start a pipeline business, the majority hastily dismissed the notion. Pablo and Bruno heard the same excuses over and over: 'I don't have the time.'*

*'My friend told me he knew a friend of a friend who tried to build a pipeline and failed.'*

*'Only the ones who get in early make money on pipelines.'*

*'I've carried buckets all my life. I'll stick with what I know.'*

*'I know some people who lost money in a pipeline scam. Not me.'*

*It made Pablo and Bruno sad that so many people lacked vision. But both men resigned themselves to the fact that they lived in a bucket-carrying world…. and that only a small percentage of people dared to dream pipeline dreams.*

## Personal Leadership Qualities

*'The task of leadership is to align strengths in ways that make weaknesses irrelevant.'*
Peter Drucker

Before you write up your own vision/mission statement, here are some key personal leadership qualities I've compiled from reading autobiographies of great leaders, books on leadership and from my own observations:

- ❖ The essence of leadership is the ability to **translate a vision** or mental picture into reality. It is to lead people by communicating to them their true potential in such a way that they can clearly see it for and in themselves.
- ❖ Leaders are guided by correct **principles/morals** and well thought-out self-chosen **values.** By focussing on correct principles we create balance and have a foundation for all decisions and relationships. What principles are important to you?
- ❖ Leaders are **visionary** and keep their eyes on the horizon, not just the bottom line.
- ❖ Leaders stay **flexible,** adapting to new realities ahead of the pack rather than reacting to the current crisis.
- ❖ Leaders have a sense of **responsibility, contribution and service** to others, and see life as a mission, not a career.
- ❖ Leaders **believe in other people**, and want to help them achieve their full potential, seeing the oak tree in the acorn.

- ❖ Leaders are prepared to **continually learn**, by reading, attending training courses, and seeking knowledge from other people.
- ❖ Leaders live life as an **adventure,** and love the challenge and excitement of something new.
- ❖ Leaders embrace **change** and find a way of making change work. They work smart as well as hard; building on strengths and compensating for weaknesses, especially when working within a team.
- ❖ Leaders are **positive** and say *can* rather than *can't*. They have constructive and motivated desires and aim high. How positive are you?
- ❖ Leaders keep in **balance** their life, views, communication, the way they treat others, and their actions and attitudes.
- ❖ Leaders exercise **humility**, and do not need to *make an appearance*, play mind games, or try to be all things to all people.
- ❖ Leaders are **honest** and act with **integrity**, exhibiting soundness of character.
- ❖ Leaders exercise **compassion** balanced by the **courage** not to be manipulated and to stand their ground when needed.
- ❖ Leaders **invest in themselves**, realising that they are the most valuable asset they have.
- ❖ Leaders focus on their **character** before their personality. Rather than trying to change other people, they try and change themselves.
- ❖ Leaders live through their **conscience,** and exercise honest living. They can return kindness for offensive behaviour, go the second mile, and feel no need to justify themselves.
- ❖ Leaders live to the **future**, overcoming the pull of their past, and realising that they can take responsibility for their own life. They can imagine and visualise their **vision** and **mission** in life.
- ❖ Leaders know that **comparisons with others** are dangerous, because real security is internal, not external.
- ❖ Leaders are **self-aware** and realise to improve they must start from their current base, not from where they should be, or where someone else is.
- ❖ Leaders **listen** to others and respect different opinions.
- ❖ Leaders understand **wealth comes from work**, and that something for nothing is a fallacy.

- ❖ Leaders understand that business and **ethics** can come together, and that economic and political systems can be based on a moral foundation.
- ❖ Leaders understand that **technology** is a **servant** of **humanity**, and there is a need to develop humans as well as technology.
- ❖ Leaders know that **image** is less important than substance of character and principle, recognising that no amount of money spent creating the right image can compensate for a flawed fundamental character.
- ❖ Leaders exercise a **legitimate leadership style** based on others believing in them and trusting and respecting them. They exercise self-discipline and therefore are an (and can lead by) example to others.
- ❖ Leaders exercise **patience** with both procedures and people, and are able to **persuade** by using reason and communication to find mutual benefit outcomes.
- ❖ Leaders are **sensitive** to the thoughts, feelings, and needs of others.
- ❖ Leaders are **open to new ideas** and acknowledge that they do not have all the answers.
- ❖ Leaders are prepared to do noble things **anonymously** without the need to boost their self-image.
- ❖ Leaders take **responsibility** for their life and do not blame others for their circumstances.
- ❖ Leaders do **not give up, or give in** and generate the will to see things through.
- ❖ Leaders strive for **total quality** in all that they do, recognising that the results can be revolutionary.
- ❖ Leaders are not **afraid to try new things** and will take calculated risks. *'A ship in harbour is safe, but that was not what ships were made for.'*

Before going further with your vision and mission statement, you also need to be aware of a *swamp* – the obsessions that can indirectly control us and deflect us from our purpose. When looking through the following list (and I am sure you can think of more), ask yourself two questions:

1. How much of an obsession is this to me?
2. If it is an obsession, what would happen to my self-worth if it were not there anymore?

Do I have an obsession about?

- My spouse or partner?
- Money?
- My family?
- Myself?
- My ex-partner, ex-business partner, or anyone else I regard as an enemy?
- Friends or a particular friend?
- My religion?
- My material wealth and possessions?
- Work – Am I a workaholic?
- Having a good time – instant gratification?
- Peers and peer group pressure?
- Eating, smoking, or drinking?

Connecting to our values helps us keep things in perspective, and identify what should guide us, giving us the power to say, 'NO.'

*'Decide what you want, decide what you are willing to exchange for it. Establish your priorities and go to work.'*

H. L. Hunt

## Visioning Your Future

The secret with visioning is to vision whatever it is you want as though it has already been achieved. As though the life you want is already here. See yourself *having* what you want, *doing* what you want to do, and *being* the person you want to be. You *don't need* to vision the steps to get there – your conscious mind does that for you.

*'Vision is the capacity to believe in what my heart sees, what others can't see. Vision is seeing positive possibilities where others see only negative probabilities.'*

Carl A. Hammerschlag

Now let's do a simple visualisation. First, relax physically, perhaps by listening to relaxing music or whatever suits you best. Secondly, visualise an important future birthday, taking time to really imagine the scenario – it could be your 40th, 50th, 80th, 90th or 100th! Now picture a group of your closest work colleagues in a corner of the room. They are talking about how you helped and inspired them, and what you have been like to work with. What are they saying?

In the next corner there are a group of your friends, and they are saying what you have done for them, and the things they really like about you. What are they saying?

In the next corner are closest family members talking about their relationship to you, what you have done within the family, what they think about you, and the kind of person you are to them. What are they saying?

In the final corner of the room are a group of people you socialise and possibly play sport with. Again, they are talking about the kind of person you are, how you have been to them, and how you have contributed to their lives. What are they saying?

When you have completed this exercise, think about what you would like these people to say about you in the future. It will give a good indication of the sort of person you want to be; what is important internally to you, and what will be worth striving towards.

With visualisation, when you *feel* that the picture has connected with your creative side, you may want to use an affirmation (see below) to add conviction to it. Repeat the visualisation of what you want regularly throughout the day until the visual image becomes factual for you.

When visualisations are backed up with powerful positive language, such as self-talk in the form of affirmations, and followed through with willpower, this often gives you results way beyond those you originally hoped for.

If you find it difficult to see beyond your current reality with its challenges and problems, try *pipe-dreaming* your way out of it. The Wright brothers had a pipe-dream, as some saw it, when they visualised themselves designing and flying the first aeroplane. Many people ridiculed their dream, but the brothers fortunately had the courage to persist, and gave future generations an amazing new mode of transport.

## Using *Affirmations* to Cement your Vision

An **affirmation** is a positive, substantive, and assertive statement. It can turn negative feelings, thoughts and emotions into positive ones; give conviction to visualisations; give you the will to tackle current challenges, and substantiate and cement your perception or paradigm changes.

A good affirmation has five basic ingredients; it must be *personal, positive, in present tense, visual* and have *emotion* attached to it. Here's an example: 'I am *(personal)* extremely excited *(emotional attachment)* that I am *(present tense)* fulfilling my dream *(positive)* of helping people less fortunate than myself and I dream and picture *(visual)* myself continuing on my quest with endeavour, pride, accomplishment, commitment and dignity.'

A powerful technique to use when repeating your affirmations is to say them whilst looking into your own eyes in the mirror. You may experience some limiting thoughts and self-doubt about what it is you are focusing upon and affirming, but persevere, and the seed of the affirmation **will** be sown deep within you. Use affirmations regularly and consistently for each experience you want to manifest. They do not need to be complex: 'I am very generous,' 'I am very content,' 'I am happy, vigorous and successful in the pursuit of my goals.'

Now write and practice a few affirmations for yourself, including your purpose. Here's one to get you started: 'I am happy, successful and always do the best that I can, using everything for my advancement.'

Here are a few more examples of affirmations:

My ideal self is loving towards all in all situations.
I am courageous and experience security and peace in all situations.
I am confident of my ability to deal with life situations and events.
I am resourceful in dealing with changes and problems.
I am freely creative in all situations.
I enjoy whatever I do.
I play and enjoy laughter.
I enjoy working, producing, and creating.
I enjoy freedom of expression – writing, singing, dancing, and celebrating life.
I care about my friends, and support them.
I do what is good, nurturing, and beneficial for both others and me.
I take care of my body and mind with healthy food, exercise, and relaxation.
I am understanding, kind and gentle with others – as I would like them to be with me.
I forgive other people as I would like them to forgive me.
I forgive myself as I learn from my mistakes.
I recognise that I have many faults and much room for improvement.
I am comfortable with and accept pain, weakness, need and negativity in others as well as myself.

I experience unity with all beings – human, animals and plants – and am interested in their well-being.

I am generous with my resources.

I share my time, money, energy and life force with others seeking the benefit of the whole.

I need little for myself, and thus have an abundance of time and energy for others.

I am honoured to be able to serve others in various ways.

I experience a steady feeling of inner self-worth as an expression of the divine.

I am humble without need for recognition or affirmation.

I experience unity even with those who disagree with or criticise me.

I make time to meditate and experience my inner source.

I perceive all situations and events as opportunities for growth and learning.

I take total responsibility for my reality – remembering that others are simply actors in the play I have written and am writing for myself.

I perceive my loved ones and others as fellow souls in the process of evolution.

I work for the joy of creation – bettering the world around me.

I am a happy person.

I share my happiness with others.

I am happy for other people's happiness.

Athletes and sports people have used this process for many years. They visualise themselves achieving the best they can in their chosen sport and support the images with affirmations. In fact, research shows that almost all world-class performers use visualisation – they see, feel, and experience their desire before they actually achieve it.

## What is a Vision and Mission?

Martin Luther King, Jr. said, 'I have a dream,' and what followed was a vision that changed a nation. That famous speech is a dramatic example of the power that can be generated by a person who communicates a compelling vision of the future.

For a company or organisation, management author Tom Peters identified a clear vision of the desired future state of the organisation as an essential component of high performance. Widely-read organisational development author Warren Bennis also identified the ability to create a vision as a key factor that made leaders great.

But what is the difference between a vision and a mission? Winston Churchill, Great Britain's Second World War Prime Minister had the **vision** of a free Europe. His **mission** was to win the war.

*'Some see things as they are and say why? And others see things as they are, and say why not?'*

J F Kennedy

Saying, 'Why not?' is vision. How things COULD be done better rather than staying with the status quo.

There is one universal rule. You will never be greater than the vision that guides you. No Olympic athlete ever got to the Olympics by mistake; a compelling vision of his or her stellar performance inevitably guides all the sweat and tears. Your vision statement should require you to stretch your expectations, aspirations, and performance. Without that powerful, attractive, valuable vision, why bother?

## How a Vision is Used

John Bryson, author of *Strategic Planning for Public and Nonprofit Organisations*, says that, typically, a vision is 'more important as a guide to implementing strategy than it is to formulating it.' This is because the development of strategy is driven by what you are trying to accomplish. A mission statement answers the questions: Why do I exist? What am I all about? What values will guide me? A vision, however, is more encompassing. It answers the question, 'What will success look like?' And it is in the pursuit of this image of success that you are motivated to pull out all the stops in your quest.

A vision statement should be realistic and credible, appropriate, ambitious, and responsive to change. It should orient your energies and serve as a guide to action. It should be consistent with your values. In short, a vision should challenge and inspire you to achieve your goals.

## The Impact of Vision

The impact of having a vision and mission will be substantial. A vision/mission statement will enable your life to be more cohesive, and become your rock, a solid foundation for the building of the rest of your life.

Living by your mission takes you towards a higher purpose, and the world *can* become a better place because you are being directed by your mission. A mission can be built upon the principle of contribution: getting follows giving, rewards follow giving service, and leaving a legacy follows making a difference. Put another way, before determining what it is we want, we need to know what it is we have to offer.

In an amazing study on goal setting, Yale University in the USA surveyed the graduating class of 1953 to determine how many had written goals for their future lives. Only 3% had such a vision. In 1973, the surviving members of the class of 1953 were surveyed again. The 3% with future vision had accumulated greater wealth than the other 97% combined.

## Shared Vision

To a leader the genesis of the dream is unimportant. The great leader is the servant of the dream, the bearer of the myth, the story teller. 'It is the idea (vision) that unites people in the common effort, not the charisma of the leader,' writes Robert Greenleaf in *Leadership Crisis*. He goes on to write:

> *Optimal performance rests on the existence of a powerful shared vision that evolves through wide participation to which the key leader contributes, but which the use of authority cannot shape…. The test of greatness of a dream is that it has the energy to lift people out of their moribund ways to a level of being and relating from which the future can be faced with more hope than most of us can summon today.*

## The Process for Creating a Vision

Like much of strategic planning, creating a vision begins with intuition and dreaming.

If the vision is for your organisation you may mindstorm with your staff or your board what you would like to accomplish in the future. Talk about and write down the values you share in pursuing that vision. Different ideas do not have to be a problem. People can spur each other on to more daring dreams and visions that they are then willing to work hard for.

The vision may evolve through a strategic planning process. Or it may be formed in one person's head in the shower one morning! The important point is that members of an organisation without a vision may toil, but they cannot possibly be creative in finding new and better ways to get closer to a vision without that vision formally in place. Non-profit organisations, with staff and board members actively looking for ways to achieve a vision, have a powerful competitive and strategic advantage over organisations that operate without a vision.

When visioning possible changes, ask, 'What is the preferred future?' and:

- Draw on the beliefs, mission, and environment of the organisation.
- Describe what you want to see in the future.
- Be specific.
- Be positive and inspiring.
- Avoid assuming that the system will have the same framework as it does today.

It is exactly the same for individuals. If you really want to achieve something memorable or contribute to the world in a worthwhile way – create a vision.

## Benefits of Visioning

The process and outcomes of visioning may seem vague and superfluous. However, the long-term benefits are substantial.

## Visioning:

- Breaks you out of boundary thinking.
- Provides continuity and avoids the stutter effect of planning fits and starts.
- Identifies direction and purpose.
- Alerts us to needed change.
- Promotes interest and commitment.
- Promotes laser-sharp focus.
- Encourages openness to unique and creative solutions.
- Encourages and builds confidence.
- In organisations vision builds loyalty through involvement (ownership).
- Results in effectiveness and encourages *doing the right things* rather than just *doing things right*.

## Vision Killers

As you engage in the visioning process, be alert to the following vision killers:

- Tradition
- Not believing in the power of a vision
- Fear of ridicule
- Stereotypes of people, conditions, roles etc.
- Complacency of some stakeholders (in an organisation)
- Fatigued leaders (in an organisation)
- Short-term thinking
- 'Nay Sayers' and negative energy drainers.

What is your personal vision?

## Mission Statement – What is It?

A mission statement is a personal and powerful statement which sets out your intent for your future. It gives a purpose and direction to your life and future based on your values and beliefs. It is a broad outline of how you will accomplish your vision and purpose. To produce a valid statement of intent you need to be creative and go beyond your current reality. Your statement also needs to be flexible, so you can update, change and enhance it when necessary.

A mission statement encourages you to think deeply about your life as it is, and as you would like it to be.

Think about what is really most important to you?

What are your deepest thoughts, feelings, values and beliefs?

What are you all about as a person?

What qualities of character, leadership and personality do you want to have?

How do you want to be remembered?

If you could change anything, what would it be?

# Creating your own Mission Statement

To start creating your mission statement look at what you want out of life, what you want to do with your life, and the kind of person you want to be.

To the question 'What you would like to have?' beware of answering, 'I want it all.' Because if you had it *all* where would you put it? If you find yourself thinking like this you probably need to take more time to explore what you really want.

Some would say that you can have anything you want, but you live within physical limitations; you can only be in one place at any one time, there are only 24 hours in a day and 7 days in a week, and your life expectancy is limited!

However, history is full of people who have sought the so-called impossible and achieved it. Bear in mind, that the more unobtainable what you want is, the more you will have to sacrifice in order to obtain it. You only have so much time to spend, so spend it well.

Imagine the analogy of being in a large superstore (the planet in which we live) where you are given enough money (time) to buy anything, but not everything, in the superstore. You may decide to put a *want* in your shopping cart such as a new career, car, or house, but you don't consider its cost, which is the time it will take to obtain and maintain the want. You could even find yourself out of time!

Some say time is money, so with money you can buy time. But you can't buy people to do the things you want to experience – fly your own plane, climb Everest, trek across the Sahara, or drive a Formula One racing car. And can you hire people to spend time with your family and friends? The point is that the wants will always outnumber the hours in a day, so choose carefully at the outset.

**What are the things in life you would really like to have?**
**What are the things you really want to do?**
**What sort of person are you striving to be?**

*'Ever more people today have the means to live,*
*but no meaning to live for.'*

Victor Frankl

These are the things that are going to be most important to you. They may be possession–led (a type of house, for example) or non-possession–led (such as freedom to travel or enough surplus financial income to give to your favourite good cause).

Some things you want because you really want them. Other things you want are because you think they will give you what you want. The first category is intentions or desires – the second, methods or behaviours.

You might say, 'I want a sports car,' but discover that your true desire is to have adventure and fun. Instead you could simply write a list of things you consider fun to do. In this example, fun is the desire, and the activities listed are your methods or behaviours.

In order to get what you want, you need to know what you want. If you don't know where you want to go, you are not going to get there. If career choice is more important than finding a romantic relationship, that's fine as long as it is what *you* want. If *you* want a relationship, and family is important to you, your career orientated friends may not understand, but does that matter?

It helps to recognise therefore that wanting the house, car, better body, career, money, even perhaps the perfect relationship or spiritual path are simply the method or behaviour to get something else. Something inner and experiential such as security, fun, satisfaction or inner peace.

It is helpful to know this so that you can write lists of methods and behaviours to achieve the experience you seek. What you might find is that you can fulfil most of your desires and intentions without much help from outside at all. And much of it you can give yourself straight away. Want fun? Be fun loving. Want love? Love yourself.

Ironically, once we give fully to ourselves, possessions and symbols often become less important. Who would you rather be around – a fun loving, joyful, happy person or a miserable, needy, unhappy (and rich) person?

When you are genuinely *up* because *you* are the source, inspiration and reason for that feeling, people pick up on this. Of everything external you want, get into the habit of asking yourself, 'What experience am I looking for?'

Who is wealthier – the person who is addicted to material possessions, or the person who is free from this? Truly wealthy people carry their riches with them. The less they need of this physical world, the wealthier they are. They may or may not have large sums of money. Their security comes from within – the sign of true inner wealth.

True wealth is to have health, happiness, abundance in life, to be loving and able to accept love, being caring and sharing, being able to learn, knowing what you want and what you want to do with your life, enjoyment, balance, giving back and helping others. Truly wealthy people make a real difference.

*Make your life extraordinary and leave a legacy. Life is a mission not a career. A mission is a cause. A Career asks, 'What's in it for me?' A mission asks, 'How can I make a difference?'*

These are the words of *Gandhi* whose mission was to liberate 350 million people! But we can all do small things in a great way.

## Writing your Vision and Mission Statement

*During the early stages of the building of Liverpool Cathedral, an American visitor approached a workman and asked him what he was doing. The man replied, 'I'm mixing mortar.' The visitor asked a second man, 'And what are you doing?' and received the curt answer, 'Carrying bricks.' He asked the question again and this time drew a proud response from a brick layer, 'I am building a Cathedral.'*

Think big. Gather as many of your ideas and thoughts as possible and put them down on paper. Write for as long as you can – you can edit it later. When you do write your initial draft of your own vision and mission statement, start with 'I am…' as this will give it the positive pull of a visual affirmation.

Here are some powerful statements that people have included in their personal mission statements:

- I will ensure my life is balanced, honest and honourable.

- I will place family before business.

- I will develop a new skill or proficiency every year.

- I will never compromise on my ethics, principles, and values.

- I will concentrate on my immediate tasks.

- I will always think deeply before making decisions.

- I will always consider the feelings of others in everything I do.

- I will act with compassion, understanding and integrity in everything I do.

*'Often people attempt to live their lives backwards; they try to have more things, or more money, in order to do more of what they want, so they will be happier. The way it actually works is the reverse. You must first be who you really are, then do what you need to do, in order to have what you want.'*

Margaret Young

Take some time and firstly write your personal vision statement (your picture of your ideal life, your purpose).

Then write your mission which will be a broad outline of your journey towards your vision and also detailing what you want to have in your life, what you want to do and the person you're going to be. Make them exciting, inspiring and meaningful.

Now you know what it means to have a purpose in life. Most importantly you recognise what steps to take to find your purpose. You know what it means to be the leader of your life, how to shape your future and how to acquire the characteristics of a true leader. The power of affirmations and visualisation will help, as you have now detailed what you *want* in your life, what you want to *do* as well as what kind of person you want to *be*. Now you have written your own vision and mission statement you are all set to determine your future.

The journey continues…

# Action 4

## Take Control

*'A vision without a task is but a dream. A task without a vision is drudgery. A task with a vision is the hope of the world.'*

Inscription on a church in Sussex, England, circa 1730.

To achieve your mission and vision to take you toward your purpose you need to make changes, decisions and commitments. And you need to identify your goals. In this chapter you get to do just that. In many respects this is the self-management chapter as the results you get here act as a catalyst for your future achievement, growth, happiness and internal satisfaction. However, to achieve all this there is one vital quality you need – willpower!

### Developing Your Willpower

*'I have a woman's ability to stick to a job and get on with it, even when everyone else walks off and leaves it.'*

Margaret Thatcher

To achieve *true* success you need to develop willpower. Willpower does not cost anything, and the moment you say, and mean, 'I will!' it works. Results demand action, and goal-orientated people know that action is the *only way* their goals and dreams will be realised. It may be tempting to delay until you are completely sure that success is guaranteed, but if you always wait for assurances or for the time to be right, you will never take any action.

In the cup final one team wins, another loses. If both sets of players waited for assurances that they would win, there wouldn't be a cup final. You too have to act and use your talents to accomplish your goals.

*'So many of our dreams at first seem impossible, then they seem improbable, and then when we summon the will, they soon become inevitable.'*

Christopher Reeve, died 2004

One word of caution here, however, and that is the negative effect of too much effort. Ambitious striving and expectation are great, but be aware of over-exertion, of straining your mind and being unable to see the wood from the trees.

A musician was asked what happened if the strings on his instrument were too tight. The musician replied that it would be out of tune. He was then asked what would happen if the strings were too loose, and he gave the same reply. In the same way, our efforts when *over-strung* will end in agitation and tension, and when *too lax* will end in sloth and frustration. The quality of our energy must neither be too tight nor too loose; only then will it become the root of all of our achievements.

Pen Hadow, an explorer based in Dartmoor in the South West of England, was the first person to walk without support to both the North and South Poles. When he spoke about the formidable target that had dominated almost every day of his life for 15 years, he said, 'To achieve my eventual success required an exceptional degree of *FOCUS,* a preparedness to *SACRIFICE* things that some would find uncomfortable to live without, and a commitment to *PERSEVERE* until the job was finally done.'

> *'True courage is not incompatible with nervousness*
> *and heroism does not mean the absence of fear*
> *but the conquest of it.'*
> Van Dyke

**The will is a** *changer,* enabling us to stop a chain of thought and say, 'Hold on, I don't have to think this way!'

**The will is also a** *developer* and while the patterns of the mind are governed by the past, the will is directed toward the future. This is why we need to develop our willpower before we tackle our goals.

**The will is a** *chooser,* choosing the focus of attention, so that our attention will follow our will rather than following the path of habit.

**The will is** *directional.* The mind patterns energy, the will directs it. The will gives us the impetus for growth and evolution.

**The will can also be an** *individualiser,* distinguishing our true self and our individuality.

**The will is also a** *guide,* selecting our choices and the creative function of our mind.

**The will can also exist in** *opposition to the mind* and is powerful when we want to change the habits of our mind.

We need to balance the use of willpower with the art of reflection. Pascal, the seventeenth century philosopher and mathematician, wrote, 'Most of the problems in the world would be solved if people could learn to sit still in a room.'

*'What this power is, I cannot say. All I know is that it exists…. and it becomes available only when you are in that state of mind in which you know EXACTLY what you want… and are fully determined not to quit until you get it.'*

Alexander Graham Bell

## Looking at Failure

*'The greatest pleasure in life is doing what people say you cannot do.'*

Walter Bagehot

There is no such thing as a hopeless situation, only hopeless people. Failure is only temporary. And failure helps us reach our goals if we allow it to teach us where we need to improve.

Of his remarkable feats on the battlefields of Europe, General Bradley said: 'A second-best decision quickly arrived at and vigorously carried out is better than the best decision too late arrived at and half-heartedly carried out. In everyday affairs, as in battle, we are given one life to live, and the decision is ours whether to wait for circumstances to make up our mind or to act and in acting to live.'

*'Nature gave men two ends – one to sit on and one to think with. Ever since then man's success or failure has been dependent on which one he uses the most.'*

George R. Kirkpatrick

## Developing the Will to Take Action

Disraeli once said, 'Action may not always bring happiness, but there is no happiness without action.' If you are motivated, and have the will to achieve your goals and give 100% but, for reasons beyond your control, you do not achieve it, you may not be happy, however you will be *satisfied* that you have given it your best.

*'Determination is born out of purpose, knowing that you are gifted for something and this something must be attained. It is never enough to rely on luck or natural talent. You must, above all, believe in yourself, face your goals, and then fight as if your life depends on it, then go over, go under, go through, but never give up.'*

The world is full of opportunities just waiting to be acted upon, and new ones turn up every day. The only way to make the most of these opportunities is through *action*. Have the courage to act on your ideas, take decisive action towards your goals, and you will certainly change your life. And, as **The 10 Actions**® reveals, it is not the extraordinary, once-in-a-lifetime effort that ultimately brings you success – it is how you use your willpower when making everyday decisions.

To develop the will to take action, you need discipline from within. As E. M. Gray said in his essay, *The common denominator of success* – hard work, good luck and astute human relations are all important, but the one essential factor is that the 'successful person has the habit of doing the things failures don't like to do. They don't like doing them either necessarily. But their disliking is subordinated to the strength of their purpose.'

> *'If you look at most of the success stories from any walk of life they've all had to pass the persistence test.'*
> Peter Ebdon, World Snooker Champion 2002

Continually referring to your completed vision and mission statements is essential if you are to visualise your ideal future so vividly that it becomes compelling. Its power will then become your power, a far better option than just gritting your teeth and hoping.

If you make a tight fist and hold it until your arm begins to ache, and then try to hold it a little longer, where is the will? The decision to keep your fist clenched is an act of conscious willpower, whilst the aching is involuntary. The willpower to keep the fist closed requires you to decide to keep exerting that effort.

Now imagine that a robber is trying to prise open your fist to steal an extremely precious family heirloom. In this case your fist will clamp shut like a door that won't open. The discomfort of holding your fist closed is now secondary. The power to keep it clenched is drawn from your subconscious will's determination to hold on to the valuable object. Your imagination created a reality, and your will responded accordingly – this is an automatic response! You did not need to decide to use willpower to keep your hand closed.

However, you do need to be prepared for self-doubt when visualising goals, for as your imagination soars, doubt can creep in. You must be prepared to ignore the self-doubt, and summon the belief that you WILL accomplish what you set out to do.

> *'There is no challenge too great for those who have the will and heart to make it happen.'*

Another important principle for success is contribution. Many people get little because they give little. This is why the so-called success of many people is shallow and unfulfilling. If you are faithful to the principle of contribution, you will be amazed at what comes your way, and often find that you receive far more than you have given, even if it is not monetary.

For many people the fear of failure is too difficult an obstacle, perhaps because it involves stepping into an unknown future. If this is the case for you, change your perception to one of viewing the unknown as an exciting movement in the direction of your dreams, purpose, vision and mission. Make the decision now to never let fear hold you back; tackle it head on with courage and willpower. Remember, *It takes guts to leave the ruts!* Willpower is the ability to say *I will, I will, I will!* If you begin to automatically say *I will* rather than *I won't*, you find solutions rather than problems.

> *'You said but. I've put my finger on the whole trouble. You're a but man. Don't say, but. That little word but is the difference between success and failure. Henry Ford said, I'm going to build the automobile, and Arthur T. Flanken said, But…'*
>
> Sgt. Ernie Bilko, *The Phil Silvers Show*

As we learned with **Action 2**, we influence the outcome of our life. Successful people are not lucky – they design, plan, and work hard to put plans into action, and believe that success breeds more success. Make a vow now to never be envious of other people's success. Instead summon up the drive, enthusiasm, and commitment to take charge of your own future and create your own good fortune. Make that vow and write it down!

> *'When people say to me: How do you do so many things? I often answer them, without meaning to be cruel: How do you do so little? It seems to me that people have vast potential. Most people can do extraordinary things if they have the confidence or take the risks. Yet most people don't. They sit in front of the television and treat life as if it goes on forever.'*
>
> Philip Adams

No one else can lead you – they may help point you in the right direction, but you have to do the *walking and talking. I will* puts steam in your engine, and turns sluggishness into motion, whereas *I won't* paralyses the engine, and dampens enthusiasm and initiative. It doesn't matter how big or small – if your vision and goals are worthy to you, they are great. *To you* is the key in that last sentence.

For one person being Prime Minister is the goal, to another it could be taking a year out in a remote part of the world to write their long-envisioned book. Always be true to yourself.

We all know that there is a difference between the ordinary and extraordinary person. The difference is the word EXTRA. Extraordinary people put extra effort into whatever they do.

We have looked at the virtue of patience before, but as Denis Saleh, a contemporary poet and author once said, *'I have been hard at work now, longer than I like to remember, on a novel set in ancient Egypt. I've found out how the pyramids were built: slowly. Almost anything can be done, it seems, if one proceeds slowly enough, but we moderns cannot grasp this.'*

Often we are discouraged by the enormity of a task or the length of the journey, and become impatient with the challenges we face. We then can lose faith in the project or ourselves. Patience reminds us that what is in front of us is just one step, one further step towards our vision and mission, giving us the internal energy, will and power to go forward.

*'Learn the art of patience. Apply discipline to your thoughts when they become anxious over the outcome of a goal.*
*Impatience breeds anxiety, fear, discouragement and failure.*
*Patience creates confidence, decisiveness and a rational outlook, which eventually leads to success.'*
Brian Adams

## Identifying your Goals

To successfully achieve our goals we must differentiate between *efficiency* – getting the job done *right,* and *effectiveness* – getting the *right job done.*

At school I was never taught how to design plans for life and set goals. For many people goals are just an elusive wish list, rather than something clear, decisive, and as definite as day and night. Less than 5% of the population have written goals and less than 1% review and rewrite them from time to time.

Goal setting is a formal process for personal planning. By setting your goals on a routine basis you move step-by-step towards their achievement. By knowing precisely what you want to achieve, you know what you must concentrate on to do it.

Goal setting is a standard technique used by top-level athletes, successful business-people and achievers in all fields, giving long-term vision and short-term motivation. By setting sharp, clearly defined goals, you can see progress in what might previously have seemed a long pointless grind. The process of achieving goals also gives you the confidence to aim for higher and more difficult goals.

Goals are set on a number of different levels: First, you decide what you want to do with your life (your vision and mission) and what large-scale goals you want to achieve. Second, you break these down into smaller targets that you must hit in order to reach your lifetime vision and mission.

It makes sense to plan your future, as the rest of your life will be spent there! What are your goals for 5 years from now?

There are a few important points that you need to consider before setting your goals:

1.  Make them **action orientated** and **specific**. The more precise your targets, the more likely you will be to hit them.
2.  Make sure your goal is **measurable**. Rather than say *I want to be happy* or *I want to spend more time reflecting and reading*, actually define what will make you happy, or state the number of books you will read, otherwise you will not know when you have achieved your goal.
3.  Your goals need to be **challenging** but also **achievable**, slightly out of your immediate grasp, but not so far that they are totally out of reach.
4.  The goal must be **yours,** and not someone else's – follow your own heart rather than another's advice.
5.  There should be a **timescale** attached to each goal, so that it will keep you focused. The timescale should be realistic for the goal to be achieved.
6.  Have **more than one goal**, so that you do not become obsessive and include personal, family, career, financial, health and making-a-difference goals. Also make your goals compatible: For example, a goal of becoming the Managing Director of your company at any cost would not be compatible with a goal of being compassionate to others. Also remember the formula; *WIGS* – Wildly Important Goals – some of us have too many goals to ever achieve, so some success gurus suggest you set fewer, bigger, and wilder goals to be truly effective.
7.  Have a **plan** to achieve each of your goals, but make it flexible to allow for future change. Begin each day, week, month and year with a challenge towards your goals.
8.  **Write it down** to make it tangible, and state each goal as a positive statement:

Another helpful device to remember for setting goals is **SMARTER**: **S**pecific, **M**easurable, **A**chievable, **R**ealistic, **T**imed, **E**xciting, **R**ecorded.

We often do not think broadly enough when setting our goals. We get consumed with work, and neglect our health and fitness goals, or focus on professional and career success at the expense of precious personal relationships. To avoid this, look at the important roles of responsibility in your life: for example, personal and family role responsibilities such as father/mother/son/daughter. You will also have work/business/career roles of responsibility such as colleague, manager and business owner, and you may have roles of responsibility in the community including membership of neighbourhood groups.

Setting your goals around your important roles of responsibility will give you a sense of greater balance in your life. Your roles of responsibility will obviously change with time as you could be a son today and a father tomorrow! So you need to be flexible in your goal setting and return to this exercise often.

An effective goal focuses on results rather than activity, and helps you determine what you need to do to achieve it. A by-product of this process is that you will know where you are at the moment. Your goals also need to be translated into daily activities, so that each day you do something, no matter how small, towards achieving them. Working at your goals (and identifying your roles of responsibility) gives structure and direction towards your mission. Identify what you want to achieve at the end of one year, five years, and ten years (**The 10 Actions**® **Workbook** will help you here).

Now you have identified your goals and set one, five, and ten-year targets, how do you feel? Overwhelmed? Underwhelmed? Review your list, and eliminate any goals that can be identified as unachievable fantasies or ones which do not excite you. Your goals should stretch you, but not towards breaking point – there is a fine line between healthy pressure and stress. If you have more than one goal in each of the categories, you may want to prioritise them.

Take time to reflect on your goals and assess the intensity of your desire to achieve each of the goals you have written. If you have any doubt about your willingness to commit to achieving any of the goals, stop right there. Question whether it is the right goal for you. You must feel strong, committed, and ready to make big decisions if you are to achieve these goals.

Do you feel excited? Fearful? Quietly satisfied? Accept these feelings and take ownership of your goals. Will all your goals stretch you rather than defeat you? Do you have the patience and persistence to reach them? Are you guaranteed to reach all of them? Probably not if they are all challenging. But one thing I can guarantee is that you will never attain goals that are not set.

## Prioritising your Goals and Setting an Action Plan

Are you ready to commit to the daily committed pursuit of your dream? The world is full of people with good intentions, but what makes a dream come true is positive, energised, goal-orientated action. Work smarter, not harder is a valuable concept. If you are to achieve more than a fraction of your potential you still have to put in a lot of effective hard work. The key to making this hard/smart work enjoyable is to love what you are doing.

Many of your goals will be similar to something that has already been done. There is a wealth of *qualified* experience out there that we can learn from. However, avoid so-called helpful advice from people who have not done, or are not willing to do, what you are going to do. Also be wary of people who always see the *grass as greener on the other side* – those who constantly change jobs and appear to be working hard towards something only to wander off to another *greener* looking pasture. In contrast, those who are climbing the mountain of success have purpose, continuity, and consistency underlying all their actions. Decide who you want to spend your time with – the *watchers* or *doers,* the *green grassers* or *mountain climbers?* And always trust in yourself, especially now you have a well thought through vision and long and medium term goals.

Repetition is another useful tool to ensure you follow through on your vision with the necessary action. Advertisers use repetition all the time to get a message across and the most successful people hold their goals constantly in mind. Continual repetition of your visions, goals and plans acts upon the subconscious mind, stimulating the creativity and willpower to produce the desired results.

How much of a price in both sacrifice and effort are you prepared to put in to achieve your goals? Are you prepared to overcome any and all obstacles to your will, drive, determination and creative power? Do you truly realise you can't get something for nothing? You must give out in effort to receive. Do you have faith in yourself and your ability to succeed? If you use the enormous power of repetition in the right way – a positive, affirming way – there will be no other outcome than success.

## How to Manage your Time to Achieve your Goals

What would you do if you were given an extra hour every day? This section discusses time management (personal management) skills. These are essential skills for effective people. People who use these techniques routinely are the highest achievers in *all* walks of life. If you use these skills well you *will* function effectively, even under intense pressure.

## The 80:20 Rule

Many people spend their days in a frenzy of activity, yet achieve little because they do not concentrate on the right things. At the heart of time management is an important shift in focus:

*Concentrate on results, not on being busy.*

This is neatly summed up in the Pareto Principle, or the 80:20 Rule. This argues that typically 80% of unfocused effort generates only 20% of results. *The remaining 80% of results are achieved with only 20% of the effort.* Is 20% of your current effort achieving 80% of your results, and 80% of your effort producing 20% of your results?

Whilst you cannot create more time, you can make the best of the same time that is available to us all by managing yourself effectively. How much is your time worth to you? Even if this 80:20 rule were only partially true, imagine what would happen if you started taking time and effort from the less effective 80% of activities and moved them to the highly *effective* 20% – 1% more *effective* action might produce 5% more results.

This concept is becoming increasingly important with work pressure, rising stress levels, and more people heading towards burnout. So what can you do? Watch, look and listen and become self-aware of how effective you are by keeping track of what you do and assessing your results. You may notice patterns emerging, and that the same amount of time will produce twice as much when spent on one thing rather than another. Take time and effort from the least effective thing, and see what happens.

## How Much Does your Time Cost?

The first part of your focus on results should be to work out how much your time costs. This helps you to see if you are spending your time productively and profitably. If you work for an organisation, calculate how much you cost it each year. Include your salary, payroll taxes, the cost of office space you occupy, equipment and facilities you use, expenses, and administrative support. If you are self-employed, factor in the annual running costs of your business. To this figure add a guesstimate of the amount of profit you should generate by your activity. If you work normal hours, you will have approximately 200 productive days each year. If you work 7½ hours each day, this equates to 1,500 hours in a year.

From these figures, calculate an hourly rate. This should give a reasonable estimate of how much your time is worth – this may be a surprisingly large amount! When you are deciding whether or not to take a task on, think about this value – are you wasting your or your organisation's resources on a low yield task?

## Key points:

Calculating how much your time is worth helps you to work out whether it is worth doing particular jobs. If you have to spend much of your time doing low-yield jobs, then you can make a good case for employing an assistant, for doing something else or learning to delegate more effectively.

> *'The key is not to prioritise your schedule,*
> *but to schedule your priorities.'*
> Stephen R Covey

In the time management matrix on the next page, identify tasks that fit into each of the boxes, thinking carefully about the description of each box. The top left, for example, is both **important and urgent** and the top right is **important and not urgent**.

- Where do you spend most of your time and effort? In the small squares in the centre put in the percentage of time you spent in the last week in each of these areas.
- What would it feel like to be constantly in the Important/Urgent box?
- When you are not in the Important/Urgent box, where are you?

Where is it best to spend your time? View each box in turn.

**Not Important and Not Urgent.** You should not really spend any time at all here as even leisure activities can be classed as important for relaxation.

**Not Important, but Urgent.** If these activities are Not Important to you, it is because they are Urgent to someone else. This is a section where you can really implement change.

|  | URGENT | NOT URGENT |
|---|---|---|
| **I M P O R T A N T** | | |
| **N O T  I M P O R T A N T** | | |

**Important and Urgent**. It is difficult to get away from these as they are Important (to you) and also urgent. However, these tasks can cause burnout and stress, so you need to control the amount of time you spend here fire fighting.

**Not Urgent but Important.** These are things you may not be doing at the moment (Not Urgent), but would have a big impact if you did (Important). So it is here that you can be really effective with time. The more time you spend here, the less time will be needed in Important and Urgent (prevention rather than cure!).

To spend more time with the **Not Urgent but Important**, you must take time from the Not Important (to you), but Urgent (to others) box, and to do this you need to say, 'No,' to less important matters.

*'I do not know the key to success,
but the key to failure is trying to please everybody.'*
Bill Cosby

If someone throws a ball at you, you don't have to catch it. For example, you are really busy and a friend rings to chat. If you don't explain that it is inconvenient to talk at the moment, you catch the ball, and as a result become stressed and resentful.

Have you ever not answered the phone when you are busy with something else? If you choose not to answer it, you are taking responsibility for your own peace of mind. The same applies to criticism and destructive comments. When someone throws a comment in your direction, you can catch it and feel hurt, or drop it and get on with your day.

How often do you catch unnecessary balls? Not catching the ball simply because it is thrown your way is a powerful tool to regain control of our life.

*'A No uttered from deepest conviction is better and greater than a
Yes merely uttered to please, or what is worse, to avoid trouble.'*
Mahatma Gandhi

Here are some ideas to help you manage your time in order to achieve your goals:

- **Live in the present.** Your future is determined by the decisions and choices you make today. Focus on the immediate time you have at your disposal rather than living in the past.

- **Place a value on yourself and what you do.** If you feel yourself as valuable, you will see your time as valuable.

- **Clarify your goals.** Be very clear about your aims and ambitions, both short and long term. By now you will have written them down, making it easier to make decisions about what needs doing, and plan accordingly.

- **Write down your daily schedule and priorities.** Not simply ones related to your work – include others such as relationship and health goals. Work on the basics first, and set aside a realistic block of time for priorities.

- **Prioritise your day around the important tasks rather than the easiest or most pleasurable ones.** Do the toughest (and most rewarding) tasks first when you have most energy. You will then feel good about doing them and find the rest of the day's tasks easy in comparison.

- **Be consistent and effective with short periods of time.** Just 15 minutes a day devoted to a subject could make you a master of it in 5 years!

- **Be aware of how others will try to have you commit to what they want.** Always check your schedule before making a commitment to anything new. Don't allow others to divert you from your objectives. Learn how to say No.

- **Delegate.** Effective delegating saves time in the future.

- **As well as working hard, work smart.** Ask: Am I doing what is most important? Am I doing this task or activity in the most efficient way? Can anyone help me achieve this either quicker or better? Am I seeing the wood for the trees? Am I using technology as my servant rather than my master? Will my current activity have a positive outcome, or am I doing it to avoid something else? Will doing this take me towards my goal?'

> *'There is nothing so useless as doing efficiently that which should not be done at all.'*
> Peter F Drucker

- **It's your personal productivity that matters.** People are usually only productive for just over 50% of the time. FACT: About 30% of your time is lost through ambiguity, poor self-discipline, or trying to sort out problems.

- **Be decisive.** Now is a three-letter word that often separates success and failure. Make it a habit to do things now, rather than procrastinating and see how organised you become. What strategies and techniques can you employ to keep you effective and focused?

- **Balance your life.** Don't forget to allow time for family, friends and fun, as leading a balanced life reduces stress and increases energy levels. Time management is really life management. And your overall health and wellbeing require attention in the following six important areas:

**Physical** (exercise, nutrition, sleep)

**Intellectual** (cultural, aesthetic)

**Social** (intimate and social relationships)

**Career** (school and career goal directed work)

**Emotional** (expression of feelings, desires)

**Spiritual** (quest for meaning)

- **End the day well.** At the end of the working day, tidy your workplace, make notes about what needs doing tomorrow and prioritise those tasks so that you are prepared and focused for the next morning. And a final thing – don't say you don't have enough time! We all have exactly the same number of hours per day – the same that were given to Helen Keller, Margaret Thatcher, Michelangelo, Mother Teresa, Gandhi, Leonardo da Vinci, and Einstein.

Three Questions to Ask Yourself Three Times a Day:

1. What have I done?

2. Where do I stand relative to what I wanted to get done?

3. What should I do now?

The three benefits of monitoring your progress relative to your activities are:

1. You get more done

2. You get more of the right things done

3. You avoid days when you don't get much done

# Procrastination, Distractions, and Other Problems

If you are having a problem with time management, consider the following suggestions:

- Review your long-term and intermediate goals often.
- Continually try to eliminate those unnecessary tasks which are unrelated to your goals, or to you maintaining a balanced life style.
- Take advantage of your natural cycles. Schedule the most difficult activities when you are sharpest.
- Learn to say No!
- Reward yourself for effective time management.
- Solicit cooperation from those around you.
- Attend to your needs for spontaneity.
- Do not set yourself up to fail. Be realistic and work toward an individualised approach that makes sense for you.
- Record things – the process of putting schedules, priorities, and plans on paper is helpful in itself.

## Instant Gratification

I once heard *A Shortcut* described as the longest distance between two points (e.g. it often turns out to be a longer route because you get lost). That's a great way to describe instant gratification. How would your life change for the better if you no longer gave in to all those short-term temptations that you know will kill your long-term success? What would it be like for you to become the kind of person who automatically chooses to do today what you know will be good for you tomorrow?

## Preference questions

A great way to make this change is to use preference questions. Preference questions help you replace the urge to do something counterproductive with the urge to do something productive. For example, imagine your ultimate desire is to lose three stones of body weight in six months, but your immediate desire is to have a delicious hot fudge sundae. Chances are you'll be inclined to satisfy your immediate craving at the expense of your ultimate goal. Instead, why not ask yourself this preference question: *Would I rather be at my ideal weight right now, today, or have a hot fudge sundae?*

If you choose being thin instead of eating that sundae, you turn your ultimate desire (being thin) into an immediate desire, and given yourself the leverage you need to replace the urge to do something wrong with the urge to do something right.

## Procrastination

The next step is to use procrastination in a positive way to turn the urge for that hot fudge sundae into something you can put off indefinitely. The beauty of procrastination is that instead of saying *No*, you're saying, *later*. And when *later* comes, the urge may have passed. If not, just put it off again. Keep putting it off and *later* never comes.

## Perspective

Another powerful tool to make the change from instant gratification to delayed gratification is simply to change your perspective. Instead of saying: *I want to buy this big screen TV today because it costs only £75 a month for the next five years*, say *I want to put £75 in the bank each month, earning interest, so that I can buy a big screen TV as soon as possible.*

## Overcoming negative procrastination

However, procrastination can also be a negative force that we employ for a number of reasons, including:

- Overestimating the amount of time left to perform a task, and underestimating the amount of time required to complete it.
- Believing you will have more motivation if you put off the task to the future.
- Believing you need to be in the right mood to be successful in completing the task.
- Being a perfectionist so you are fearful of doing the task badly.
- Being disorganised with time and resources.
- Being fearful of making mistakes, experiencing failure, or letting someone else down.
- Black and white thinking (all or nothing).
- Holding the false belief that other people's success has come easy.
- Having unreachable goals.
- Having a tendency for self-criticism and self blame leading to low self-esteem.

Here are a few suggestions to overcome negative procrastination:

- Don't beat yourself up over it, but commit to creating a new habit.
- Realistically estimate the amount of time it takes to do tasks.
- Remember that *motivation* often comes *after* you have started something.
- Stop making elaborate excuses such as, I need to be in the right mood, or it's too late to start now, or I perform better under pressure.
- Keep a journal, particularly of your thoughts and put together rational responses to limiting thoughts, for example:

| Thought | Response |
|---|---|
| 'I'll start work on that project tomorrow because today is so glorious that I am just going to relax.' | I'll spend 2 hours working on this project, and still have some time to enjoy the beautiful day. |

- Get better organised. Use an appointment book or an organiser, and keep your desk/office tidy.
- When planning, work backwards from when the goal needs to be accomplished, and break it down into manageable tasks and milestones. Start each week with a review of what is important and keep a daily to do list.
- In your breaks, take time to reflect on your success in overcoming procrastination.
- If you have been successful, celebrate your success.

### Deciding Your Work Priorities – Finding Out What to Spend Your Time On

An important part of focusing on results is working out what to focus on! This section concentrates on three areas – clarifying what you enjoy, understanding your strengths and weaknesses, and working out what constitutes excellent performance in your job.

**Do what you enjoy** – work out what elements you like and dislike, so that you can focus on the things you enjoy.

**Concentrate on your strengths** – maximise your skills by doing a job that suits your strengths.

**Understand how to be excellent at your job** – ensure that you concentrate on the right things by agreeing them with people you need to such as your employer, business partner, or co-directors.

Always ask the following questions:

- *What is the purpose of the job?*
  If possible, express this in a single sentence starting with the word To: *To ensure effective distribution in the South East...* for example.

- *What are the measures of success?*
  Find out the key targets to be achieved, and how these achievements will be measured. If you are self-employed or run your own business you should know what success looks like for you.

- *What is exceptional performance?*
  Find out what this is considered to be, and work out how to achieve it.

- *What are the priorities and deadlines?*
  You need to know this so that when you are overloaded with work you know what to focus on.

- *What resources are available?*
  This ensures that you are using all the tools at your command.

- *What costs are acceptable?*
  This lets you know the boundaries within which you can move.

- *How does this relate to other people?*
  What is the broader picture within which you have to work?

If you have answers to these questions, you will know how to achieve excellence in your job.


## Activity Logs

Keep an Activity Log for several days to help you understand how you spend your time and when you perform at your best. By analysing your activity log you will be able to identify and eliminate time-wasting or low-yield jobs, and know the times of day at which you are most effective.

## Action Plans – Small Scale Planning

Whatever you want to achieve, draw up an action plan. An Action Plan differs from a To Do List in that it focuses on the achievement of a single goal and consists of a list of tasks that helps you achieve your objective, allowing you to concentrate on the stages of that achievement and monitor your progress towards it.

## To Do Lists

Remember To Do All Essential Tasks in the Right Order.

Prioritised *To Do* Lists are fundamentally important to efficient work. If you use them ensure that:

- You remember to carry out all necessary tasks.
- You tackle the most important jobs first, and do not waste time on trivial tasks.
- You do not get stressed by a large number of unimportant jobs.

To draw up a Prioritised *To Do* List, list all the tasks you must carry out, breaking large tasks into manageable segments. Mark the importance of each task with a priority from A (very important) to F (unimportant). Redraft the list into this order of importance.

## Goal Setting

Use the important process of goal setting to:

- Decide what is important for you to achieve in your life
- Separate what is important from what is irrelevant or urgent
- Motivate yourself to achievement
- Build your self-confidence based on measured achievement of goals

Enjoy the achievement of your goals and reward yourself appropriately. Draw lessons where appropriate and use these to improve your future performance.

- If you achieved the goal too easily, make your next goal harder
- If the goal took a dispiriting length of time to achieve, make the next goal slightly easier
- If you learned something that would lead you to change other goals, do so
- If, in achieving the goal, you noticed a deficit in your skills, decide whether to set goals to fix this.

Remember too that goals will change as you develop and mature. Adjust them regularly to reflect this growth in your personality. If goals do not hold any attraction to you any longer, let them go. Goal setting is your servant, not your master and should bring you pleasure, satisfaction, and a sense of achievement.

## Delegation and Sharing Workloads

Transferring **responsibility** enables you to put your energy into things that take you towards your vision and goals. Effective delegation is a key principle of self management. Consider the following two types of delegation: The *Go and Do* or *Gofer* delegation. 'Go for this, do this, do that, and tell me when you have done it.' This type of delegation is limiting and doesn't empower those you delegate to. This usually ends up therefore with comments such as: 'You didn't tell me to do that.'

In contrast *Motivational ownership delegation* includes an element of choice. To be really effective, this type of delegation needs to follow the five steps listed below:

1. Focus on what *results* need to be accomplished and agree the results between you both, so the other person becomes committed to the outcome.

2. Share *standards/parameters/guidelines* drawing on your experience of factors to avoid, and the tried and tested ways of achieving good results. However, make sure that the responsibility remains with them, not with you.

3. Identify the *resources* the person needs to achieve the results including *you* but not do it for them as this can be de-motivational.

4. Identify a benchmark for the results to be achieved and agree a *performance review* time if it is a long-term task. The aim here is to create answerability and agree who is *responsible for what.*

5. Identify and agree either the *reward* or *negative consequences* when you evaluate the success at the project's conclusion.

This process can be empowering, rewarding and nurturing of responsibility for all involved, and can work just as effectively within a family as within an organisation.

# Self-management Checklist

1.  *Specify a clear-cut goal you want to accomplish.* Be specific. For example: 'I'll write for four hours a day.'

2.  *Specify when you'll do it.* 10.00 a.m. on Thursday, for example.

3.  *Record your success.* Make a record of your successes and your failures. This could be a graph showing the numbers of hours completed per day.

4.  *Make a public commitment.* Tell someone (monitor) your proposed goals and your deadline, and ask them to check to see if you achieved it.

5.  *Add an explicit penalty for failure if necessary.* For example, tell your monitor that you'll buy them a drink or take them out to lunch each time you fail.

6.  *Think small.* If you've got a hundred letters to write, don't try to do them all at once. Going for too much too soon is why so many people fail at self-management.

7.  *Specify the amount of product you will produce.*

8.  *If you find yourself drifting, get a timer that beeps every five minutes to chart whether you're on task.*

9.  *Arrange for regular contact with your monitor or coach, daily or weekly as needed.*

10. *Arrange for a friend to help you monitor your goal attainment.*

11. *Get rid of distractions.* Try to do your work when and where no one can bother you. Watch out for that phone and other diversions, such as sorting through junk mail.

12. *Recycle.* Your self-management project may not work the first time you try it, and will certainly fall apart from time to time, so be prepared to adapt and innovate.

Remember, you do not demean yourself by using these explicit self-management techniques. Use them, and you'll be in the company of some of the world's most productive people.

You know that to achieve your life's vision and to live with purpose you need to make changes, decisions and commitments. Not always easy at the outset, I agree, yet essential. Willpower is an essential tool for your success and in this chapter you've discovered ways to develop it. You identified your goals too, as with no destination in mind, no route is favourable. And once identified, you could prioritise them and develop a plan of action.

More than merely planning however, you discovered that self-management is another key to success. To manage your time well you have to be aware of where you procrastinate, distract yourself (sometimes deliberately) and adjust any other potential problem areas. All done? Let's continue!

# Action 5

## Build Character

*'Success is to be measured not by wealth, power or fame,*
*but by the ratio between what a man is and what he might be.'*
H G Wells

It could be said that successful relationships with other people is what all life is about. For this reason it is essential to concentrate on the three following areas:

- How to build your inner character by developing key qualities and skills

- How to create and sustain highly effective relationships with others, *and*

- How to establish high trust levels in others by using the model of the *trust bank account*

Truly successful people are at ease with themselves, comfortable in their relationships and connected to their personal values. Their success is not short-term, gained at the expense of others, or by using short cuts.

While a person who manipulates others may achieve a small measure of success through sheer determination and seemingly clever techniques, ultimately they will fail because dreams need the co-operation of others. Their external success will be shallow and empty – and inside they know it!

To become the person you would like to be, you must first see yourself as the person of your ideal. To do this you must learn to value yourself highly which in turn leads to a positive self-image, the generation of self-belief, and, most importantly, respect for yourself. Mother Teresa's mission allowed those in the last desperate period of their lives to end their time with dignity. It is never too late to discover who you are. Self-value is the foundation upon which your future needs to be built. It will have an enormous impact on your relationships as you learn to appreciate, respect, and believe in yourself and others.

# Increasing your Self-value and Worth

No matter what age you are, the essence of who you are has probably been muddied by years of negative conditioning about yourself and others leading to an accumulation of limiting beliefs about what is possible in your life. However, those assumptions are only true if you believe them. So how can you make yourself worthy and value yourself highly? Here are a few suggestions:

- Be **flexible** with your **character, personality and temperament.** If you ever hear yourself saying 'It's just the way I am.' Stop! Your personality and temperament are not fixed in cement. We are all born with a certain personality type, but we can change. For example, I completed the same personality tests twice, once under my former employers, and once as a self-employed person and I achieved markedly different results – the result of my learning new values and endeavouring to change. You can escape the temperament trap – if things in your personality need improving, improve them!

- **Become resilient, yet flexible and examine your assumptions.** One of the things peak performers do best is to interpret people and situations in ways that liberate rather than limit them. The tree that is most flexible will remain standing in the wake of hurricane force winds while more rigid trees snap.

- If you have character or personality traits you want to change, learn to **do and act the opposite** as a positive discipline.

- **Let go of your past.** Leave behind past mistakes, unsuccessful relationships, and things you are not proud of. By all means learn from the past, but do not battle with it.

- **Learn the art of reflection.** Develop the ability to stand back, and look at yourself objectively – to see who you are and who you want to be. Ask yourself self-examining questions about your personality, health, appearance, the way you treat others and reflect on your inner motivations using techniques such as contemplation and meditation. One insight gained during a reflective exercise could save you *hours, days, weeks, months* or even *years* of work and time.

- **Develop the ability to get along with people.** Build healthy, productive relationships with everyone you meet. Listen to and affirm them – the results can be amazing with problems eliminated or put into perspective. And the spreading of goodwill helps you in the pursuit of your vision.

- **Become a problem solver, not a problem creator.** Don't try to win the battle, try to solve the problem.

- **Be positive with yourself and others.** If you find yourself being negative, change your attitude immediately as a positive mind counteracts negative energies, makes waves of compassion and understanding, and it heals. It is always a good idea to surround yourself with positive people – like a disease, it's contagious.

- **Have belief in your ability.** Have the belief that **you will** make a difference. Don't fall into the trap of doing just enough to get by – mediocrity has been described as the cancer of the soul.

- **Exercise personal discipline.** If you exert good self-discipline it shows in your attitude – you will get jobs done, avoid procrastination, and enjoy what you do. Here are some helpful ways to exercise self-discipline:

  o Block out time each day to do a *chore*

  o Involve other people – it makes you more committed

  o Keep a record of things such as exercise and score yourself

  o Reward yourself – for big things and put a picture of the reward somewhere prominent

  o Use a gimmick to make boring routines more interesting

  Establishing solid self-discipline patterns takes time but releases consistency and the ability to perform at a high level. A member of the audience meeting a talented pianist after a concert said, 'I would give half my life to play the piano like you do.' To which the pianist replied 'That's exactly what I have given!' *Real* success does not happen overnight.

- **Exercise self-honesty and be true to yourself.** *'I have nothing to teach the world. Truth and non-violence are as old as the hills.'* Gandhi.
  Can you admit that you have been selling yourself short in life? Can you open your eyes to the huge possibilities and alternatives available to you? Here are some ways to develop more self-honesty:

1. Take the blame as well as the credit for your position in life honestly and openly.

2. Become curious about everything – discover the wonder of nature, read good books, listen to educational CDs, talk to successful people.

3. Stop feeling sorry for yourself! If you are alive and well, you've got it made!

4. Get out of any rut – unplug the TV for a month, go to the opera, go to Peru on holiday rather than the Costa del Sol.

5. Look through other people's eyes to see yourself honestly. Look at yourself as if you were your brother/sister, parents, children, wife/husband or friend.

6. Use the affirmation: *My rewards in life will be in direct reflection to my service and contribution to others and our planet.*

7. Listen to others with empathy.

8. Look for and speak the truth – don't be misled by the media's mixed messages.

9. Self-evaluate regularly (the tools are in Action 1).

10. Invest in your knowledge, skill and attitude development. As Benjamin Franklin once wrote, *'If an individual empties his wallet into his head, no one can take it from him.'*

11. Set aside time to reflect alone each day. Use the time to ask honest questions of yourself and as an opportunity for personal growth. Remember we get out of life exactly what we put into it – *'Whatever a man soweth, he shall also reap.'*

- **Project a modest image**. Project your success without flaunting it. Do, however, reinforce past successes, as this builds confidence, and success breeds success.

- **Don't compare yourself with others**. View yourself in terms of your own ability, potential, vision, and goals – they are individual and unique.

- **Eliminate envy**. Once envy gets a grip on us, it grows like a virus, eating away at our self-esteem and poisoning our relationships when we are drawn into competing rather than making an emotional connection. If you are in the vicious circle of envy, opt out now. Contentment is being happy with what you already have. So, if you can't get what you want, try to want what you can get. Ask yourself if the person you envy most is fundamentally more content than you.

- **Radiate a simple charm**. Project inner warmth and transmit your confident self-image with a smile – it can save hundreds of words. As well as showing you are comfortable with yourself, it creates a lasting first impression.

- **Self-Accept!** Accept the way you are at this moment! The perfect human being has yet to be discovered, so ignore little faults, and accept yourself as an imperfect, changing, growing and worthwhile person. You are special. This applies also to situations you are not happy with. Learn to accept the situation and everything about it. Why? Because that's the way it is, whether you like it or not and it is only by accepting a situation that you can change it.

- **Base your decisions and actions on rational thinking rather than emotion.** Reacting only to emotion nullifies wisdom, creativity and rational thought. Enjoy your emotions as children do, but make decisions through common sense and logic. It's good to make important decisions when the adrenaline flow is steady!

- **Practise positive self-talk and affirmations.** Feed your self-image with nourishing food through positive self-talk.

- **See yourself as worthy.** Remember the work we did in **Action 1** about our perceptions? We behave not in accordance with reality, but our perception of reality. All that you do or aspire to do is based on your self-image so try to develop positive self-image pictures. Napoleon said, *'Imagination rules the world'* – the way you see yourself and your world is the world in which you live.

- **Read a biography.** Read the life story of someone who inspires you, and imagine yourself as that person. Nelson Mandela's *Long walk to freedom* has inspired me and fuelled much of my work on character and personal development.

- **Write a 1 – 2 page journal of your professional and person qualities**. Do it as if you are going to apply for the job of your dreams. List your maximum current and future potential. Read it regularly.

- **Watch stimulating and inspirational shows, TV and DVDs** rather than watching TV as a habit, which can make for tunnel vision and inhibit your creativity.

- **Be relentless and persistent in achieving your vision and goals.** Winning is a learned habit. And it takes constant practice to overcome limiting and self-defeating ways of living! Excellence is not, however, synonymous with perfection – it is doing it right most of the time. Practice makes perfect should read practice makes improvement. We need to keep learning new knowledge, mastering new skills, and developing our character, personality and attitude to develop successful habits. It's not necessarily what you do, but how well you do it that determines its real value – anything worth doing is worth giving your best shot. Give it 110%.

> *'Our deeds determine us, as much as*
> *we determine our deeds.'*
> George Eliot: 1819–1880

- **Develop positive self-expectancy.** True self-belief is in partnership with your level of commitment, purpose, and burning desire. Become dissatisfied with the status quo. Want and embrace positive future change. Expect to win. Winston Churchill was a poor student but he had expectation, as did Beethoven who was deaf!

- **Associate with winners, optimists, and success stories.** You can be realistic and optimistic at the same time, by realistically examining all the facts, but remaining optimistic about your ability to succeed. Associating with other optimists creates a positive, creative, and results-orientated atmosphere.

- **Cultivate the ability to be natural.** Be a person that others feel comfortable with. If you have a sincere interest in other people, they will like you.

- **Develop your self-esteem.** Say, 'I'd rather be me than anyone else' and learn to like and be comfortable with yourself. How do you accept a compliment? People with low self-esteem often talk themselves down, and lack the ability to accept value paid by others. Those who know who they are do not need to be defensive or prove anything – their self-esteem is enough.

*'My work will be finished if I succeed in carrying the conviction that every person is the guardian of his or her self-respect and liberty.'*
Mahatma Gandhi

- **Be grateful when you are feeling good, and gracious when you're not!** Even the happiest people on the planet have their fair share of low moods, problems, disappointments and heartache. However, when depressing times come, they accept it with the same openness and wisdom as the good times.

- **Believe in your own worth.** Make excellence a lifestyle move for yourself. Quality is not just a word you see on a certificate on your wall, it is something that resides within you. Think of one or two people you know who are known for their high quality exceptional work, and there is a good chance they have made excellence a lifestyle. How? By believing in their own worth.

The above list of keys to self-worth and excellence is meaningless unless you take action. Look at the list and identify your weak points. Decide to strengthen them until they become a solid and strong part of your character make-up. Excellence and self-worth are lifelong commitments that are worth making. Now write down your weakest areas, and what you will do to strengthen them.

## Character Development

What is the difference between character and personality?

Our personality success focuses on developing our public image – dressing for success, using communication (and other) techniques to influence people, even faking interest in people to get them to like us. However, if we use just personality to create our success without developing our character it is like reaping without sowing seed and such success will be shallow and short-lived.

There are also people who have a sound character, but lack the necessary personality or communication skills of success and this can affect the quality of their relationships. Take a few moments to consider the following:

- Think of someone who used their personality or some kind of communication technique to get their way with you. Later you found out they lacked character. What was the situation? How did you feel?

- Think of someone you know who has a sound character and is always true to their word, but doesn't have outward success due to their personality skills. How do you feel about this person?

Ultimately, what we are says more about us than anything we say or even do. All of us know people we trust without question, regardless of their human relation skills, because we *know* their character.

## Sound character

So what constitutes good character and what areas should we focus upon? Research conducted in this area continually identifies certain traits that constitute good character and character strength.

- **Integrity.** Building integrity is about dealing fairly and openly with people, telling it as it is, as well as how it could be, and understanding that trust is a vital foundation for good relationships with others. People with integrity make and keep promises to others and themselves. Your word is one of the most precious things you own, so do not give it lightly. You may ask, 'Does one broken word matter?' Well, one broken word is like one grain of sand. In a lake one grain is not much, but as more grains are added it becomes a swamp (bogged down), and eventually a desert (barren). Make only agreements you plan to keep. By keeping your word, you keep it powerful to you and to others. Do you keep secrets?

- **Humility.** True humility is being honest, first, and most importantly, with yourself. Do you have enough humility to apologise to yourself for mistakes you make, and are you modest enough to do the same with others? Would you rather be *right* or *happy?*

- **The *choices* you make define the kind of person you choose to be.** You make (conscious and subconscious) choices about everything in life, so it makes sense to exercise these choices with care and thought. Choose to rise above the mediocre behaviour of others and be a figure of transformation and inspiration to others.

- **Do the right thing.** Doing the right thing even when it appears risky or costly (in the short-term), develops morals that have meaning to you and help shape your character.

- **Sincere motivation.** The prime mover of every action is motivation and when that is sincere you reach a satisfying outcome. Inner motivators such as passion, fear, love and greed are so powerful it is vital you spend time in reflection to ensure you choose positive motivators.

- **Understanding that what you do does matter.** One person *can* make a difference in making the world a better place. Ask the question, 'Will what I am doing make a difference to others?'

- **Respect.** Do not pre-judge others, but acknowledge that there is something to respect in everyone – even if you have to look hard! People with sound character treat others as they would like to be treated themselves, and respect the person rather than their position.

- **Responsibility.** People of strong character take responsibility for their own lives, and do not blame others for what happens to them. You can choose to exercise self-control and make a considered response rather than merely react to situations.

- **Fairness.** Be fair to yourself and others in *every* area of life. Play by the rules and do not abuse the power of position by taking advantage of others. Be just and treat all people equally regardless of race, age, sex and beliefs.

- **Care.** Demonstrate caring by trying to understand other people's beliefs and their reasons for doing things. Care too about your community, society, and the environment on a global scale. Show care by offering compassion, express gratitude, forgive others, and go out of your way to help others in need.

- **Loyalty.** Be loyal to people, including those not physically present. Loyalty shows in what you say and do, and in your intentions.

- **Reliable.** Be true to your word. When you say you will do something, see it through. Keep promises and be reliable to yourself and others (as with integrity above).

- **Honesty.** Regard honesty as a virtue without compromise. Even when the going gets tough and dishonesty seems the easy way, know that honesty is the real foundation for building trust based relationships with others.

- **Forgive and forget.** For (in favour of) giving (to give) – in forgiving, we sometimes *give* to the other, but always to ourselves. How do you feel when you genuinely forgive another person? Also, forgive yourself for the way you judge yourself. Try this simple, but effective exercise, when you find yourself judging someone or something. Say to yourself (out loud if you can), 'I forgive _____ (name of person judged) for_____ (what they did to make you judge them). I forgive myself for judging _____ (the person) for _____ (what they did). However, once forgiven, you must also forget – the best way to heal memories is to forgive the past, forget it and let it all go.

- **Take your citizenship seriously.** Demonstrate real character strength and do your share to make your community and society better. Be a good neighbour who obeys the laws of the land, respect legitimate authority, and care for the greater environment in which you live.

- **Laugh!** Even if you weren't born with a sense of humour – you can develop one. Laughter helps you enjoy better health and is one of the best antidotes to depression – an *internal massage* that gives the muscles of the face, chest, abdomen, heart and mind a workout. People who laugh live longer.

### How can you grow your sense of humour?

1. Don't wait for others to smile first. *A smile is the shortest distance between two people.*
2. Enjoy the company of those who have humour to share.
3. Enjoy *playtime* and rediscover the inner child. I include a section to help you reconnect with our natural childlike behaviours! (on page 104)
4. Develop the gift of spontaneous laughter. Being able to laugh at yourself reflects both self-acceptance and humility and keeps your little self (the ego) in proper perspective.

As well as an ability to laugh, people with a sound character learn to enjoy what they do. *Enjoy* is an interesting word, because it has no opposite (Unjoy! Disjoy!). When life seems grim, you can either moan over your fate or *choose* to face it with joy.

*'With coarse rice to eat, with water to drink, and my bended arm for a*
*pillow – I still have joy in the midst of these things.'*
Confucius

Humour can also play a part in physical healing. Norman Cousins in his book *Anatomy of an Illness* relates how he was cured of terminal illness through doses of laughter whilst watching hours of comedy.

Research has confirmed that humour can act as a natural painkiller, while laughter strengthens the immune system. Strong laughter increases the rate of deep breathing and exercises the abdominal muscles, decreases physical tension and stress and helps you relax. Truly, laughter is the best medicine.

- **Learn true happiness.** Since we are not solely material creatures, it is a mistake to place all our hopes for happiness on external development alone. To be truly happy we need three core elements in place – something to look forward to (a vision/mission and worthy goals), a readiness to share, and a drive to make others happy – you can't fail to be happy yourself if you are making other people happy.

  Five simple steps to being happy are:

  1. Free your heart from hatred – forgive

  2. Free your mind from worry

  3. Live simply and appreciate what you have

  4. Give more

  5. Expect less

  *Do not take lightly small good deeds,*
  *Believing they can hardly help,*
  *For drops of water one by one,*
  *In time can fill a giant pot.*
  Patrul Rinpoche

- **Enthusiasm.** As a boss once said 'If you are not filled with enthusiasm, you will be fired with enthusiasm.' One of the unquestioned qualities that separate the successful from the also-rans is the inner fire of enthusiasm. When you bubble with positive personal energy, people will love being around you. All of us have had our natural enthusiasm extinguished over the years, but we can rekindle the flame and even relearn enthusiasm until it becomes a permanent part of us. My greatest fear for many years was public speaking, but by generating enthusiasm for my work and facilitating workshops, I now love the chance to speak. As I discovered, our greatest fear can become our greatest joy. Once you have generated enthusiasm, don't allow others to stifle it, and be wary of falling into negative thoughts and attitudes. To keep your enthusiasm levels high, keep focused on new dreams, goals, action plans and success – this will be better than any external motivation.

- **Graciousness and gratitude.** People with true character strength are quick to express appreciation. A humbling example of this occurred in Arnhem, Holland where thousands of British paratroopers sacrificed their lives during WWII to capture the crucial Arnhem Bridge, immortalised in the film A Bridge Too Far. Ever since the war's end the children of Arnhem have tended the graves in the Allied cemetery at Oosterbeek, and every year the anniversary is marked as 1,000 children, aged 9 to 13, lay flowers on the 1,760 graves, and escort returning veterans around the cemetery in a moving ritual that leaves even the toughest veterans speechless with emotion. In Arnhem, gratitude really does go beyond the grave.

- **Generosity.** Generosity becomes stronger and more delightful the more you engage in it, and demonstrates the quality of non-greed with its willingness to give and share. To strengthen this trait, practise acting on your impulse to give – give time, energy, resources or love for the welfare of others.

## Learning from our childhood

Learning to draw strength from our childhood experience is an awesome tool in our character development. I have put into *italics* key words that I believe differentiate our childhood from adulthood – areas that can make adulthood much more enjoyable.

As small children *time* barely exists for us – it is vast, fluid and *easily shaped.* We live in the *moment,* are intensely *curious* about the world we inhabit, and fully absorbed by everything we *see, hear, touch, taste and smell* (are you in touch with your senses?). As a toddler, a short stroll is automatically a walk with *attention.* Not a stone, flower or tree is passed without minute inspection. We *see* faces in trees and clouds, and the moon in puddles, and we want to *play* with and *interact* with it all.

Everything we do *exercises our senses* and *expands our perception* of our environment. We take *play very seriously*, usually playing in nature which is an adventure including tree houses, river crossings, building dens, squelching through mud, tasting snow, and splashing in the rain! We feel *naturally connected to the beauty of nature*, and our *view of reality* has not yet *been fixed by the demands and rules* of our society and culture. We love to hear or tell a story, and our fantasy life is rich and varied. We *laugh at almost anything*, or, as babies, point or look at empty space with interest.

Also as children our *self-expression is encouraged through creativity*; we draw *without any concern for perspective or reality,* and revel in bright colours, shapes, and patterns. Being totally unselfconscious, we make up our own songs, even our own language. Our *creativity and view of our reality is indulged* and we have a *vivid imagination* until with maturity we are taught that we are just being silly. As a result we learn to forget about our imagined friend, the angel by our bed, the face on the tree and the voice in the river.

Perhaps we should seek to *reconnect with our childhood* through nature, try to bring back our innocence, *trust and sense of real freedom* and the experience we enjoyed as children, and also the *fun, creativity and sheer ecstasy of the childlike adventure* of our world.

Can we nurture our childhood by respecting the stories of the children around us, listen to them, see the world through their eyes, play with them, blow bubbles with them and *just make time stretch?* Maybe we should walk with attention, *live in the beauty of the present* and *honour the child within us*.

## Developing our character strength

One way to grow character is to study great men and women who have made a positive difference to the world such as Nelson Mandela, Gandhi, Martin Luther-King and Mother Teresa. We can learn a great deal about true character from these people, and also seek to develop these sound character traits and philosophies into our own lives.

Another way to grow our character is to attempt to develop good character values, perhaps by seeking out role models in your personal, family and career/business life as sources of inspiration. However, when seeking the advice and knowledge of others, be cautious as this story warns:

*The General and the Boy:* A General waiting to cross a river asked a little boy how deep it was, and whether his horse could cross safely. The boy looked at the size of the General's horse and replied confidently that there would be no problem. However, the river was actually very deep and the General almost drowned. Bedraggled and furious, he threatened to punish the boy. 'But General,' the boy innocently replied, 'I see my ducks crossing the river every day, and their legs are far shorter than the legs of your horse!'

Napoleon Hill wisely says that 'Opinion is the cheapest commodity on earth' but we must review the character of others before we act on or emulate their advice. Demonstrate your character through what you do, not your opinions.

The way to develop genuine humility, for example, is to practise it. A man out with a group of friends had the opportunity to brag about a recent promotion where he had been promoted ahead of another friend of the group, but chose to resist the temptation. Choosing not to gloat not only made him feel good, but impressed his friends who admired his judgement and humility.

In developing our character we need to be aware that there is a clear distinction between thinking and feeling. The *cognitive* domain and our analytical side comes from the mind, while the affective domain involves the heart and emotions. To native people wisdom comes from the heart, and the heart is the bridge into the spiritual and the divine in creation. The world can truly be a beautiful place when your heart gets involved. As the great composer Igor Stravinsky said, *'I haven't understood a bar of music in my life, but I have felt it.'*

One emotion that seems to be taboo in our society is *crying,* but like laughter it can be a wonderful natural release. Have you ever heard someone coming out of the cinema sobbing, but saying it was the best film they had ever seen? Tears are a natural part of both the healing process and the enjoyment process, and people can be moved to tears by intense feelings of gratitude, humility, sorrow and compassion.

Another emotion we are encouraged to dispel is the emotion of fear. In our society fear is viewed as weakness, and it can be considered taboo to show or teach a child about fear. As a child waking up from a nightmare, how many times did your parents tell you that you were silly, or that there was nothing to be afraid of? Ironically, parents often respond poorly to a child's fear.

More often than not the child learns:

*If he speaks the truth about his uncomfortable feelings, he distresses his parents*

*If he acknowledges fear, either his own or his parents, he distresses his parents*

*He/she learns that it is much better to lie or hide their feelings than to talk about or acknowledge them*

*It is obviously wrong to be afraid or people would acknowledge and talk about it.*

These are not good life lessons to carry into adulthood; however, they are powerful and pervasive in our society. By learning to ignore this instinctive, intuitive voice, we actually suppress and distrust an incredibly valuable survival tool. So what can you do to reawaken and use our inner intuitive skills? The key thing is to acknowledge and talk about your feelings even when you are uncomfortable, afraid or confused. By speaking the truth about how you feel, you allow for freedom of emotional movement away from those negative feelings into clear understanding and enlightenment and begin to trust your voice of inner certainty.

For many people one of the most basic fears is the fear of being seen as stupid. Nowhere is this truer than in the corporate world and, as a result, people often suppress their own ideas, intuitions, and creative insights for fear that they may appear foolish. This particular fear is often learned at an early age, but can be combated by simply speaking out anyway – not only will other people start to express their feelings, emotions and thoughts, but it is another sure way to grow character.

Make your decisions based on what is on the inside – that's what counts. When your commitment comes from your heart you will mean it, and be in real control of your emotions, decisions, and actions.

We all have loving hearts, but like any muscle, if we don't use it, we'll lose it. Mother Teresa once said, 'Love is a fruit in season at all times, and within reach of every hand,' while George Washington

Carver commented, 'How far you go in life depends on being tender with the young, compassionate with the aged, sympathetic with the striving, and tolerant of the weak and strong. Because some day you will have been all of these.'

Our heart may be like a car that is clean on the outside but filthy on the inside. However, love and forgiveness will clean us on the inside, and when you have a clean heart, you can face any problems with self-respect and courage.

Try this quick heart MOT:

- Do you always treat people as you want to be treated?   YES/NO

- Are you willing to forgive people who have wronged you?   YES/NO

- Can you forgive yourself?                                YES/NO

- Can you accept forgiveness from others?                  YES/NO

- Do you really care about other people?                   YES/NO

- Are you compassionate towards the struggles of others?   YES/NO

- Do you always treat people with the respect they deserve?   YES/NO

If you feel anger in your heart, cleanse it with forgiveness, if envy, cleanse with charity, disrespect with respect, disregard with appreciation, conflict and stress with relaxation and peace. A clean engine always delivers power – a clean heart is no different, and will give you the power of courageous transformation. Harmony within will create harmony without. **The longest journey you ever make could be from your head to your heart!**

Have you ever found yourself in a tussle between heart and brain? Your heart often wants to go in one direction and your brain another, but most of us have been taught to distrust our heart – a teaching that stems from the patriarchal philosophy that has dominated our world thinking for the past 2000 years where intellect is honoured over emotion.

To hear your heart, you need to be a good listener. When you find yourself engaged in an activity that allows your head to take a break, and the experience brings you a sense of joy and passion that you haven't experienced in years, that's your heart talking. For example, you travel somewhere that causes you to slow down, and immerse yourself in the beauty of a region, and suddenly you feel alive. Or you participate in a hobby or new activity and find that you love the experience, losing all track of time. The experience itself is uplifting, and you feel happiness and have more energy. That's your heart calling you.

When your heart calls you to bring more passion and joy into your life, you have several choices:

1. Ignore it, and keep on living as you are
2. Move to a monastery
3. Develop awareness and clarity about what it is you really want in your life – and then take action and get support to live the life of your dreams.

Which is right, the heart or the brain? Your heart speaks in metaphors, analogies and images of possibility – the possibility of you fulfilling your potential and becoming who you are meant to be. Your head tries to find the rationale to make that picture a reality, but in figuring out how to solve this challenge, inevitably fears, limitations and doubts surface. Your head is not against your heart – it's simply trying to protect you from getting hurt by going through a logical, rational thought process.

When is the time to listen to your heart? It's a very individual process, but two key things often awaken us:

1) The pain of where you are becomes greater than the fear of change
2) The signs and signals around you can no longer be ignored, and you begin to take note of the coincidences

Reasons people are afraid to listen to their heart include:

- 'What will others think?'
- 'How will we succeed?'
- 'How will we prosper?'
- 'This is not logical/rational/practical.'

Yet anything you fear losing – money, status, position, reputation, for example – comes from the ego's need for external power symbols. What we really fear when following our heart is the increase in our vulnerability, because the kind of power we are embracing is INTERNAL, and not normally recognised in the outside world.

As a colleague once said, 'My heart always spoke to me and captured my attention, helping me to follow my life's journey. This was often to the disappointment of my family and friends who wanted me to be more rational.'

How tragic that our society has taught us to distrust the callings of our heart. We often work when we need to rest, eat when we are not hungry, and laugh when we want to cry, remain angry when we need to forgive. It is our intellect that drives us to prove ourselves when our heart may be broken. If we listened to our heart, we, and our world, would be very different.

The process of forging our character does not happen overnight, but is a lifelong task. Begin by choosing a character trait to work on for a month until it becomes an automatic habit, telling other people as this makes a *social statement* about your intentions and instils moral responsibility. For example, if you talk to your loved ones about integrity, you will be more committed to act with integrity!

We must always remember that values can be morally good, bad, or neutral, and that they do not necessarily command our actions; for example, we can value one thing and do another. However, while our views represent our intellectual position rather than acting as a moral compass, our virtues such as diligence, personal responsibility, perseverance, sincerity, honesty and courage actually underpin our character and allow us to conduct our life and work better.

We find these ideals represented across history and cultures, most frequently appearing as the Greek cardinal virtues of wisdom, justice, self-mastery and courage. They are called cardinal, from the Latin *cardo* meaning *hinge* – that on which something depends – because most of the other virtues are related to one or more of them.

**Wisdom** is the virtue that enables you to exercise sound judgment, and take the right course of action in your pursuit of good. **Justice** is an outward or social virtue that enables you to be fair and give each person what he or she rightly deserves. **Self-mastery**, by contrast, is an internal virtue. It gives you intelligent control over your impulses and fosters moral autonomy. A teenager who spends six hours a day in front of the television and cannot complete his homework, or an adult who continually blames other people are examples of individuals who lack self-mastery. **Courage** is not simply bravery, but also the steadfastness to actively pursue what is good and right even when it is not convenient or popular.

To summarise so far, we have looked at:

- What you can do to value yourself
- The development of sound character traits
- Suggestions for ways to develop your character.

Let me reinforce once more that although you may have been told many times that your character is a part of you that you cannot change, I am here to tell you that you can.

# Your Personality

People form an opinion about us within the first few seconds of meeting us, but these are often misleading. At my first social function on joining a healthcare company I formed opinions about two people, one a negative 'I can't understand him' and another 'We will get on great!' Both were completely inaccurate. When I got to know the first, I found him to be a person of immense honour, trustworthy, and a responsible colleague, while the other I thought I'd really get on with turned out to be a complete fake.

This is why I suggest we focus on our *character* strength before our outward *personality* so we portray our true self.

Through our personality we communicate ourselves to others, both verbally and non-verbally. During the early days of a romantic relationship the couple communicate feelings without the need for words, and this non-verbal communication is evident in every human encounter. We can tell whether a person is happy or sad, enthusiastic or worried or depressed – the person's personality communicates it to us.

There is a very simple formula if you want someone to like you – like them. The way we would like others to react or respond to us is the way we must express ourselves to them. There is no other way to be successful on the interpersonal front.

How can you portray your personality? Adopt a confident manner and be aware of the way you walk and move as your physical actions express your mental attitudes. Shoulders bent and drooped = heavy burdens. Head down = pessimism. Shoulders back, bold steps, and eyes up and out towards a goal = confidence.

If you want to be successful, you need the help of other people, but to get that you must *find out what it is they want and how you can help them get it,* not just as a technique but because you *really* want to understand them. Once again it is helpful to cultivate positive character qualities:

- **Gratitude and manners**. We all like to be thanked *genuinely* for what we do, and few forces break a friendship more quickly than a lack of gratitude. You also need to express gratitude in your daily life so why not get the gratitude habit by making a list of everything, big and small, that you are grateful for?

- **Honesty**. Honesty cancels out many other personal shortcomings and is strongly valued by others.

- **Humility**. This allows you to admit mistakes, accept criticism that is constructive, avoid cover ups, and give credit where it is due.

As Winston Churchill once said, *'I do not resent criticism, even when, for the sake of emphasis, it parts for the time with reality.'* Constructive criticism can plant a seed that, when nurtured, brings about a transformation in your career or personal life.

- **Wit and humour**. Be with people who have a fun personality – they recharge your batteries. Life is meant to be lived, and your personality should convey that message.

- **Forgiveness, fairness, caring, loyalty, enthusiasm, respect, acting with integrity, modesty, not comparing yourself with others and trying to be real.** All these character areas can be developed and will shine through your personality when you meet others.

How do you avoid a bad first impression? Actually, the truth is that other people and the world form their opinion of you based largely on the opinion they have of themselves. If you act like a nobody, the world will take you at this value. Act as a somebody, and the world will treat you as such. One of the best ways to impress other people is to forget about creating an impact on them, and simply ask about their favourite subject – themselves.

## Reputation

If you focus on developing character followed by personality, reputation will be a natural by-product. However, here are some key areas to consider when projecting your reputation:

- Maximize Your Most Powerful Assets
- Know Thyself – Measure Your Reputation
- Learn to Play to Many Audiences – be flexible, have many friends, treat all people fairly
- Live Your Values and Ethics
- Be a Model Citizen
- Convey a Compelling Vision & Purpose
- Create Emotional Appeal – Are people happy & content around you?
- Recognise Your Shortcomings – the sooner you do, the sooner you can fix them
- Stay Vigilant – a reputation can be ruined in one conversation, one phone call, one unconsidered response.
- Make other people's Reputation important

- Speak with a Single Voice – be consistent
- Beware the Dangers of Reputation Rub-off: Birds of a feather flock together. When two or more people enter into a partnership their reputations may be attributed to each other.
- Manage Crises with Finesse
- Fix It Right the First Time – if for any reason your reputation suffers, acknowledge it and fix it straight away
- Never Underestimate people's cynicism
- Remember – Being Defensive Is Offensive

## Trust and Trustworthiness

Trustworthy people have integrity and the moral courage to do the right thing even when it is difficult to do so, and trust is essential to the formation and maintenance of a civil society. But what does trust mean? What makes us feel secure enough to place our confidence, even at times our welfare, in the hands of other people?

*'The glory of friendship is not the outstretched hand, nor the kindly smile, nor the joy of companionship; it is in the spiritual inspiration that comes to one when he discovers that someone else believes in him and is willing to trust him.'*
Ralph Waldo Emerson

In *Trust and Trustworthiness,* political scientist Russell Hardin addresses standard theories of trust and articulates his own new and compelling idea: that often what we call trust is better described as *encapsulated interest.*

Hardin argues that we place our trust in people whom we believe to have strong reasons to act in our best interests. He claims that we are correct when we assume that the main incentive of those whom we trust is to maintain a relationship with us – whether it is for reasons of economic benefit, or for love and friendship.

*'Few things can help an individual more than to place responsibility on him, and to let him know that you trust him.'*
Booker T. Washington

*'One falsehood spoils a thousand truths.'*
Ashanti Proverb

Effective and successful relationships with other people are built on two main elements:

- Having your own house in order.
- Having a foundation of trust with the other person.

Trust is perhaps the area that causes the greatest frustration and pain. The world is full of broken relationships between individuals, communities, races, religions and countries where trust has been broken. So how do we build trust and create open and honest communication with other people?

One of the most powerful metaphors I have come across is the **Trust Bank Account.** A *Trust Bank Account* is similar to a financial bank account except that we deposit and withdraw trust instead of money. We have a *trust bank account* with everyone we have a relationship with, and deposit trust into that relationship through acts of kindness, keeping our word, honesty and commitment.

Just as a healthy financial bank account holds more funds, so a healthy *trust bank account* reflects the amount of trust you have deposited with that person. As the other person's trust towards you increases, not only does it make communication easier, but the more you can call on that person if you need to. With a high reserve of trust, you can even be forgiven if you make a mistake.

On the other hand, if you constantly make withdrawals of trust from the *trust bank account* through being unkind, dishonest, ignoring, threatening, and breaking commitments, your trust bank account becomes overdrawn. In fact, mistrust prevails and the relationship is tense with constant watchfulness to see where the next unworthy deed will come from.

Successful interpersonal relationships need a basis of sustained deposits of trust to form an enjoyable, successful, and fruitful working relationship. However, we may unintentionally make withdrawals from a *trust bank account* because of differing expectations. When I run workshops and we discuss this metaphor, I ask the delegates in whose eyes is the *trust bank account* – is it ours, the other person's, or both? Answers are usually fairly evenly split.

I then ask them to think about the following hypothetical scenario: 'On leaving the last in a week-long series of workshops attended predominantly by females, I am driving home and realise I have not phoned my partner at home all week. I decide (completely out of character, as I don't usually do this!) to stop at the petrol service station and buy the biggest bunch of flowers I can get my hands on. Is this a deposit of trust or a withdrawal from the *trust bank account* I have with my partner? The answer is that it depends upon what she sees it as. If she sees it as a show of my affection, then it's certainly a deposit of trust. However, if she sees it as a means of trying (using a technique) to cover up for forgetting to phone home during the week, or even something more serious, then it is certainly a withdrawal. So the long answer to this question is that ultimately it rests in the heart of the other person. We may think we are making a deposit of trust, but if they see it as a withdrawal, then that is what it is.

This difficulty is common in relationships between parents and children, especially teenagers. Because of the age and culture difference, there can be a difference in wave length and parents often resort to demands such as 'Clean your room now.' 'Be in by 10 p.m. or else.' Or, 'Do you have to go around dressed like that?' Ask yourself if these (exaggerated) statements are deposits or withdrawals of trust? Will they form the basis for open, honest and fruitful communication?

Why not instead make a genuine offer to do something with them that they enjoy such as watching a football match, or going to see the new blockbuster film? But remember it's not a quick-fix solution and needs to be followed up with other deposits of trust and kindness.

Before I ask you to identify some key relationships, and then some major deposits of trust you will make into those relationship *trust bank accounts,* here's a reminder of some things that enable us to make fruitful major deposits.

- **Be straightforward and clear.** Lack of clarity is a major cause of breakdown in communication and relationships, and can lead to withdrawals of trust from the *trust bank account.* Don't assume your expectations will be the same as for other people, as they will often be completely different. Ask them for their opinion. You will also need an element of courage to address differences rather than just sweeping them under the carpet and hoping it will all work out.

- **Acknowledge when you make a mistake.** Although some people think that an apology gives an impression of weakness, 'Sorry' said from the heart can be a deposit of trust. To sincerely apologise for your mistake is a sign of strength, and personal integrity, and shows that you accept you are not perfect.

- **Remember names!** Names are our identity and are important to us all.

- **Act and behave from character, integrity, and values rather than ego.** Nobody likes the ego driven individual who is just out for themselves.

- **Keeping promises and commitments.** This is a major deposit in the *trust bank account* as one of the biggest withdrawals of trust is a broken promise or commitment. I suggest making promises sparingly and only after careful thought – have people say of you, 'When they make a promise it is as good as done!'

- **Show people you really care.** Develop a genuine caring attitude to show others you regard them as important. When you really care about another person you develop an understanding that enables you to do things that really comply with their deepest needs or interests.

- **Forgive and forget.** Forgiving and forgetting shows that you care enough to genuinely want to actively engage to resolve past conflicts. Forgiveness builds bridges that you can one day pass over.

- **Think other people are important.** How do you feel when someone notices you? It can be a real morale booster, and scientific studies have found that people work much better when the boss treats them as though they are important. If you constantly make an effort to notice other people, let them know and show them they are important, you will make huge deposits into their *trust bank account.*

- **Let them know they impress you.** The temptation is to impress your own importance upon them. Yet one-upmanship is a huge withdrawal from the *trust bank account,* because expressions such as, 'How wonderful BUT let me tell you what I did...' make the other person feel small or can annoy them.

- **If you're not impressed, appreciate them.** Appreciation is the opposite of depreciate (lower the value) and raises the value of another person. Accepting and believing in someone else is the best way of allowing them to change for the better.

- **See people's problems as opportunities.** Our ability to see problems as opportunities develops transformational relationships with our children and others — not only will it change your attitude, it will also change theirs. Being a solution thinker is a powerful style of thinking. When I was in a sales job my exceptionally competent boss told me to embrace customer complaints and look at them as an opportunity to create a more loyal customer. It worked, because if we could sort out a complaint over and above the satisfaction the customer was expecting, it was as if the complaint never existed, and the deposit into their *trust bank account* developed a loyalty very difficult for competitors to break.

- **The small courtesies are often the big ones!** We are all tender and sensitive inside, and small courtesies and perceived small things are big deposits into the *trust bank account,* touching our innermost feelings and the emotions of our heart.

- **Practise unconditional love with those you truly care about.** When you offer love without strings you affirm the other person's worth and develop their self-esteem and self-belief. Although developing deep, meaningful relationships requires immense personal strength, courage, and digging deep into your character strength reserves, a more rewarding and profound experience is difficult to find.

Now you know the importance of building character and its vital place in successful relationships. You have the key qualities and skills to develop your inner character and create and sustain highly effective relationships with others. And you can establish high trust levels with others using the *trust bank account* method.

If you have thoughtfully worked through the issues you are ready to progress further in the exciting arena of developing deeply meaningful and rewarding relationships. Ready?

# Action 6

## Interact with Skill

*'The need for cooperation can only strengthen humankind, because
it helps us to recognise that the most secure foundation for a new
world order is not simply broader political and economic alliances,
but each individual's genuine practice of love and compassion.
These qualities are the ultimate source of human happiness,
and our need for them lies at the very core of our being.'*
Human Rights and Universal Responsibility.

Cooperation is an example of interacting with skill, as in going for a win/win result instead of trying to have everything your own way. Being assertive is another example, not to be confused with being aggressive. Remember how in one study it was found that only 15% of a business person's success can be attributed to their knowledge and technical skills. The remaining 85% is determined by attitude and the ability to deal with people. That's why it's essential you develop the right attitude and develop the skills necessary to deal well with people in all situations at all times – and **Action 6** reveals how.

*'The job is dealing with customer needs.
70% is about fixing the person, 30% about fixing the car.'*
The R.A.C.

Our lives are interconnected with others as Robert Thurman, a Tibetan practitioner and scholar demonstrates. He asks us to imagine a scenario where we are on a train full of people for the rest of time! Some people on the train just sit reading their newspapers and eating lunch, others are agitated, upset or angry, while still others are busy enjoying themselves. How would everyone else's moods and behaviour affect you and the other passengers? How would it affect your behaviour if you knew you were on this train for the rest of time? Would you compete or co-operate with them? Would you try to create conflict or prevent it?

As the global economy becomes increasingly integrated, the results of an election in one country affect the stock markets in many others. Nowadays we cannot think only in terms of my nation or my country, let alone my village or my town. Universal cooperation and responsibility is the key to overcoming the problems the world faces in the 21st Century. Could the same be true for us as individuals?

Universal cooperation and responsibility is paramount to long-term human survival. It is also the best foundation for world peace, the equitable use of natural resources, and the proper care of our environment.

Your inter-relational style is crucial if you are to create a smooth train journey. Do you have a style that gets the best out of others? Or do you have a style that inhibits creativity or irritates others? Can you change your style?

*'I look forward to a time when we can mature like other species from competition to cooperation, and build a human society in which the goals of individual and community, of local and global economy, of economy and ecology are met. This will shift us out of crisis and into the happier, healthier world of which we all dream.'*

Elisabet Sahtouris, evolution biologist

Any act of kindness toward a fellow human being rewards you with positive inner feelings that material possessions cannot give, and reminds us of the all important aspects of life such as service, kindness and love. If we all do our part, we will soon live on a more cooperative planet.

*'An eye for an eye makes the whole world blind.'*

Mahatma Gandhi

When working in the healthcare industry, my colleagues and I went on a course that involved using the principles of win/win (a way of finding internal and external solutions where all parties involved feel their needs are met). We learned that to achieve win/win in the workplace we needed to have certain processes in place. After attending the course we went to our senior management team and asked what our corporate strategy was and what the goals were for the following year. We then asked for a system to be put in place where the whole company could be rewarded rather than just an individual or individual team if the company goal were achieved. Our senior managers agreed and the target was not only achieved, but surpassed. We were successful in creating a cooperative, creative, result-orientated working environment where everyone wanted everyone else to succeed. The financial results were astounding, our staff retention rate improved by over 20%, motivation and commitment levels improved markedly and it became a truly enjoyable place to work.

We all know we live in an ever-changing world where technology is changing at a rapid pace. In the same way we adapt to new discoveries, it is vital that we apply the same flexibility when dealing with people. This means starting from where the other person is currently at, and working from that position.

Being an effective leader requires the same skills, whether leading a business, school, community group, expedition or even with your friends or at home. However, before people can be won around to your ideas, they must be won to you – remember the trust bank account?

What is your self-chosen strategy in attracting people to you? Is it authoritarian – do this my way or else? Or have you learned the fine art of leading committed and motivated people to a desired destination?

Many people who are self-conscious, shy and feel inferior fail to realise that the underlying problem is a failure to deal effectively with other people. But bossy, domineering types also have something missing as they have to rely on force to get people to do what they want and are often disliked because they have never learned how to get on with people.

People are here to stay, so learn how to take them into account! The doctor, solicitor or car mechanic who is the most successful is not necessarily the most intelligent. Nor are the happiest couple necessarily the most beautiful. Successful people are those who have learned about cooperation, even if they haven't come across the concept of win/win. One helpful method is to think of everyone as a potential customer and think like a true customer service professional: View all customers as a beautiful garden that must be cultivated and watered frequently because they're worth it. Remember that service is the lifeblood of any organisation. Everything flows from good service and is nourished by it. Customer service is not a department, it is an attitude and you need to treat every customer as if your world revolves around them, because it does!

William James, the psychologist and philosopher, called the discovery that human beings can change their lives by changing their attitudes a revolution. People with the right attitude achieve goals. We are going to look at developing a cooperative attitude rather than the competitive attitude our society instils in us from childhood. At school the exam system judges our performance by the grade we achieve – compared to other students, rather than how well we performed compared to our own ability. Then on leaving formal education we enter the dog-eat-dog world of work where we are not only aware of external competition – the companies and organisations we compete against – but also internal competition for promotion and pay rises.

Can you change your conditioning? Consider first how you currently interact. Are you currently aggressive, passive, or somewhere in between when dealing with others?

Mark McCormack in his book, *What They don't Teach You at Harvard Business School*, explains how to make bargaining and negotiation a win/win for both sides. Win/win outcomes in your dealings with other people is the result you are looking for using **Action 6**.

Why is this Action so important? In Dr Wiggam's column, Let's Explore Your Mind, he reported that of 4,000 people who lost their jobs in one year, only 10% lost them because they could not do the work. The remaining 90% lost their jobs because they were unable to deal successfully with other people. Before you start to look at the different ways we interact, it is worth considering the following:

- Many people are hungrier for their ego to be filled than their stomachs. Hungry dogs are mean dogs. Hungry egos are also mean.

- Most people are more interested in themselves than anything else.

- Everyone has a desire to feel important and be something.

- To approve ourselves, we crave other people's approval.

- People with big egos suffer from too little self-esteem, not too much.

- To be petty, you have to stoop to very low levels.

- Winning the argument often loses the sale.

- Little things very often trigger big things – it takes one small spark to set off an explosion!

- People hate not being given credit for what they have done, or not being encouraged. They also hate being criticised in front of others or being ignored and not asked their opinion.

- 95% of the cases where someone acts unreasonably, we asked for it!
- If you decide before the meeting that the person is going to be difficult, guess what? You set the stage for them to act upon! Your own attitudes are reflected back to you in other people's behaviour.
- Speech research shows that when a person is shouted at, it is almost impossible not to shout back even if we cannot see the speaker. The louder we talk, the angrier we become. What happens, therefore if you lower the tone of your voice?
- You won't sell anything to anyone else, until you are sold yourself. Others will not be enthusiastic until you are. If you don't believe in yourself other people won't either.

In the UK, ritual humiliation from surly servers is often the order of the day. It's amazing how the average British person can make the innocuous phrase 'How may I help you?' sound like a curse. Signs too often also communicate a negative message – for example: You break it. You buy it.

How refreshing then, to walk into a branch of *Richer Sounds*, a leading hi-fi retailer, where every sign in the store conveys a positive message. Instead of saying *No dogs allowed*, they have a polite notice that reads: *Guide dogs welcome,* which implies simply that other dogs are not. Are shoplifters deterred by signs that say: *Shoplifters will be prosecuted*? Probably not. Richer Sounds shops have one that says: *Free ride in police car – for shoplifters today only.*

It conveys the desired point, and makes honest customers laugh. As founder Julian Richer says: 'We like amusing signs because we think that if we can get customers to smile, we are halfway there.' Even more enticing is the example of a shop selling mechanical toys in San Francisco where their *Guide to Fun* reads:

- *Please do touch the merchandise*
- *Feel free to play with anything in the store, except the employees*
- *If you break it... relax, we know you didn't mean to*
- *Because we care... share demo toys with others!*
- *Food and drinks allowed – enjoy!*
- *Speak any language – except foul*
- *If you're under 18, you must be with someone older*

- *Our toys carry a lifetime guarantee – the lifetime of the TOY, not YOURS*
- *All sales are final (more or less)*
- *Most importantly, our employees are instructed NOT to say:* Have a Nice Day.

## Communication/Interpersonal Leadership styles and their implications

| High | **PASSIVE BEHAVIOUR** | **ASSERTIVE BEHAVIOUR** |
|---|---|---|
| THOUGHT & CONSIDERATION GIVEN TO OTHERS | I do not express my needs, wants and opinions directly. I put other's needs above my own.<br><br>I LOSE, YOU WIN | I clearly express my needs, wants and opinions in a way which is considerate of others.<br><br>I WIN, YOU WIN |
| | **NO/LOW STANDARD BEHAVIOUR** | **OPENLY AGGRESSIVE BEHAVIOUR** |
| Low | I do not express my needs, wants and opinions and I do not care much for other people's either.<br><br>I LOSE, YOU LOSE | I am direct in expressing my needs, wants, and opinions and I give no thought to other people's.<br><br>I WIN, YOU LOSE |

Low    COURAGE TO PUT MY POINT OF VIEW ACROSS CLEARLY    High

*'Adopt the attitude and action you want the other person to express.'*

Now let's look at these more closely, starting with the bottom right – the *openly aggressive style* which comes from the mindset of *I win and you will lose*. It is the authoritarian approach, 'I will get my way at any cost, but you will not get yours.' These people are prepared to use their position, power, qualifications, material/financial wealth, personality or physical intimidation to get their own way.

Unfortunately, most of us have been programmed with this win/lose way of thinking. Imagine having two children and at Parents' Evening you are told, 'Johnny is doing really well, in the highest group for most subjects, and he should get a place in one of the best Universities – you should be very proud of him. Whereas Jayne is struggling, particularly with the academic studies – she will need to improve her grades to even get into sixth form.' What would you be thinking?

What this kind of comparative information does not tell you is that Johnny is a natural gifted type who is coasting through school and getting results by putting in little or no effort, whereas Jayne, although not getting the grades, is working really hard and her improvement since this time last year is exemplary. Competition lies at the core of this type of system. But grading against other people rather than against our own potential is dangerous because it can give out inferiority vibes.

Most of life is not one big competition. Do you have to compete with your spouse, work colleagues, friends, family or children? In most relationships, if we are not both winning, we are both losing. If you want results that depend on the input of others, leave the win/lose mentality at home, it is counter productive for achieving any form of cooperation.

So is there a need for *win/lose* thinking? This approach where people are programmed to go out and get what they want from the prosperity there is for all, is fairly common and relies on being tough (so-called), focussed and driven. However, tough, focussed and driven does not make us happy.

A group of western economists (as reported in Summer 2004 issue of *Positive News: www.positivenews.org.uk*) suggest that rather than measuring economies by Gross National Product, the measure should instead be Gross National Happiness as in Bhutan, led by King Jigme Singye Wangchuk. This unorthodox approach questions the values of unbridled economic progress and the perception/paradigm that if we have enough material goods, we will be happy. Instead they suggest a model that embraces the totality of life and includes emotions, feelings and other softer values that don't show up in current economic and business models. Is this the way forward, creating real value?

## Aggressive behaviour is based upon the beliefs that:

- Your own needs, wants and opinions are more important than other people's
- You have rights, and others do not
- You have something to contribute, while others have little or nothing to contribute

## The goals of aggressive people are:

- To win! To dominate! To intimidate! To overpower! To get what they want when they want it! They often obtain their goal by belittling, degrading and humiliating others.

## The basic message of aggressive people is:

- You will never have to wonder what I think – I am going to tell you! You will never have to wonder what I feel – I am going to tell you! And I guarantee that you are going to do what I want you to do, even if I have to use fear and intimidation in order to get you to do it! You are even more stupid than I thought if you disagree!

## The thought patterns of aggressive people include:

- I'm OK – you're not
- I have rights – you don't
- People should do what I want without questioning me!
- Personnel don't send me good people any more!
- If more people were like me, we wouldn't have the problems we have
- I am never wrong!
- My feelings are more important than yours!
- I don't need to listen to you. You have nothing to offer me

## Aggressively handling criticism entails:

- Being defensive
- Making counter attacks
- Resenting the criteria
- Stubbornly refusing to change

Some people rather than having a win/lose attitude, develop a win attitude, where they go out just for themselves, not necessarily so others will lose, but so that they win every time.

One interim measure you can take if you fall into either of the above two categories is that if you 'win' or accomplish a task better than someone else, then show the other person how you did it.

Now let's have a look at *no/low standard behaviour*, or lose/lose thinking. The first common type is when you have no standards, values, desires, dreams or aspirations for yourself – your attitude is that if you go through life losing, so be it. At the same time you don't really want to cooperate with anyone else, believing that if nobody wins, being a loser is acceptable.

The other type of lose/lose mentality is where your energy is totally focussed upon an 'enemy' with a vindictive get-even type of attitude. An example of this is the dissolving of a business partnership through dispute where one partner sells all the stock and company assets for a fraction of the real value, totally blinded by the acute desire to make them lose, even if it means personal loss as well. Can you think of divorces where this type of thinking prevailed?

Now let's look at *passive behaviour* or *lose/win thinking*. In its extreme this is martyrdom saying: 'Walk all over me, use me as your door mat, everyone else does.' You are easily intimidated by others because you have little internal value and therefore no courage to stand up for what you believe. In fact, you are often not even prepared to express your feelings for fear of being ridiculed or contradicted. In any form of negotiation you are the one to give in because you are seen as, and see yourself as, permissive and passive.

Because you feel constantly downtrodden, you bury a lot of unexpressed feelings, which ultimately leads to resentment, anger and frustration. Sometimes these buried emotions result in out of character outbursts or surface later, more seriously, in severe chronic illnesses and disabilities such as heart disease, nervous disorders, stress and mental illness.

**Non-assertive** or passive behaviour is based upon the beliefs that:

- The other person/people's needs and wants are more important than your own
- The other person/people has rights and you do not
- You have nothing or little to contribute, and the other person has a great deal to contribute

**The goals of passive people are:**

- To be liked. To be nice. To be a friend and appease others. Permeating these goals is the desire to avoid conflict at all costs.

**The basic message of passive people is:**

- What I think doesn't matter. What I feel is unimportant. Please read this sign, 'Walk all over me'. I don't respect myself, and I don't expect you to either.

**The thought patterns of passive people include:**

- I'm not OK – I'm not sure about you.
- Everyone has rights but me.
- I can survive if everyone likes me and approves of what I do, say and feel.
- Nice people don't disagree.
- Don't make waves. Don't rock the boat. People won't like you.
- Peace at any price.
- What I think is unimportant.
- I won't offer my opinion. People might laugh at me.
- It's not my place to speak up.

**The non-assertive, passive recipient of criticism:**

- Whines
- Cries
- Pleads
- Makes excuses
- Engages in self-pity
- Hates themselves
- Blames others

## Being Assertive

We have saved the best to last – the *assertive behaviour* of the person who thinks *win/win*. More than an interpersonal or communication technique, this concept of win/win is more a philosophy, seeking shared benefit in every interaction you have. As an *Assertive, win/win* person you are naturally solution, rather than problem orientated and always look for equally satisfying and jointly agreed outcomes. You operate with an attitude of fair exchange, and make it your business to take care of the needs and wants of others.

As an assertive person you understand you can achieve more by adopting a cooperative attitude. Because you have values, true character strength, vision and worthy plans, you do not need to borrow any power from another's position or other external influences. You don't believe your success has to be at the expense of someone else, but you also don't necessarily capitulate to other people's demands. Often you look for a solution that perhaps neither of you had thought of before; one that is therefore creative and better than either could have come up with on their own. This is exciting human interaction. Have you ever been part of a team, be it a sport, work or other type, where there was a natural understanding between people and a spirit of support where all cooperated for the common good? Feels good, doesn't it? To develop your cooperative social skills:

- Share ideas rather than keeping them to yourself.
- Understand that the one common denominator to success and happiness is other people. Success with people gives you an 85% chance of success in your chosen profession, and about 99% in your road to personal happiness.
- Give genuine and sincere compliments to other people.
- Offer help and encouragement to other people, particularly in areas where you have experience or expertise.
- If you need to recommend changes or suggestions, doing it in a pleasant way.
- Embrace diverse viewpoints.
- Exercise self-control, particularly when those around you do not.
- Develop a problem solving mentality, rather than a problem creating mentality.
- Realise you have in abundance many things that other people want.
- Recognise that a happy human being is more likely to spread happiness than an unhappy one.
- Work with human nature rather than against it. Just as a bad golfer blames his clubs, someone who does not work with human nature blames other people for their misfortune.

Here is another helpful extract from Mark McCormack:

*'I find it helpful to try to figure out in advance where the other person would like to end up – at what point he would like to do the deal and still feel he's coming away with something. This is different from, 'How far will he go?'... A lot of times you can push someone to the wall, and you still reach an agreement, but his resentment will come back to haunt you in a million ways.'*

You need to be flexible rather than rigid in your approach when negotiating or bargaining so there are no bad feelings.

## Assertive beliefs

When thinking about situations in which you ought to be assertive, be aware that:

- You have needs to be met
- The other people involved have needs to be met
- You have rights and so do others
- You have something to contribute as do others

## As an assertive person your goals will be:

- To get the work done at a level of excellence, while enhancing the growth and development of those doing the work. To communicate in a style that is accurate and respectful of the dignity of all persons involved. And to encourage those you work with to do the same.

## The basic message of assertive people is:

- You will never have to wonder what I think – I will tell you. You will never have to wonder what I feel – I will share that with you. And I guarantee that I have no interest in being critical of you for what you think or feel. Indeed, I invite you to share these things with me. We are here to get the job done, and to contribute to a positive work environment.

## The thought patterns of assertive people include:

- I'm OK and you're OK.
- I have rights, and so do you.
- It is all right to learn from mistakes.
- I am a valuable and worthy person, and so are you.

- I have choices in nearly all situations, and I am responsible for the consequences of my choices.
- I trust you, and you can trust me.
- I am not a helpless victim.
- I will not allow others to decide for me how I will behave.
- Conflicts provide opportunities to grow and should not be avoided.
- I want to find a way we can all win.

## Elements of Assertive Communication
- Visual    =    Look assertive!
- Vocal    =    Sound assertive!
- Verbal    =    Use assertive language

## Visual elements of assertive communication
- Eye Contact
- Facial Expressions
- Gestures
- Posture

## Vocal elements of assertive communication
- Voice Volume
- Speaking Rate
- Tone of Voice
- Fluency

## Verbal elements of assertive communication
- Statements should be direct, clear and concise.
- Sentences should be complete.
- Avoid intensifying words, such as *extremely, very* and *incredibly.*
- Avoid qualifying words such as *sort of, kind of, somewhat* and *it's just my opinion.*
- Avoid evaluative labels and name calling, such as *stupid, lazy, inconsiderate* and *selfish.*

## People who are assertive:
- Are generally calm and relaxed
- Hold good eye contact
- Can be firm when necessary
- Have a positive attitude towards people and situations
- Recognise responsibility for their own behaviour
- Have confidence
- Are open and honest
- Sharing is in their nature
- Listen well
- Communicate well

## Examples of Assertive Situations
1. Praising the work of a subordinate.
2. Telling someone about the good things they are doing at work.
3. Asking for clarification of something you do not know or understand.
4. Admitting that you are nervous or afraid.
5. Admitting you have made a mistake.
6. Disagreeing with your boss.
7. Giving an opinion at a meeting.
8. Dealing with critical customers.
9. Criticising another's work (in a constructive way).
10. Asking subordinates to do unpleasant work.
11. Terminating someone's employment.
12. Getting information from experts.
13. Asking others not to smoke.
14. Asking for a pay rise.
15. Applying for a new job.
16. Receiving an appraisal from your boss.
17. Being asked to do something beyond your scope at work.
18. Responding (rather than reacting) to personal attacks in a calm way.

19. Responding to sexist or racist remarks (rather than ignoring them).
20. Stopping a conversation that is time wasting.
21. Dealing with another's personal problems.
22. Responding when someone else takes the credit for things you have done.

## What to do to be Assertive

- Know when to leave things alone.
- Work within your abilities. Do not exaggerate your strengths and weaknesses.
- Do not act helpless if you can act independently
- Once you've decided on a particular subject or to follow a particular pattern, say so, being specific and direct.
- Stick to your statement. Repeat it if necessary until you get a satisfactory response.
- Being silent after saying something says a lot; it indicates to the other person that you're waiting for an answer.
- Listen carefully when others are talking even if what is said does not alter your opinions.
- Be positive, focus on solutions, and check everyone understands by summarising.
- Make eye contact.
- Relax.

## Handling common assertive situations

Most assertive situations you face will fall into one of the following categories:

- Making requests
- Saying no
- Giving critical feedback
- Accepting criticism

## Making Requests

The assertive style of making a request asks specifically for what you want. By taking responsibility for your requests, you allow others freedom to grant or refuse them.

Assertively making a request means:

- Stating a need
- Asking for action
- Giving a reason for the request

If your request is honoured, always express gratitude. If your request is denied, be a gracious loser.

## Saying no

Assertive people say 'No' directly without hesitation, and without giving lengthy excuses or apologies. Being clear about your priorities and goals makes saying 'No' easier.

## Giving feedback

Giving feedback in a straightforward, assertive style focuses on work-related behaviour rather than people's personalities. Both parties can come away from the feedback feeling positive, and the problem that engendered the feedback is likely to be solved.

## Accepting criticism

An assertive individual can listen to criticism, objectively examine the feedback, and state their position without becoming defensive.

The assertive approach to receiving criticism involves:

- Patiently listening to the criticism without interrupting
- Paraphrasing the feedback
- Asking for specifics to ensure understanding
- *Acknowledging the parts of the message with which you agree*

An extension to this assertive, *win/win thinking* is *win/win* or *no deal thinking* where if we cannot find an outcome that benefits us both, we agree to disagree agreeably – no deal. Use this concept at the outset of the relationship, negotiation or formation of anything that involves people.

So is assertiveness or going for a win/win or no deal always possible?

Probably not, for example, if you are discussing something with a friend and the issue is more important to them than to you, you may decide to go for a lose/win outcome to preserve the relationship with that person. Lose/win can also be an option if the time, effort and resources needed for any kind of win is just not worth it, or if it violates other principles, values or priorities. If your life is in real danger I suggest just going for win and maybe forgetting about other people, although in survival situations co-operation with others is the best option.

The best choice, therefore, depends on the situation with the key word being *choice*. However, cooperation – being assertive rather than aggressive or passive and going for a win/win (or no deal) outcome – is really the only viable option for long term successful relationships.

If we look at the different styles of those involved, we can see that the outcomes will be different. Two assertive win/win people will, without doubt, develop really creative outcomes which they both feel good about, while two openly aggressive people will probably end up with a lose/lose outcome as neither will be prepared to compromise.

The aggressive type however loves the passive type as they can feed off them, manipulate them and always get their way (in the short-term), achieving a win/lose outcome. Two passive types together will probably end up with a lose/lose as neither will go for what they really want and all the time will be spent trying to give the other person what they want. The no standard type of person will probably end up with either a lose/lose or lose/win outcome whoever they are dealing with because they simply don't care.

An assertive person however, has the true character strength and internal power to achieve win/win outcomes. They will do this without subordinating to the intimidation of the openly aggressive type, but by leading through example with the passive and no standard type. They also give the passive and no standard types the power to achieve things beyond their current realm of reality. And because of their character strength can even influence the aggressive types to soften their approach because the aggressive type will recognise that intimidation does not work with assertive people.

If you briefly return to the diagram depicting the four types, you will see that to achieve these win/win outcomes you need a balance between your own internal courage to put your point of view across and thought and consideration for the other person. If you have this balance, it is the first real step.

Can you see the power of adopting this approach with interpersonal relationships?

## Dealing with aggressive people?

Firstly, you must come with a cooperative win/win attitude and be clear about no deal up front, so the other person is in no doubt about where you are coming from. You can't expect a yes response if you set a negative stage, so create a positive and affirmative atmosphere and reinforce the calm assumption that the other person is going to cooperate with you.

Let them state their case without interrupting so that they feel you understand their viewpoint and be prepared to concede something to find a point of agreement. State your case moderately and accurately, calmly presenting the facts and leaving out any counter threats or force. It is natural with these types to try to persuade them with argument, but if you can, use any third person speak such as testimonials or recommendations to prove your point. Rather than saying to your boss, 'I deserve a pay rise,' say, 'I believe my record here will show I deserve a pay rise.' If you attack the ego of this type of person you will lose – it is again about working with human nature rather than against it – find a way they can escape from their previous hard line view without losing face.

## Achieving win/win outcomes

Now identify one relationship in your personal life and one in your professional life where a win/win outcome would be the ideal to aspire towards. Write down the name of the person, where you think the relationship currently is, and what *you* could do to generate a win/win outcome.

Personal relationship:

Current reality:

What I can do to achieve a win/win outcome:

Professional relationship:

Current reality:

What I can do to achieve a win/win outcome:


What ideally needs to be in place to achieve win/win?


Interpersonal leadership is the key factor here. To express assertiveness and achieve win/win outcomes, you need to introduce a *shared* attitude and character so you offer *shared* influence and achieve *shared* outcomes and benefits.

It is about being nice and tough all at once – you don't have to be either/or. It's about having the character to listen empathically to others, but remaining confident yourself, and being considerate and sensitive as well as bold and brave. If this balance is not there, you will fall back into either passive or aggressive behaviour. If you are highly courageous and brave, but lack any element of consideration for others, you will be aggressively going for a win/lose outcome, often based on fulfilling your ego. Whereas if you are extremely considerate and sensitive but lack personal strength you'll be thinking a lose/win mentality because you have little or no courage to express your own views.

Having this balance right allows you to listen to understand, but also gives you the power to politely confront. However, you also need to develop a sharing attitude, where you genuinely want to share recognition, rewards, credit, power and happiness.

You need to be *really* happy for the success of other people, especially those closest to you, rather than perhaps eating your heart out at another's success. Our sense of worth must not come from comparisons with other people, but from an inner sense of security, personal worth, and self-belief.

It is a real test of your ability to make deposits of trust into the trust bank accounts of other people when you deal with an aggressive win/lose person. The key is to separate the person from the issue and still focus on making small and regular deposits into their trust bank account by being understanding, respectful, courteous, and not defensive and judgemental.

The more you exercise your own integrity and character strength, the greater your influence will be with people, even the openly aggressive ones who will begin to realise that shared benefit or win/win with you is the only way to get more of what they want. When the trust bank account is high, people will even support decisions they don't necessarily agree with, because these people will want to support you – with high trust they may even work with you to make the decision happen.

You won't need to abandon any old friends, but you may wish to expand your range of friends or contacts to help you climb your mountain. We need different people in our lives to allow us to achieve our true potential – it is important to have contacts who help you achieve shared benefit win/win outcomes.

The *process of working through issues* is also essential to achieve these shared benefit win/win outcomes and includes formal performance agreements between work colleagues and partnership agreements between two or more departments or organisations, or even customers and suppliers.

A helpful tool in this process is the following Five Stage Agreement to clarify what is expected, define roles and identify who and what is available to accomplish the results.

- Identify the agreed and shared *results* to be achieved. This keeps everyone focused on the big picture and results, rather than the methods.

- Once you have identified the results, you need to agree the *standards/parameters/guidelines* to operate from. For formal agreements this could be in the form of policies, procedures or manuals, while informal agreements could ensure you draw on your strengths, compensate for any weaknesses, and identify what has worked and what has not in the past.

- Next you need to identify the *resources* available and make sure they are in place to achieve the results. This could include financial, technical, IT, specialist or human resources.

- Next, agree the benchmark to which you are working, agreeing between all parties involved *who is responsible for what,* and time scales for achieving outcomes to take you towards the results. The standard of work to be produced should also be agreed at this time to ensure a high standard is achieved throughout.

- Finally, identify the *reward or negative consequences* for achieving or not achieving the results identified at the beginning of this process.

Basically you agree what will happen as a result of evaluation, and for a lengthy project you may have many evaluations before the results are achieved. The rewards could be financial such as salary increase, allowances, recognition, credibility, training or development opportunity, or an increase or decrease in areas of responsibility. The important thing once again is that it is clear at the beginning, so everyone's expectations are unambiguous. Effective reward is a motivational power and can establish a positive bond with the leader that encourages effective cooperation. It should not just be tangible performance that should be rewarded, but other factors including such things as good communications.

This process can be extremely powerful in the workplace through motivating employees, allowing them to be part of the creation of criteria for success and providing a standard from which they can measure their own success. When people are given a chance to be part of this process, not only will they engage, but they will work to far higher standards than under traditional authoritarian supervision and management gofer methods. Being focussed on jointly achieved results will release creativity, personal energy and power that you would never have thought possible in people.

## Achieving Win/Win in Organisations

The final thing we need to have in place to achieve mutual benefit or win/win outcomes within the context of performing within an organisation is having systems in place to support it. You may ask, 'But how can I change the *systems* within the organisation that I work?' But actually by being proactive and focussing on those things you can do something about, there is always something you can do. Put together a proposal, for example, to show how changing the system could benefit company and customers, motivate staff, aid staff retention rates, lower overhead costs, improve sales/turnover, and improve the efficiency and effectiveness of the working culture. Would it work? Not sure, but surely it's worth a try.

Companies with win/win systems in place do not need a motivational speaker to give their workers a temporary boost. That motivational boost is generated naturally as a consequence of having the right systems in place to allow it to happen. It will also be more permanent, rather than temporary.

This is not to say competition does not have a place as you will be naturally competitive in the marketplace against other companies who operate in a similar field. However, cooperation can be applied here too through developing the common marketplace, for example, or applying and developing industry standards. One example is the airline industry that must cooperate with its competitors in areas of safety as a general deterioration in the industry's safety record would affect all the airlines.

Competition can also be valuable as a comparison against the previous year's performance. Yet cooperation systems implemented in organisational planning, training, interdepartmental communication, rewards, strategy development, and sales and marketing systems facilitate an environment where mutually beneficial win/win outcomes flourish.

If a person has always got results by trampling over other people and dictating what they do, this may be related to a system where people are rewarded purely on financial results. Changing the reward system so that how he or she is perceived by their team is also a factor may be all that is needed to change this person into a cooperative team leader and people developer.

However, sometimes the problem is the system rather than the individual. If it sets people up for win/lose, the natural consequence is that openly aggressive types will arise, even if this is not their natural style. If the culture within an organisation is changed to be cooperative, people will find ingenious ways to create joint benefit win/win outcomes. It can work in families, education, law, business, and local and national government.

One cooperative organisation I worked for combined the quarterly team meeting with a session at the bowling alley, where, instead of competing against each other, each team would compete against their previous score. As a result the attitude changed from competition to open encouragement as those players with better skills shared their techniques to increase the score.

Achieving win/win outcomes actually places more responsibility upon the individual because focusing on a joint outcome fosters mutual responsibility between team members. In addition, when you have clear guidelines, have identified the available resources, know the standard of performance required, and the reward or consequence (as a team) for achieving or not achieving, you set yourself up for success rather than failure.

This employee notice board summarises what we have done so far:

The six most important words in the English Language are: 'I admit I made a mistake.' Huge deposit into the trust bank account!
The five most important words are: 'You did a great job.'
The four most important words are: 'What is your opinion?'
The three most important words are: 'If you please.'
The two most important words are: 'Thank you.'
The single most important word is: 'We.'
The least important word is: 'Me'

This is the essence of what we have done in this Action. We have gone from me to we thinking, to seek agreement rather than disagreement, to be responsive rather than resentful, to bend without breaking, and to win without anyone losing.

*A boss says, 'Get going!' A leader says, 'Let's go!'*

*'The essence lies not in the victory, but the struggle.'*

In the first five Actions of this series we looked at becoming the master, but now we are beginning to look at the importance of becoming the servant. The highest goals in life, health and wellbeing, personal success and happiness, are reached by those who choose to serve.

Many leadership studies have identified that for the leader the most important concern is the people he or she leads. Studying the behaviour of other people can be a key to interacting with them effectively and discovering how you can get the best out of them individually and as part of the team. Research and behavioural science has suggested that the successful leader and communicator will learn all he or she can to increase their effectiveness through their understanding of human nature.

*'Problems become opportunities*
*when the right people come together.'*

Becoming servant orientated requires character strength, courage, and a heart filled with devotion, empathy, kindness, consideration and compassion.

Will your decisions over the next week benefit others more than yourself? Will you give more than you receive? Will you avoid blaming others? Will you be part of a winning team? Will you forgive yourself and others? Now write down what you can and WILL do in the next week in these areas.

## Increasing your Cooperative Power

*'Either all human beings have equal rights, or none have any.'*
Annie Besant (1845–1933), British Social Reformer

Ask, 'Can you help me with this?' or seek advice. 'This is what I want to accomplish, what do you think? What ideas do you have? What is your opinion?' These statements nurture cooperation. *It is psychologically impossible for a human being to give us 100% of their commitment unless they are allowed to give their ideas.* The brain and body work together as a team.

People support what they help create. If people feel part of a problem they will come up with ideas to become part of the solution. In the work scenario it could be seen as *participative management*. The ideal of *multiple management* in an organisation will enlist both the brains and the brawn of all the workers. This is where all ideas are valid with suggestion boxes, rewards, and recognition for ideas that are implemented. And shared responsibility for success, as well as challenges with ownership of the problems encountered. What a work environment!

*'The best minute you spend is the one you invest in someone else.'*

Sometimes you may need the support of another person for one of your own ideas. Instead of saying, 'I wish you would help here and approve my idea.' Consider: 'If you were me, how would you go about getting this idea across to our colleagues and approved?' This approach asks them to become involved in your idea or problem, and makes your problem their problem. If you want other people's help and recommendations, try this approach.

The key with this principle is the intent with which you ask. If it is just a technique or a way of getting people to feel sorry for you, it will not work and you could be seen as a nuisance. You could also lose friends if you are just doing it to make your candle glow brighter or for a pat on the back. You must ask for advice, ideas and suggestions and *really mean it*, not just when you want assurance that you are right, or when you want sympathy.

*'Meeting people halfway is the most significant trip we can take.*
*We don't work for each other, we work with each other.'*

Another powerful principle you can apply is **praise**. Have you ever noticed how if someone pays you a sincere compliment or praises you it automatically lifts your spirit and gives you new zest for life? The lift we get from praise is not illusionary, and works equally well when we give it to other people.

Science has shown, even if it does not really understand it, that physical energy is released when praise is given. An experiment using a machine called an erograph to measure fatigue showed that when praised, children showed an immediate increase in energy. The opposite was true when they were criticised.

The video by teacher Jane Elliot, *A Class Divided*, also showed how children when praised and uplifted performed much better in written and oral tests, but under-performed the following day when criticised and picked on.

*'Great achievements are nurtured with the cooperation of many minds with a common vision working toward a common goal.'*

Many studies have shown that praise and recognition is number one on the list of the things that are most important to an employee. Most of us, whether it be at home, at work, at school or amongst friends are hungry for praise, appreciation and attention. If most people are hungry for this praise and we give it to them, do you think they will be more generous in giving us what we want, whether it's their cooperation, genuine input, skill, knowledge or ideas?

Again the key here is the intent, and the praise must be genuine, but if you do this every day you will see a transformation in people as they become more friendly and cooperative. As well as looking for good things in other people to praise, also look for good things in your own life that you can really be thankful for – there will be a great deal! The deliberate looking for the good in others helps take our minds off ourselves. It will help make us less self-conscious, less self-righteous and more tolerant and understanding. If we stop finding fault and find the good, our own happiness will be greatly increased. There is some good in everyone!

*Coming together is a beginning, keeping together is progress, working together is a success.*

Take time to make a short list of the people who are important to you and where you will make a conscious effort to look for the good within in order to offer genuine praise.

## What if we Have to Offer Criticism?

There are times when you need to point out something to another person, but the key is to do it in a way that builds them up rather than beats them down. It's about helping them to improve rather than hurting their feelings. It should not be about the personalities, it

should be about the act, not the person. So how can you criticise in a positive way?
Here are some guidelines:

- Criticism made in front of other people will cause resentment. Do it in private.

- Try to preface the criticism with a compliment. It will create a friendly atmosphere and put them more at ease, preventing defensiveness from both of you and open up an environment for receptive dialogue. Compliments and praise will open up the other person's mind.

- Criticise what the person did, not the person. This makes it impersonal. You can build them up whilst pointing out their mistakes. 'I know from past experience this error is untypical of you, what in your view happened?' Let them also know they are better than the mistake they have made and give them a high expectation to live up to. Avoid phrases such as, 'You are terrible at...' or, 'Of all the stupid things you could have done...' or, 'Why didn't you...?' instead try statements such as: 'This work is not up to standard, what can we do to improve it?' or, 'The report did not get to me on time, what happened?'

- Help them with the answer, and be part of the solution as well as the problem. It is about correcting the mistake and finding a way to avoid it happening again. As you saw earlier with *performance agreements*, make sure expectations are clear. As well as telling people what is wrong, tell them also what is right. Give them a target to aim toward.

- Ask for cooperation, rather than demand it. 'Will you?' gets more cooperation than, 'Do this.' It is not a slave/slave driver relationship you are forming. Participation gets more cooperation than force. 'Here's what we are aiming for, and I can help by doing ...' will work much better than, 'This is the way we are going to do it, whether you like it or not.'

- Don't drag up the past and past mistakes. This is especially true in our personal lives – what good does dragging up the past do anyway? Remember it is about changing an action rather than winning an ego fight.

- Finish the criticism on friendly terms. Don't leave things in the air, so it can be brought up later – face it and settle it. Finish it with something like, 'I know I can count on you,' or,

'I know this was a one-off.' If you finish on friendly terms, it will be buried.

*'Life's most urgent question is: What are you doing for others?'*
Martin Luther King

Now you can interact with skill. You've discovered how cooperation and going for win/win results raises you head and shoulders above those who simply try to have everything their own way. You know how to be truly assertive, as opposed to simply being aggressive. And you know that 85% of a business person's success is determined by their attitude and their ability to deal well with people. Now you can do just that – with all people, in all situations, at all times.

# Action 7

## Communicate with Ease

*'To be able to listen to others in a sympathetic and understanding manner is perhaps the most effective mechanism in the world for getting along with people and tying up their friendship for good.'*
Justice Oliver Wendell Homes

Leaders and successful people communicate with ease. They communicate in a way that has *everyone* listening, understanding and engaging positively. Now discover how this can be true for you. Make communication breakdowns a thing of the past, and see how you can use *Performance Coaching* to ensure *everyone* improves their performance and enjoys their success.

Have you noticed how some people seem to radiate genuine love, kindness and understanding? They share the unique ability to make us feel the most important person in the world – not because of who we are or what we have done, but simply because we are fellow human beings. Their openness of heart doesn't expect something back. But because their *intent* is to focus on what is good in the other person, and to respond with gratitude, this enables them to feel genuine good will towards all. Are these qualities you could aspire towards?

Medieval philosopher Thomas Aquinas taught that when you want to convert someone to a different point of view, you must metaphorically speaking walk to where they stand, take them by the hand and guide them, rather than ordering them to come to you.

Jack Welch, ex-CEO of the General Electric Company, famously summed up the secret of his successful management skills in three little words: *'Communicate, communicate, communicate.'* It sounds simple, but when industry captains plot a new course, most leave the crew still standing on dry land. Why?

Many successful entrepreneurs believe responsive communication is the key to good relations with both employees and customers, and will pay big dividends.

## Is your communication clear?

And for good communication you need to develop the art of good listening.

> *Arthur Dent: 'You know, it's at times like this, when I'm stuck in a Volgon air lock with a man from Betelgeuse, about to die of asphyxiation in deep space, that I really wish I'd listen to what my mother told me when I was young'*
>
> *Ford prefect: 'Why? What did she tell you?'*
>
> *Arthur: 'I don't know; I didn't listen.'*
>
> The Hitchhiker's Guide to the Galaxy

Imagine you go to your doctor because you're worried about the continual headaches you're having. Without listening to you, without making a physical examination, or without expressing concern, your doctor immediately seizes upon the word *headaches* and says, 'I get a lot of this. Here let me give you a prescription for some strong pain killers.' How much confidence would you have in his prescription? Yet how often do we behave in the same way, rushing in with advice or our own prescription.

Do you ever say, 'I know exactly how you feel,' and then go on to explain your circumstances? Or have you heard yourself saying, 'I don't understand him/her – they just won't listen to me.' Have you listened to them first?

The people you meet every day make constant judgements about you and frequently that judgement is based on something you said (talking rather than listening!). Most of us think that if we talk a lot the other person will be impressed and see us as intelligent, but actually we quickly tire of people who always make smart remarks.

One of the greatest desires of the human soul is simply to be understood. Sometimes a person comments that another is a great conversationalist, but actually that person has not said very much, just listened in depth. You are far more likely to make mistakes when you talk, rather than when you listen. Have you ever heard anyone accuse someone of listening too much?

> *'Help me never to judge another*
> *until I have walked a day in their shoes.'*
> H Jackson Brown Junior

*Why were we given two ears and one mouth?* Should we be listening more than talking? For true communication, *listen* with intent to the speaker to really understand them.

> *Let me drop everything and work on your problem*
> Seen on a T-shirt

When you attend a seminar or workshop facilitated by someone you respect for their expertise, you listen intently regardless of their communication skills. You also listen more because they are the teacher and you are the pupil. This is a useful role to remember in conversation, although it requires our willpower as we would always rather be the teacher/ talker, than the pupil/listener.

> *'When we seek to discover the best in others,*
> *we somehow bring out the best in ourselves.'*
> William Arthur Ward

An accountant once researched how much a company loses because its people do not listen. He found that the typical employee spends three-quarters of every working day in verbal communication, nearly half of which they spend listening. But that same average employee is only about 25% effective as a listener.

Take a few minutes and reflect on the cost of ineffective listening in your own life. What's the intangible cost? Dale Carnegie, in his book, *How to win friends and influence people,* wrote, 'You can make more friends in two months by becoming more interested in other people than you can in two years by trying to get people interested in you.'

## If Listening is so Powerful, Why is it so Hard?

There are four basic methods of communication; reading, writing, speaking and listening. However, perhaps the reason that listening is so difficult is that our past training concentrates on the first three.

To listen better, we must change our perceptions of others. If we are prepared to understand them as unique human beings in an environment of openness and trust, most people are only too willing to tell us their points of view. The problem usually lies not in them, but in us as we tend to shut off our receiver.

The real key to your ability to influence me is your *intent*. If you want to really understand me and show that in your conduct, you will be successful even if you are not a particularly good talker.

In conventional communication models both speaker and listener share responsibility for seeing that communication lines run smoothly, but this is not always the case. A door-to-door salesman calls, and you decide whether you want to listen. The onus is on them. However, the market researcher must coax a response from you by being an effective listener.

At home or in everyday encounters the responsibility for making communication work is more evenly distributed between speaker and listener but there's more potential for crossed wires as familiarity can lead to you mistakenly thinking you know exactly what the other person is going to say before they open their mouth. Instead of listening, people more often take turns in not listening to each other.

## Accepting criticism and other people's opinion?

Most of us have a natural tendency to defend ourselves in the light of criticism; but it is wise not to react in a knee-jerk fashion. Ask yourself if there is any truth in what has been said and, if so, use it to learn something new about yourself. What criticism have you received that could be valid?

You can also compare another person's opinions with your own, and if it disagrees you can either dismiss it or find fault with their opinion. However, almost every opinion has some merit, so look for the grain of truth there and learn from it.

## Do we say too much when talking?

*'The less men think the more they talk.'*

Montesquieu

When involved in negotiating a contract, who has the most information to make an informed decision – the person who talks most or the one that listens most? Many so-called big businessmen who have reputations for making great deals simply encourage the other person to talk while they keep silent and gauge the other's position. In talking, feelings and motives will undoubtedly surface, especially if you watch the body language as well. If you don't want to give your position away first, it is very simple – shut up and listen.

*'You ain't learning nothing when you're doing all the talking.'*

Notice on an office wall.

Most of the time people just wait for their chance to speak and don't listen to the other person properly which creates a breeding ground for misunderstanding and conflict. However, if the other person feels listened to, they will appreciate this and listen to you with the same attitude. This is the essence of real, rather than superficial, conversations.

## How our Automatic Responses can Prevent Another Person from Feeling Understood.

*'Listen, or thy tongue will make thee deaf.'*
Native American proverb

We often respond automatically to another person based on our own experience of the past or for our own motives, rather than with the intent to really understand another person. Some of the ways we do this include:

Giving *advice*
Asking *questions and probing from our own point of reference.*
*Judging* then either agreeing or disagreeing
*Explaining and interpreting* based on our past experience.

In the statements below, identify the type of response being used – in some there may be more than one.

'I think you should do it this way.'

'Why did you file the report in that way? It would have been easier to put the summary at the beginning.'

'What do you hope to gain by doing it that way?'

'You are right – he should never have spoken to you in that way.'

'If I were you, I would log everything said at these meetings to cover your back.'

'It seems every time you attempt to get these reports in on time, you fail.'

'I can see why you said that, but you are not looking at the big picture.'

Listening carefully to everything someone says, including their tone of voice, what is not said, and by looking at their body language, gets your focus of attention off you. By listening with the *intent* to understand and appreciate you will find that when you do speak it is more likely to be informed and insightful speech.

*'Good communication is as stimulating as black coffee
– and just as hard to sleep after.'*
Ann Morrow Lindberg

Do you know couples where one says, 'If only he/she would listen to me.' Or an employee who complains of his boss, 'He just will not listen to anyone.' Or children who say to a parent, 'You just don't understand me!' Think of any area of conflict and then think of how it would improve if both parties truly understood it from the other person's point of view. A lot of misery, conflict, failure and bad decisions are due entirely to a lack of listening and understanding.

## The Five Levels of Listening

Let's look at the following five levels of listening of which the first four are most commonly used.

- *Ignoring.* We make no attempt to listen and focus on something else.
- *Pretending.* We make out we are listening, but nothing actually registers with us.
- *Selective listening.* We listen only to the bits we want to hear and as a consequence sometimes lose the most important part of the message.
- *Attentive listening.* We listen carefully to the words said so that we pick up clearly what the other person is saying to us.
- *Empathic listening.* Effective empathic listening has the *intent* to *understand the other person by also seeking the real meaning beneath the words* including looking at tone of voice and body language – we really want to understand how they feel.

*People don't care how much you know,
until they know how much you care.*

These five levels of listening can be used for different circumstances, but remember the more you want to really understand another person, the more deeply you need to listen. True listening and a total concentration on the other, is always a manifestation of love – the essential part is the discipline of putting ourselves to one side, totally accepting the other, and stepping into their shoes.

*'Before I walk in another's shoes, I must first remove my own.'*

Unknown

### The Attitude and Skill of Empathy

To become a more effective empathic listener you must develop both the attitude (intent) and the skill, understanding how meaning is conveyed from speaker to listener.

Communications experts split communication between three key areas; the actual words, how we say them, and our body language. This pie chart represents the percentage of communication for each of these areas.

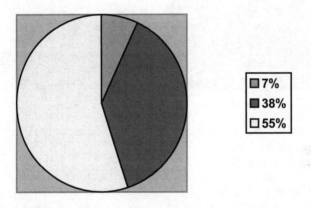

7% actual words
38% how we say the words
55% body language.

## Why is empathic listening so powerful?

Whenever I work to solve organisational problems, in approximately 80% of cases the blockage comes down to communication. Effective empathetic listening results in very accurate information leading to accurate and confident decisions.

Empathic listening is also a major deposit into the *trust bank account* of the other person. All of us like psychological air where we can express ourselves, and our need to be valued and understood. By listening with the clear *intent* to understand you create this psychological air and the result is good communication, creative solution finding, and effective team working.

Empathic listening gives people an open space in which they can explore feelings and feel understood without being judged. The skills include capturing the feelings expressed and non-verbal cues, and phrasing empathic responses clearly, supportively and with sincerity. However, above all these skills, attitude – the real *intent* to understand is most important as illustrated by the iceberg picture and diagram. If you have the attitude without the necessary skills, you can still listen empathically. But if you have the skills with the wrong attitude, you will have few, if any, chances to listen at this deep level.

 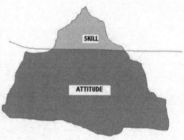

When you have listened at this deep empathic level in the past? What was the outcome?

Useful phrases to reflect back the underlying emotion to the other person include:

'If I am right, you felt that…'

'I sense this is something you feel very strongly about…'

'I can see that it upset you a great deal…'

## Taking in someone's messages and influencing them

To influence others you must make conversations work for you rather than against you. What you say, how you say it, how you listen and convey that you are doing so, and how well you read the messages portrayed by body language will partly determine your influencing skills. As will a clear understanding of 'office politics' and individuals motivation in achieving their and/or the organisations goals, as illustrated in the following diagram.

| POLITICALLY | SKILLED |
|---|---|
| High political skill used to achieve their own goals<br>CLEVER – The 'Fox'<br>Pursues own goals | Uses positive skill to achieve the organisational and their own goals<br>WISE – The 'Owl'<br>Aligns organisational & personal goals |
| INEPT – The 'Donkey'<br>Low political skills as they only pursue their own goals<br>POLITICALLY | INNOCENT – The 'Sheep'<br>Low political skill – pursues own goals & organisational goals<br>UNSKILLED |

Understanding other people's reasons enables us to choose the right tactic for influencing the situation. For example:

1. **Reasoning.** *'There are two very good reasons you should adhere to our health & safety procedures, the first is...'* Reason uses fact, logic and argument to make your case.

2. **Inspiring.** Where reasoning focuses on logic and the head, inspiring focuses on the heart and appeals to the emotions as in Martin Luther King's speech, 'I have a dream.'

3. **Questioning.** *'Would you like to be promoted into the new vacancy?'* Using good questions helps the other person find their own way to a desired destiny.

4. **Making them feel good.** *'You're a great employee.'* If people feel positive towards us, they are more likely to agree with us.

5. **Dealing.** *'If you work late tonight for me, I'll do it tomorrow.'* This appeals to our sense of fairness, but the terms of exchange need to be clear as some people will take, take, take without any feelings of guilt.

6. **Asking a favour.** *'Can you please help me out with this project?'* Simply asking for help because you need it is hard for people to resist if used sparingly.

7. **Testimonials.** *'The experts in our industry say...'* referring to acknowledged views from people with expertise or best practice models is particularly useful if the other person is concerned about the risk or keen to fit in.

8. **Using authority.** *'It is our company policy to…'* This uses our position of power, but is more likely to result in compliance rather than true commitment. A useful last resort, but not always effective early on. If it does not work, you will find all the others difficult.

9. **Forcing.** *'Do it or else you're fired.'* Using threats and warnings apart from emergencies and disciplinary meetings is seldom effective, and is the root symptom of many broken relationships.

Tactics or combinations of tactics vary according to the situation and the person you are trying to influence. Look over the list and decide which ones you use the most and least, and then consider which ones you could use to be more effective in influencing other people.

## You are skilled at handling conversations if you:

- Listen in a positive way at the right time. Listen to the entire message before accepting or rejecting it. Listen to understand rather than to win an argument.

- Understand the importance of effective communication – no problem is solved until both sides communicate.

- Talk meaningfully when it is your turn, speak the truth and get to the point.

- Be aware of your personal prejudices and do not allow them to influence your judgement.

- Know how to alter the direction of the conversation acceptably.

- Keep communication moving at a comfortable pace.

- Build on the key points the other party raises.

- Deal with differences of opinion, and use them to sharpen debate and locate creative solutions.

- Find out what people think and respect their point of view.

- See as well as listen. Look at the body language, listen to the tone of voice – it can convey much more than the actual words spoken.

- Listen to feeling as well as reason. You are trying to get inside the other person's head.

- Be alert to what the other person is not saying. Very often what is missing is more important that what is being said.

- Provide positive feedback.
- Have the right word for the right occasion and ask the right questions.
- Treat the other person as special and give them your full attention.
- Relax. Tension and anxiety reduce our effectiveness for listening.

*Good communicators often become great leaders.*
*Remember: A boss says, 'Get going!' A leader says, 'Let's go!'*

Other people should ideally see you as someone who understands them and is sensitive to their feelings and what they say. Those in the workplace who report directly to you expect you to be genuinely interested in helping them perform well. You can help do that by demonstrating that you listen to them, and respect what they say. Research confirms that we all tend to hear what we want to hear (selective hearing). When you take the trouble to really listen to other people's messages you:

- Discover what is happening, and the nature of current problems.
- Learn how problems have altered.
- Learn how to deal with people, how their minds work, and how they approach problems.
- Access a rich source of ideas for improvements.
- Convey the message, 'I care.'
- Gain clues as to how to avoid future problems.
- Give people a chance to express their feelings about things including their life and work.
- Increase the chances of other people listening to you.

If you are not devoting your full attention to listening, people soon realise that you are merely waiting for your turn to speak. We must listen properly to:

- Understand
- Remember *and*
- Recall

Two powerful questions you can ask yourself whilst listening are:

- What does this person really mean by what they are saying?
- How does this person feel right now?

By trying to sincerely answer these questions, your listening will certainly improve.

The average person talks at around 125 words a minute. Yet you think at up to 500 words a minute. Why not use this spare capacity fully?

## Bad listening habits to avoid include:

- Branding the subject as uninteresting. If we listen with the genuine *intent* to understand, every subject can be a source of rich learning.
- Criticising a speaker's delivery or mannerisms.
- Listening only for facts.
- Listening with ridicule rather than respect. Some people who are not good with words still have important messages to convey.
- Faking attention. The talker may respond by only giving you part of the information.
- Using bargaining tactics such as, 'I'll do this, if you do that,' for example. They will not work if you want deep, meaningful communication.
- Becoming distracted.
- Taking the other person for granted.
- Avoiding difficult material by keeping to familiar subjects. True understanding (and learning) is going beyond what we currently know.
- Allowing emotion-laden words to arouse personal antagonism.
- Daydreaming.
- Communicating negativity through our body language.

## Examples of things people do not want to hear

- 'I don't think you should be seeing him or her.' – Judging.
- 'You started it.' – Blaming.

- 'Can't you ever get anything right?' – Pain-inducing statements curtail communication.

- 'Sex is not everything in life.' – Telling them how to lead their lives.

- 'I am interested in only what is going well for you, not the problems.' – Sometimes people need the psychological air space just to express their concerns.

- 'Don't feel sorry for yourself.' – Telling them how they should feel!

- 'No wonder you're lonely, you need to get out and meet people.' – Help them find their own answers, rather than jumping in with well intentioned advice.

- 'You can get by, I know you can.' – Gives the impression you want them to cheer up for your sake.

- 'Sure, but tell me as quickly as you can.' – Tells them that you have no time for them.

Be honest – which ones in these two lists do you use? Can you see why communication breakdown is the cause of so many personal, work, business and organisational problems?

Write below in a positive tense, the ones you will avoid in the future:

For example, if you have a tendency to judge, you may state: 'When I am listening to…, I will listen to them without judging, and try to really understand what they are saying.'

*Four essentials for enhancing your listening capabilities are:*

- Energy
- Attending
- Making requests
- Expressing understanding

## Energy

Active listening means showing with your whole body that you are focused on the other person. Good listening means staying alert both mentally and physically.

## Attending

Use non-verbal methods to help show that you are giving the other person the attention they deserve. Attending behaviour includes:

- **Making eye contact.** Hold it for at least 70–80 per cent of the time. More than this may make the other person feel uncomfortable.

- **Using body language.** Position your body towards the other person, and nod regularly to show that you either agree or are paying attention. Avoid folded arms as this places a barrier between you and the other person. Mirroring the body position of the other person is another way of signalling that you are listening to them.

## Making requests for information

Asking relevant questions and seeking additional information shows that you are listening. Ask open-ended questions as part of your listening strategy to encourage the other person to expand and elaborate. For example:

- **Tell me about …**

- **What do you feel about …**

- **That is interesting, explain a little further?**

Try posing fact-seeking questions based on what you have heard so far in an encouraging way. For example, 'I find what you just said very interesting, tell me how it works.'

Probing, when carried out in a neutral manner with the clear *intent* to understand, encourages the person to be more specific. For example:

- **Can you give me an example?**

- **Tell me how I could do what you suggest?**

- **Would you like to explain how I can best help?**

Non-verbal messages including nodding, interested looks, leaning forward and smiling also show that you are listening, and help the conversation flow.

## Expressing understanding

When you convey to someone that you have been listening you help reduce the inevitable communication gaps that exist between people. You can do this by:

- **Reflecting back feelings**

- **Paraphrasing**

- **Summarising**

## Reflecting back feelings

Demonstrate your ability to truly hear by also being sensitive to and reflecting back the emotion underlying the words using expressions such as:

- **It seems you are feeling...**
- **It sounds to me as if...**
- **You must be really... (angry, pleased, worried etc)**

## Paraphrasing

Another clear sign that you are listening well is to paraphrase the content of the other person's communication in your own words, allowing them to correct misunderstandings.

Similarly, if a speaker is developing a theme you can help them by using questions that promote extensions – for example:

- **How do you mean?**
- **What makes you say that?**
- **Tell me more**

## Summarising

When you summarise what someone has said it conveys the extent of your active listening. You might introduce the paraphrase or summary with something such as:

- **As I understand it...**
- **If I've got it right...**
- **So what you are saying is...**

## Listening in a group

In these situations it is easy to switch off either permanently or temporarily and disengage from the group. For better group listening:

- Check what new ideas, goals, or solutions seem to be emerging. Can you write them down in order of importance?
- Identify what facts need further clarification.
- Specify the missing information.
- Identify what opinions, judgements, values or convictions come to mind

- Try developing an idea already expressed by someone else; attempt to explain, elaborate and analyse it. Find examples, illustrations or explanations.
- Find the relationship between the various facts you hear. Can you integrate these into a single theme, argument or point?
- Analyse what might encourage the group to greater activity, such as reminding them of the importance of the task or its deadlines.
- Keep your own set of written records to serve as the group memory.
- Watch to see whom you should encourage to speak next.
- Who is dominating the conversation or preventing others from speaking openly? Identify who is talking too much and find a way to reduce this behaviour.

By doing the above you will occupy a decisive, knowledgeable and respected role within the group.

## Body Language

We send over 750,000 body language messages, the majority conveyed by the face, which is our primary site of non-verbal communication.

| Emotion | Facial Pattern |
| --- | --- |
| Interest/Excitement | Eyebrows down, eyes track, look, listen. |
| Enjoyment/Joy | Smile, lips widened up & out, smiling eyes (circular wrinkles) |
| Surprise/Startled | Eyebrows up, eyes blinking. |
| Distress/Anguish | Cry, arched eyebrows, mouth down, tears, sobbing. |
| Fear/Terror | Eyes frozen open; pale face; trembling; hair erect! |
| Anger/Rage | Frown, clenched jaw, eyes narrowed, red face. |

Begin to watch the body language of other people, and at the same time become aware of your own. Remember 55% of communication is through body language, so to become a really effective communicator you must become skilled at picking up these signals.

What can you do about your body language? You know your moods are expressed in posture, but your posture can also affect your mood. Walking in an upbeat, proud posture elevates your spirits, while walking with your gaze on the ground and shoulders slumped makes you feel dejected and deflated. Research confirmed this in a study where two groups were trained to walk in different ways. One group were shown how to walk with confidence at a brisk pace with head held high. The other group were trained to do the opposite with heads bowed and walking in slow, small steps. Those who were in the first group were full of energy, the other group tired and down. These feelings were confirmed medically by tests including blood tests. We can give ourselves an energy boost, change the chemistry in our bodies, and prepare to master the situation by simply standing tall.

## Effective questioning

*'Nothing shapes our lives so much as the questions we ask, refuse to ask, or never think of asking. The question is the helmsman of consciousness. The questions we ask determine whether we will be superficial or profound, acceptors of the status quo or searchers. The difference between Einstein and Hitler depends on the questions they asked. What you ask is who you are. What you find depends on what you search for.'*

Sam Keen

The best way to develop the habit of intentional or attentive listening is to ask plenty of questions, and then listen to the answers. Here are some specific question types we can use.

### Opening questions
The opening question forms the first vital stage in the sequence which will lead you to a piece of evidence, and is particularly useful for interviewing.

### Open ended questions
These are questions to which the answer Yes or No cannot be given, and encourage the person to talk in more detail. You will nearly always get a higher quality answer by asking an open question, normally introduced by Who, What, Which, Why, Where, When or How.

'When do you organise your priorities?'

'What method did you use to plan that project?'

'What where your reasons for needing that information straight away?'

## Checking questions

By using checking questions, you can gather relevant information quickly, establish areas worth pursuing, or close down particular avenues of conversation.

'Do you plan your priorities on a daily basis?'

'Are you responsible for planning projects?'

'Is it correct that you need the information immediately?'

## Past tense questions

When dealing with a touchy subject, it can be useful to put your question in the past tense. Instead of 'Do you sometimes forget to…?' use 'Have you ever forgotten to…?'

## Probing questions

Probing questions dig deeper into what people are saying to establish the real meaning of the subject or gather important information and are essential in interviewing and coaching situations. Imagine aiming at a dartboard, where the bull's-eye is the target – probing questions take you steadily nearer to the bull's-eye.

## Alternative questions

These are useful when you want to reach a decision. For example: '*Would* you like to take it now or *would* you rather make an appointment for one day next week?'

## Closed questions

Can be useful to end a conversation, but always use closed questions sparingly, or you may sound like a detective or interrogator.

## THE S.A.E. QUESTIONING FUNNEL

### Situation

- What was the situation or task?
- Describe the circumstances.
- What was your responsibility?
- Who else was involved?

### Actions

- What happened?
- What did you specifically do/say?
- What problems were there?
- How did you handle these problems?

### Effect

- What was the effect/outcome?
- What impact did that have?
- How did you measure your success?
- What lessons have you learnt?

Factual Evidence

## Question types to avoid

### Multiple questions
Multiple questions confuse, or give the other person the option of only answering the part of the question he feels most comfortable with. Always ask short, direct, unambiguous questions.

### Limiting questions
This limits the other person in their choice of reply, and prevents them doing their own thinking. For example:

'Do you prefer to prepare written reports or present orally?'
'Are your strengths in managing people or in managing the task?'

### Leading questions
These lead the other person to the obvious answer:

'Do you tend to cope well under pressure?'
'You prefer being in sales, do you?'
'So it was successful then?'

Using an open question instead will provide more valuable information and the other person's answer will be more accurate, not one that you have planted in their head.

### Hypothetical questions
Hypothetical questions ask for imagined reactions to situations where the person has no concrete experience. This results in them giving you a theoretical response. Rephrased, the question's answer gives more useful hard evidence of actual past behaviour.

| Hypothetical Questions | Effective Questions |
| --- | --- |
| How innovative would you be in a job like this? | How are you innovative in your current job? |
| Would you delegate parts of your own job to your subordinates? | Do you delegate parts of your own job to your subordinates? |
| How would you handle a conflict with a customer? | How did you handle a conflict situation with the customer? |

# Listening Checklist

✓ Show you are interested by a friendly expression and maintaining eye contact.

✓ Be alert to the tone of voice being used – sometimes it is more important how something is said than what is said. Be alert to your own tone too.

✓ Encourage the talker to describe ideas and opinions freely by sticking to their subject, and using prompts such as 'Hmm.' 'Yes,' or, 'So, what happened then?'

✓ Show the talker that you empathise with his/her feelings by leaning toward the person and using their own words to reinforce your listening.

✓ Ask questions – to reassure the person talking that you are still listening.

✓ Don't take the talker's view personally.

✓ Make a habit of keeping notes – relying on memory can be dangerous

✓ Summarise your understanding by using such phrases as, 'So what I think you are saying is…'

✓ Don't be too quick to come to conclusions and give advice.

✓ Don't argue or interrupt.

✓ Remember the saying: 'You've been given two eyes to see and two ears to listen, but only one tongue, so see and hear twice as much as you talk.'

✓ If you want to listen at a deep empathic level use questions sparingly, especially the probing, past tense, alternative and closed questions. Stick to the open questions avoiding the multiple, limiting, leading and hypothetical ones. At this level you want to peel the layers from the onion to get to the soft inner core.

# How our perception can change through understanding

Listening to other people at a deep level and beginning to understand them opens up exciting new changes in perception. How does this happen?

First, you will be practising the development of your cooperative attitude (win/win) that you learned in the last chapter. Secondly, as you gain deeper understanding you benefit from vast perception shifts and become more influential and effective.

## To be Understood Effectively

*'First learn the meaning of what you say, and then speak.'*
Epictetus

How can you effectively be understood? Firstly, it depends on how well you have developed your *trust relationship bank account* with other people, and your character qualities as looked at in **Action 5**. Your interpersonal style will also determine the receptivity of the other person(s); an assertive win/win style will always succeed over an aggressive win/lose, or even a passive lose/win style.

Secondly, by understanding the other person, and getting in touch with their *feeling* for the subject, you can align your emotions with theirs.

Thirdly, you introduce your left brain using logic and reasoning, and explain it so that the other person understands.

Self-awareness and intent are also keys to the spoken part of the communication process. We often overlook what a powerful influence speech has in our lives – do we give enough importance to the words we use? We all know the destructive power of lying, so why do we lie? Could it be because of greed, desire, fear of rejection, insecurity or even jealousy? We have countless examples of people courageously choosing a path of unshakable commitment to the truth – can we emulate them? Although difficult to put into practice, speaking the truth has the power to transform and simplify our lives.

A second kind of destructive speech to avoid is harsh aggressive language. Our words have the power to harm – is this the best environment for open and honest communication? Gossip and talking behind another person's back is another unskilful type of speech. These words not only cause disharmony, but lose friends and are huge withdrawals from the *trust bank account* of the other person. Instead, tell someone something positive about them – an act of kindness that takes literally no time or effort but can provide enormous rewards, particularly in the long-term *trust bank account* of the other person.

Another form of destructive speech is heavy criticism targeted towards others. Most people get defensive when criticised (unless it is constructive) and will either retreat and disengage, or become angry and lash out. How many people have you criticised who have then said, 'Thanks very much'? Not only does it solve nothing, it exacerbates the anger and mistrust in our world.

However, even the great and noble speak without thinking as shown in this extract from Nelson Mandela's *Long Walk to Freedom*.

*In those days I was often in hot water with the Executive. In early 1953, Chief Luthuli, Z. K. Matthews and a handful of high-ranking ANC leaders were invited to a meeting with a group of whites who were in the process of forming the Liberal Party. A meeting of the ANC Executive took place afterwards at which a few of us asked for a report of the earlier meeting with the white liberals. The participants refused, saying that they had been invited in their private capacity, not as members of the ANC. We continued to pester them, and finally Professor Matthews, who was a lawyer, said that it had been a privileged conversation. In a bit of indignation, I said, 'What kind of leaders are you who can discuss matters with a group of white liberals and then not share that information with your colleagues at the ANC? That's the trouble with you, you are scared and overawed with the white man. You value his company more than that of your African comrades.'*

*This outburst provoked the wrath of both Professor Matthews and Chief Luthuli. First, Professor Matthews responded: 'Mandela, what do you know about whites? I taught you whatever you know about whites and you are still ignorant. Even now, you are barely out of your student uniform.' Luthuli was burning with a cold fire and said, 'All right, if you are accusing me of being afraid of the white man, I have no other recourse but to resign. If that is what you say, then that is what I intend to do.' I did not know whether Luthuli was bluffing, but his threat frightened me. I had spoken hastily, without thinking, without a sense of responsibility, and I now greatly regretted it. I immediately withdrew my charge and apologised. I was a young man who attempted to make up for his ignorance with militancy.*

# Coaching

## What is coaching?

Coaching sets people up for success as the coach's total belief in the individual and committed support helps the coachee clarify what they are working towards, then set and achieve goals through a *life-long* process of learning, success, and personal fulfilment.

*'Coaching is the art of facilitating the performance, learning and development of another.'*

## Coaching is about performance...

Coaching in a business context is ultimately concerned with improving performance in areas such as the delivery of a specific task or project, the achievement of business goals, or greater effectiveness or efficiency.

On the personal level, coaching helps the person create what they truly want from life. As a coach the focus is upon the other person's performance, helping them to develop real purpose, vision, balance and action in their life and a process to achieve their dreams.

*'A Coach is someone who helps you do what you don't want to do, and has you see what you don't want to see, so you can be everything you always wanted to be.'*

## Coaching is about learning...

Learning is another outcome from coaching as the future performance of an individual or organisation depends on people's ability to approach new tasks. Some people believe there are four steps to learning:

1. Unconscious Incompetence; we don't know what we don't know.

2. Conscious Incompetence; now we know what we don't know. We start to learn something new and begin to realise how much we do not know – perhaps the most frightening stage.

3. Conscious Competence; we now know what we know. As our skills and confidence grow, we realise we have achieved a certain level. We are not an expert as yet, but competent at the task in hand and aware of that.

4. Unconscious Competence; we are not aware, and we know. Have you ever driven a lengthy car journey without needing to pay attention to the skills and knowledge you use to drive? We are now really in tune with the knowing.

**Coaching is about facilitating...**

The role of the coach as facilitator enables the coachee to explore, gain a better understanding and, as a result, make better decisions than they would have done without the coaching intervention.

*'Coaching is unlocking a person's potential to maximise their own performance. It is helping them to learn rather than teaching them.'*
Tim Gallwey

## Coaching skills

*'Coaching is not merely a technique to be wheeled out and rigidly applied in certain prescribed circumstances. It is a way of managing, a way of treating people, a way of thinking, a way of being.'*
Sir John Whitmore, Coaching for Performance

There are, however, some basic skills associated with coaching that are really important to master if you are going to be an effective coach. These are:

**Build rapport and relationships** – building the trust bank account, confidentiality, getting in tune with the other person.

**Listen** – particularly empathic listening.

**Question** – questions focused on the coachee to have them think deeply.

**Raise awareness** – being aware of your own prejudices. Being aware of their body language and what is *not* being said – also being curious, but with no preconceived conclusion or attachment to any answer. Think: I wonder what they want?

**Give feedback** – honest, but encouraging (sometimes you may want to challenge them to explore at a deeper level). You may even consider giving feedback from your intuitive self, your gut feeling.

**Self management** – Believe they have the answer (not you) so hold back advice and opinions. Leave out your personal experiences, unless asked, or *if* it is really relevant and you have a development model (leadership, interpersonal styles, time management etc) that you feel is appropriate due to the flow of their conversation, ask their permission to share it first.

**Be action orientated** – a total focus on taking action to make *real* change in their life – they will also learn from this action (or inaction) by being accountable.

---

### The many benefits of coaching

Positive outcomes of coaching include:

- **Improved performance and productivity**
  Coaching brings out the best in individuals and teams.

- **Staff/people development**
  The way you manage will either develop them or hold them back. Coaching develops them.

- **Improved learning**
  Coaching is learning on the fast track, without loss of time. Enjoyment and retention are also enhanced.

- **Improved relationships**
  The very act of asking someone a question shows you value them and their answer.

- **Improved quality of life for individuals**
  Respect for individuals, improved relationships, and the accompanying success creates a better atmosphere.

- **More time for managers**
  Staff who are coached and who welcome responsibility free up valuable time for managers.

- **More creative ideas**
  Coaching and a coaching environment encourage creative suggestions from all team members.

---

- **Better use of people, skills and resources**
  Coaching uncovers many concealed talents as well as solutions to practical problems.

- **Faster and more effective responses**
  When people are valued, they are invariably willing to go the extra mile when, or even before, being called upon to do so.

- **Greater flexibility and adaptability to change**
  The coaching ethos is all about change, being responsive, and being responsible.

- **Improved self-esteem and self-belief**
  A good coach facilitates an environment where the person finds their own answers to their challenges to achieve real results, leading to growth and improved self-belief.

- **It becomes a goal orientated experience**
  Effective coaching encourages the person to identify goals and hurdles in their life, and finds ways of taking action that brings about success.

- **A cost-effective way of achieving results**
  Effective coaching is a cost-effective way of helping people achieve real results.

- **It is user-friendly**
  It is personal in a time of automated interaction when people crave good old fashioned human contact.

- **It works!**
  The results of coaching speak for themselves. It's results-orientated, achieving significant, real and measurable outcomes.

## The GROW model

The GROW model provides a structure that moves the coachee towards achieving their goals by asking powerful questions under four distinct headings:

**G**OAL – Goal setting for the session as well as long and short-term objectives

**R**EALITY – Checking and exploring the current situation

**O**PTIONS – Exploring alternative strategies and courses of action

**W**AY FORWARD – WHAT is do be done next, WHEN, by WHOM, and what is the WILL to do it?

### G – Goal

This stage is all about goal setting. Ask the coachee to phrase their issue so that it becomes a goal. Then ask them to write it down, distinguishing end goals from performance goals. Encourage them to set performance goals that move them towards their end goal, vision or purpose.

At this stage, it is particularly powerful to ask your coachee to think forward to the time when they have achieved their goal, and what it will mean for them. Check that the goal is at the appropriate level of challenge for their capability, and then move on to the next stage.

### R – Reality

This is where you clarify with the coachee where they are now. By asking powerful and open questions, you aim to raise their level of awareness about what is currently happening through questions such as, 'What obstacles prevent you from moving forward?' After checking that the goal is still relevant, move on to the next stage.

### O – Options

This stage asks the coachee what they could do to move toward their goal(s), not what they should do. By asking good questions, you encourage your coachee to come up with creative ideas to start moving forward. From their list of options, ask them to choose at least one thing to move them forward one step. Check again whether doing this one thing will move them forward, and then ask what benefit they will gain.

## W – Way forward

At this stage you encourage your coachee to turn their ideas into action, and give commitment to achieving results by asking questions such as, 'What actions do you need to take?' Ask the coachee to be as specific as possible, and write actions and dates down to reinforce their responsibility. After a final check on intention, enthusiasm and commitment, they should be ready to move forward with clarity, confidence, and purpose.

Now have a light-hearted look at what not to do as a coach or a mentor compiled by mentoring Guru David Clutterbuck, and quoted in the Brief Group *Corporate Coach* e-newsletter.

## The twelve habits of the toxic mentor

1. Start from the point of view that you – from your vast experience and broader perspective – know better than the mentee (or coachee) what's in their interest.
2. Be determined to share your wisdom with them – whether they want it or not; remind them how much they still have to learn.
3. Decide what you and the mentee (coachee) will talk about and when; change dates and themes frequently.
4. Do most of the talking; check frequently that they are paying attention.
5. Make sure they understand how trivial their concerns are compared to the issues you have to deal with.
6. Remind them how fortunate they are to have your undivided attention.
7. Don't show or admit any personal weaknesses; expect to be their role model in all aspects of career development and personal values.
8. Never ask them what they should expect of you – how would they know anyway?
9. Demonstrate how important and well connected you are by sharing confidential information they don't need (or want) to know
10. Discourage any signs of levity or humour – this is a serious business and should be treated as such.
11. Take them to task when they don't follow your advice.
12. Never, never admit that this could be a learning experience for you.

# The twelve habits of the toxic coachee or mentee.

1. Bring to the first formal meeting a long shopping list of things you want the coach or mentor to do for you.
2. Expect the coach/mentor to be available for you, whenever you want them.
3. Regard your coach/mentor as your prime source of gossip to pass on.
4. Expect the coach/mentor to always have the answer – that's why they are more senior.
5. Expect the coach/mentor to decide when to meet and what to talk about.
6. Boast about the relationship to your colleagues at every opportunity.
7. Never challenge what the coach/mentor says – s/he is paid to know best.
8. Blame the coach/mentor whenever advice doesn't work out – s/he should have known better.
9. Treat coaching/mentoring sessions as mobile – the easiest item in the diary to move at the last minute.
10. Enjoy the opportunity to have a good moan whenever you meet – especially if no-one else will listen to you.
11. Make it clear to the coach/mentor that you want to be just like them – adopt their style of speaking, dress and posture.
12. Never commit to doing anything as a result of the session. If, by accident, you do, simply forget to follow the commitment up. (Why spoil the fun of discussion with outcomes?)

By putting this chapter's Actions into practice you can now communicate with ease. You can communicate in a way that ensures people listen, understand and engage positively with you, and more importantly how you can listen, understand and build positive and fruitful relationships with other people. You have made breakdowns in communication a thing of the past. And when you add this to your new found *Performance Coaching Skills,* you can help *everyone* improve their performance and enjoy greater success.

# Action 8

## Bring About Creative Solutions

*'Orderly co-existence lies in global co-operation.'*
Nelson Mandela

This Chapter is about learning to be open to diverse viewpoints as we explore *being interested,* without judgement, in how other people choose to live their lives. And because we are all different it explores how to get the best from those people when they need to work in teams.

Although we may have different languages, styles of dress and faiths we are all part of one big human family. There is a real need for us to care for each other – even when conditions, and society, foster behaviour to the contrary. Without sharing there can be no justice, without justice there can be no peace and without peace there can be no future.

Imagine attempting a Cross Atlantic Sailing – would you rather sail single-handed or with a crew that cooperated, where all had different qualities to bring to the whole?

A group of boys playing on an old disused railway line attempted to walk along a single piece of track, but kept losing their balance and falling off. It seemed impossible, so when two of the boys bet the others that they could walk as far as the disused station box in the distance, the rest readily accepted. The two boys then demonstrated the value of cooperation by holding hands in the middle for balance from their separate rails and achieved their goal.

In nature, two plants in close proximity bring their roots together to improve the surroundings for both of them. If you and I cooperate we can achieve a lot more than if we both go it alone. It's the same when you put two pieces of wood together, you get added strength. In nature balance is reached through the natural law of existence and nature's processes.

*'Because we all share this small planet earth, we have to learn to live in harmony and peace with each other and with nature. That is not a dream, but a necessity. We are dependent on each other in so many ways that we can no longer live in isolated*

*communities and ignore what is happening outside those communities. We need to help each other when we have difficulties, and must share the good fortune that we enjoy. I speak to you as just another human being, as a simple monk. If you find what I say useful, then I hope you will try to practise it.'*

Dali Lama – Nobel Lecture, 1989

Imagine living in a world where the culture is based around service, contribution, sharing and genuinely valuing the diversity of others. Would it be more open, based on trust rather than mistrust, giving rather than taking, and peaceful co-existence rather than possessive, judgemental selfishness, defensiveness and protectiveness? What do we need for this to happen? We need a shift in perception to view the nations as one *whole* world of humans where we *value* the diverse cultures, languages, national identity and other differences. To create a world where we and everyone try to help rather than hurt. Human harmony is based on a true sense of unity regardless of whether we are educated or uneducated, Easterners or Westerners, Northerners or Southerners.

## Communicating to Find new Possibilities

The process of confronting and solving problems is a painful one, often evoking uncomfortable feelings of frustration, grief, sadness, loneliness, guilt, anger, regret, fear, anxiety, despair and anguish. Yet the process of meeting and solving problems is the cutting edge that distinguishes between success and failure, and we grow mentally and spiritually as we move through the pain of confronting and solving them. As Benjamin Franklin said, 'Those things that hurt, instruct.' It is for this reason that wise people learn not to dread, but to welcome problems.

Most of us are not so wise. Fearing the pain involved, we try to avoid problems. We procrastinate, hope it will go away, ignore it, and may even take drugs to deaden the pain. Some psychiatrists claim that this tendency to avoid problems and the emotional suffering inherent in them is the primary basis of all human mental illness, yet who among us is so self-disciplined that he or she has never said in the face of problems, 'It's beyond me.'

However, we all know that problems do not simply go away; they must be worked through or they will remain a barrier. Perhaps our first step is to solve the problem of ignoring problems! Since most problems involve other people you need to look more in depth and build on what you learned in the last chapter if you are to become creative in problem solving with other people. You need to leave your prejudices and pre-conceived ideas behind. And, although you may be unsure of the end result, you will feel excitement because it is adventurous and, ultimately, rewarding.

*'Great achievements are not born from a single vision but from the combination of many distinctive viewpoints.*
*Diversity challenges assumptions, opens minds and unlocks our potential to solve any problem we may face.'*

If you are in conversation and ask a person for their thoughts on the goals you have set, they will probably just agree they are good goals or not good goals. Perhaps they will compliment you on your ambition, or possibly ridicule you if they experience jealousy. But if you tell them with genuine intent that you really value their ideas and contributions, they may even offer suggestions that you (the creator of your goals) never thought possible. This is the power of changing your perception and opening yourself up to real creativity in your life.

To start a creative communication process like this you must believe it will result in a continuous creative spiral where everyone involved learns more, gains more and grows more than if they decided to go it alone. This concept is alien to most people. Perhaps your past conditioning has been one of defensive communication based on low trust and a belief that the person who argues the strongest usually wins. This defensive communication does not make use of the creative potential we all have, a potential even creative people do not tap into fully.

We sometimes see this creative team energy in sports teams where everyone works together for the greater good of the team rather than having an individual focus. I have seen this happen in times of adversity, when the chips really are down, and everyone pulls together for the greater good allowing ego and pride to dissolve.

*'Creative people who can't help but explore other mental territories are at greater risk, just as someone who climbs a mountain is more at risk than someone who just walks along a village lane.'*

R. D. Laing

So what is it that holds you back? Is it the unpredictable nature of the process? Is it because you have a need for structure? Is it personal insecurity? Is venturing into the unknown too risky? I believe the sense of adventure and true potential of this process outweighs anything that might hold you back. Trust me.

The level of communication in this context depends on the level of trust in the relationship and the cooperative attitude. If both are low, the communication will, at best, be defensive with one party winning at the expense of the other(s). If there is a moderate degree of trust with moderate cooperation the communication becomes respectful, but the best outcome will probably still involve compromise. However, if the level of trust and cooperative attitude is mutually high, you have a real chance of a creative *third alternative* solution where you are part of a win/win situation that is dynamic and rewarding.

## Finding the Shared Solution or the Alternative None of us Could Have Thought of on our Own.

Imagine that you and your partner (or friend) aim to have a weekend away from it all, but then find your ideal holiday differs widely. Your friend wants to go to Euro-Disney, while you would like a relaxing weekend in the South of France. The conversation could go something like this:

'I've always wanted to go to Euro-Disney – a weekend of excitement, fun and a complete distraction from work pressures.'

'Because of the work pressure, I'd prefer a quiet weekend in the South of France – it will give us plenty of time to talk and we can also have some fun.'

'I think the excitement of Euro-Disney it is what you need.'

'But I think you need to relax and chill out.'

And the conversation could go on, until one person (grudgingly) gives in, but the eventual compromise will lead to one or both feeling deflated from the initial excitement.

Now imagine the same scenario, but approaching it from a completely different perspective. Both people have developed high trust in the *trust bank account* with a framework of good open communication.

Remembering the principle of cooperative (win/win) thinking and finding shared solutions, you say: 'Let's aim to find a weekend break where we can both do what we really want to do – shall we explore the options?'

Then using the principle of effective communication, you ask them to share their thoughts first with the real *intent* to understand, before you state yours. Taking the best of both ideas and perhaps even adding to them the solution will be a weekend break better than either could have come up with alone (finding the creative solution or the higher way).

If the communication is open you go beyond the original compromise so that instead of simply being a social transaction it becomes a relationship transformation. Have you ever spent some real quality time with a colleague who then becomes a real friend? That is what this process can do – does this sound exciting to you?

So much of the success of this process is based around *involvement.* As we saw in **Action 6** it is psychologically impossible for someone to give us 100% of their effort, unless they are also allowed to give their ideas. *People will support what they help create.* This works in business as well as for us personally. In an organisation which needed to cut costs, rather than telling the various departments how much they had to cut and where, the staff were involved and asked to work on ideas for a solution. The result was a 40% increase in profits, with just a 9% increase in sales! This is true participative leadership and management.

This concept of involvement also works well in marriages with each asking for suggestions on work and running the house and asking children for their involvement rather than *telling* them what they should or should not do.

One company enjoyed a turnaround in fortunes of over 1,000% by adopting a *participative* policy, and forming a *junior board of directors* from the workforce whose remit was to find ways and means to improve anything they thought needed it. They were encouraged to write their own vision and elect who they thought worthy, and the company made the brave decision to make their financial records available and answer any questions put to them.

All suggestions needed the approval of the senior board, so control was still exercised, but the turnaround was phenomenal. It included a redesign of the company structure, improved sales and profits, increased morale and staff retentions, real promotion prospects, and more efficient and effective production. This is the difference between participative and iron fist management and leadership styles.

## If it is so good, why is it so difficult?

It goes against our years of conditioning and is at the opposite spectrum of the black and white, either/or mentality that we frequently encounter. Consider how much energy the traditional way of problem solving takes with its undercurrent of backbiting and blaming. It is like trying to play football with a rugby ball – it will end in ultimate frustration. The problem is also made worse because when people see their methods are not working they apply even more pressure to get their own way. This often involves aggressive, win/lose methods or people use their position of power. Or they adopt a passive, lose/win method and try to be popular with everyone. These people don't really want to listen or find a creative shared decision, they just want to manipulate and get their own way. But we can still take responsibility ourselves through aiming for a win/win type outcome. Easy? No! Possible? Yes!

We have also been trained to focus on developing our logical analytical left brain at the expense of the creative intuitive right brain. If you know you use your logical left side at the expense of your right, commit now to practise using your creative right side more. The two sides working together create a synergy that neither side can create by itself. Management is left-brained, for example, while Leadership comes from the right brain. Some of the greatest leaders have the ability to use their right brain to become visionary, creative, respected and trusted.

## How to Value and use Differences
## in a Positive and Creative Way

When talking about the death of the Regent in his book *Long Walk To Freedom,* Nelson Mandela quoted, *'The passing of the Regent removed from the scene an enlightened and tolerant man who achieved the goal that marks the reign of all great leaders: he kept his people united. Liberal and conservatives, traditionalists and reformers, white-collar officials and blue-collar miners, all remained loyal to him, not because they always agreed with him, but because the Regent listened to and respected different opinions.'*

On travelling to foreign countries we cannot fail to notice the vast differences between cultures and the differences between us as individuals are every bit as vast.

If we believe that only we see the world as it is we will never be able to engage in effective communication with other people let alone become creative with them. The person with real strength of character, humility and respect for others will understand the limitations of their own personal perceptions. They understand also the unique learning and resources available when engaging in meaningful communication and interaction with other people.

When faced with someone with a different viewpoint, try saying to yourself, 'Great, you see this different to me. Help me see it the way you do so I can learn from you.' If you both hold the same points of view, one of them is unnecessary, so seek out new perspectives. You will improve your own personal growth, learning and awareness, and deposit huge amounts into the trust bank account of the other person.

Do you notice how you are attracted to media, radio, TV, books and magazines that reinforce your views on life and the world? This can lead to your having marginalised or extreme views, and discourage your learning because closed minds fight to keep out alternative points of view. This stubbornness holds you back, so another suggestion is to occasionally read books, magazines, watch TV or listen to radio programmes with contrasting viewpoints. This opens you up to new ideas and gives you a broader perspective on life.

## How can we Release our Creative Powers
## to Find Creative Solutions?

We have spoken about creativity, creative cooperation, creative problem solving and creative solution finding, but what else can we do to tap into and release our creative powers? As said previously, visualisation, reflection (particularly when in a conducive environment), meditation, and changing perception all help enormously.

In addition:

- *Try putting two unrelated things together in a new way.* A simple example is using a bath as a garden feature.

- *Be a problem solver **and** a problem finder!* Seek out problems to solve. The better the problem is defined, the more creative your solutions. You will tap into your right brain allowing you to release all that creativity.

- *Use all your senses.* Become a multi-sensory observer whenever you get the opportunity.

- *Challenge concepts* to escape the old and find new ideas. Regardless of what the concept is, try challenging it.

- *Possibility thinking.* Think in terms of what's possible rather than impossible. Asking yourself, 'What if...?' opens the doors to creativity. What if there were no more wars? What if we could lead a completely stress free life? What if there were cures for every terminal illness?

- *Outrageous opposites.* Use opposites as a springboard to create new and exciting solutions by listing as many diverse opposites as possible. Imagine you have the problem of deciding where to go on holiday and you usually go somewhere hot. Start thinking of some complete opposites; trekking in Greenland, staying in a Scandinavian log cabin, visiting Asia in the monsoon season etc.

- *Use the morphological matrix.* This creativity model is based on the use of *attributes* and the items which evolve from them. This is shown in the example below of organising a company Christmas party. Bringing together the various combinations can produce literally thousands of ideas.

| Theme | Location | Music |
|---|---|---|
| 1970's | Nearby Hotel | Jazz |
| Wild west | Warehouse | Pianist |
| Medieval banquet | Boat | Tribute band |

If you want to innovate, avoid and eliminate counter-productive processes. On the other hand, if you want to crush creativity here are ten steps that will guarantee your success:

1. Criticise
   Whenever anyone comes up a new idea criticise it by pointing out its weaknesses and flaws. This will send a message that new ideas are not welcome, and that anyone who volunteers them risks criticism or ridicule – a certain way to crush the creative spirit.

2. Ban mind storms (word-storms)
   Treat mind storming as an out-dated technique that just throws up lots of new ideas that then have to be rejected. If people insist on mind storm meetings make them long, rambling and unfocused with lots of criticism of far-reaching ideas.

3. Hoard problems
   Shoulder the responsibility for solving all your or your organisation's major problems. Don't involve staff in serious issues, don't tell them the big picture, and above all don't challenge them to come up with solutions. By keeping all problems to yourself, you lose the valuable input that others could give.

4.  Focus on efficiency, not innovation:
    The current model is the one you helped develop and is obviously the best one for you or your business, so why waste time looking for different or possibly better systems? After all, if the makers of horse-drawn carriages had improved quality, they could have stopped cars from taking their markets.

5.  Overwork
    Establish a culture of long hours and hard work. Make sure that the working day has no time for learning, fun, lateral thinking, wild ideas or testing new initiatives.

6.  Adhere to the plan.
    Plan in great detail and do not deviate regardless of circumstances. Keep to the vision that was in the plan and ignore fads like market changes and customer fashions – they will pass.

7.  Punish mistakes
    If someone tries an entrepreneurial idea that fails, then blame and retribution must follow. This reinforces the existing way of doing things and discourages dangerous experiments.

8.  Don't look outside
    We understand our business better than outsiders – after all we have been working in it for years. Other industries are fundamentally different and because something works there it does not mean it will work here.

9.  Promote people like you from within
    Promoting from within is a good sign as we don't get polluted with heretical ideas from outside. It is best to find managers who agree with the boss and praise him for his acumen and foresight. And we want managers who mix with people similar to ourselves, thereby avoiding the benefit of diverse viewpoints.

10. Don't waste money on training
    Hire good people and let them learn your system. When was the last time you attended a training course?

In addition, here are some *myths* regarding creativity which can be found operating within some organisations. When reading it, put yourself in the shoes of a leader of an organisation and as the recipient of these creativity myths:

1. Creativity Comes From Creative Types. Ask a senior manager in an organisation, 'Where in your organisation do you most want creativity?' and they will typically reply 'Research and Development,

Marketing, and Advertising.' If asked, 'Where do you not want creativity?' they invariably answer 'Accounting.'

A common perception is that only some people are creative, but research in this field shows that anyone with normal intelligence is capable of a certain degree of creative work. As a leader, you don't want to curb creativity; you want everyone in the organisation producing novel and useful ideas, including your financial people.

Creativity depends on a number of things; experience (including knowledge and technical skills), talent, an ability to think in new ways, and the capacity to push through creative dry spells. People excited by their work often work creatively and are intrinsically motivated. Over the past five years organisations have paid increasing attention to creativity and innovation, but most people still do not realise their creative potential. This is partly because they are in environments which impede intrinsic motivation.

2. Money Is a Creativity Motivator. Experimental research on creativity suggests that money isn't everything. When people were asked to what extent they were motivated by monetary rewards, many considered the question irrelevant as they didn't think about pay on a day-to-day basis. And the handful of people who did spend a lot of time wondering about their bonuses were rarely engaged in creative thinking.

Bonuses and pay-for-performance plans can even lead to people becoming risk averse if they believe that every move they make is going to affect their remuneration. Research shows that people put far more value on a work environment where creativity is supported, valued, and recognised. This is why it's critical for leaders to match people to projects not only on the basis of their experience but also in terms of where their interests lie.

3. Time Pressure Fuels Creativity. In studies, people often thought they were most creative when they working under severe deadline pressure, but 12,000 aggregate days studied showed just the opposite: people were least creative when fighting the clock. In fact, it was found that a kind of *time-pressure hangover* resulted and creativity went down not only that day but the next two days as well. Time pressure stifles creativity because people can't deeply engage with the problem. Creativity requires an incubation period; people need time to soak in a problem and let the ideas bubble up.

The main problems are distractions that rob people of the time and focus to make that creative breakthrough. They need to be protected from distractions, and must know that the work is important and that everyone is committed to it.

4. Fear Forces Breakthroughs. There is another widespread notion that fear and sadness somehow spurs creativity. There's even some psychological literature suggesting that the incidence of depression is higher in creative writers and artists – the depressed geniuses who are incredibly original in their thinking.

In one study 12,000 journal entries were coded for the degree of fear, anxiety, sadness, anger, joy, and love that people experienced on a given day. The study found that creativity is positively associated with joy and love and negatively associated with anger, fear, and anxiety. Creative breakthroughs were more likely if people were happy the previous day.

5. Competition Beats Collaboration. There's a widespread belief, particularly in the finance and high-tech industries, that internal competition fosters innovation. However, surveys found that creativity is lower when people in a work group compete instead of collaborate. The most creative teams are those that have the confidence to share and debate ideas. When people compete for recognition they stop sharing information and that's destructive because nobody in an organisation has all of the information required to put all the puzzle pieces together.

6. A Streamlined Organisation Is a Creative Organisation. A 1994 letter to shareholders from a major software company stated: 'A downsizing such as this one is always difficult for employees, but out of tough times can come strength, creativity, and teamwork.' Of course, the opposite is true. Creativity suffers greatly during a downsizing.

A study of a 6,000 strong personnel division in a global electronics company charted an 18-month 25% downsizing process and recorded that creativity in the work environment went down significantly as anticipation and fear of the forthcoming downsizing caused people to disengage from their work. More troubling was the fact that even five months after the downsizing, creativity was still down significantly.

## The Secret to Effective Team Working

To be successful you need to have certain qualities that foster good teamwork. For example as a team leader, it's important to clarify:

- The team's purpose vision and goals.
- Who the members of the team are.
- Where the team can get support and resources.
- What each person's role and responsibilities are.

Determining a team's vision involves a lot more than writing a mission statement, giving it to the team, and hoping it happens. Giving a team too much direction can lead to over dependency on the team leader or resentment because they feel a lack of trust. Achieving a balance requires skill, as does finding ways of getting team members' interests aligned with those of the leader so that real progress can take place.

An exercise I often use to get a shared vision or goal is to get the team together and ask each person to write their own vision for the team. Then I get them into pairs to bring their visions together and combine them, then repeat the process until the whole team is left with just two visions which they then form into one. Everyone is involved in the creation of the vision and feels committed and part of the end vision.

It may sound obvious, but it is important that everyone in the team knows who else is in the team as this helps establish individual roles and cements commitment. By getting people to recognise that they are part of a unit, there is more chance they will take collective responsibility for a shared team outcome – the aim of any team.

As far as possible and without inhibiting creativity, all team members should also adopt a common working approach and be committed to the shared goal. At the same time, however, it's important to understand each individual person's expectations, interests, and what they can give and take from the team. It's important to assess what resources the team needs and what qualities individuals in the team have in order to achieve their own and team objectives.

It takes time before any team develops into a strong performing unit, but by creating a strong foundational structure and allowing people enough autonomy to make decisions, often these people go far beyond what is expected of them. In addition to being accountable to one another, they may reach a point where they actively encourage one another (and the team as a whole) to grow and develop. An effective team leader provides the team with an outside perspective that is neutral, whilst giving structure, guidance and encouragement. Expert coaching individually and group facilitation, providing the right level of support, are paramount to the success of a team staying on course.

Team meetings need to be productive otherwise they are self-defeating. They need to have and stick to an agenda, and not be a forum for complaint. Conflict is natural and should be resolved by good communication, trying for a win/win solution, and respecting and valuing differences. This encourages the team to develop characters that are open and honest, rather than backbiting and defensive. Collective rewards often work better than individual ones for team achievements and can be as simple as an informal social event.

## Team-working

## Belbin Team Roles

### The research

The ability to predict whether or not teams would succeed or fail was of particular interest to management trainers in the 1960s at Henley College, a leading UK management college. During the 1960s participants were placed into teams where they played simulated management games requiring the use of a range of management skills. One team member in each team was assigned the role of observer. The remaining team members were then assigned a functional role, for example, chairperson, marketing manager, financial controller.

The Henley trainers made sure the team members had similar backgrounds and levels of experience, but by the end of the week some teams had achieved very good results while others didn't. There was definitely a pattern, but at the time it wasn't clear what it was. Because of the heavy investment of time and resources in attending such courses, the trainers wanted to ensure that those attending got value for money. Therefore they wanted to find out if there was any way of predicting before the teams got together whether or not the combination of people they had selected would make a successful team.

The trainers invited Meredith Belbin and his colleagues at Cambridge University to come and investigate whether it was possible to predict which teams would succeed and why. Belbin began by asking all course members to take psychometric tests. He then began his research by putting together pure teams. These were made up of team members who had similar test scores. He tried, for example, putting all the extroverts and all the introverts together. Then he constructed teams based on individual mental ability. Later he experimented with more complex team design.

*'Teamwork is the ability to work together toward a common goal, the ability to direct individual accomplishment toward organisational objectives. It is the fuel that allows common people to attain uncommon results.'*

## Team Roles

What Belbin found was that teams selected solely on the basis of high mental ability or intro/extroversion performed significantly less well than other teams. What was more significant in predicting the success of teams was the presence of a number of team roles in addition to the functional role individual members had already been assigned.

Belbin defined team role as a tendency to behave, contribute, and inter-relate with others in a team in certain distinctive ways. He identified eight team roles:

- Co-ordinator

- Team worker

- Plant

- Monitor-evaluator

- Implementer

- Completer-finisher

- Shaper

- Resource-investigator

- (And later added a ninth: Specialist).

Most of us have a predisposition towards one or two of these team roles known as primary and secondary roles. Scoring across all team roles makes up our individual team role profile. Belbin's research indicates that trying to develop a team role for which you score less than average is unlikely to be successful, and may jeopardise the strengths of your existing team role preferences.

Generally, team role style does not change greatly over time, although the strength of preference for a role may change depending on the demands of functional role. If you have an average preference for the resource investigator role, you may find you have a stronger preference for this when you are setting up a new project team.

## Your Preferred Team Role(s)

| Roles and description | Team roles contribution | Allowable weaknesses |
|---|---|---|
| Company Worker Implementer (CW) | Disciplined, reliable, conservative and efficient. Turns ideas into practical actions. | Somewhat inflexible. Slow to respond to new possibilities. |
| Chair Person Co-ordinator (CH) | Mature, confident, a good chair person. Clarifies goals, promotes decision making, delegates well. | Can be seen as manipulative. Delegates personal work. |
| Shaper (SH) | Challenging, dynamic, thrives on pressure. Has the drive and courage to overcome challenges. | Can provoke others and hurt people's feelings. |
| Plant (PL) | Creative, imaginative, unorthodox. Solves difficult problems. | Ignores details. Too preoccupied to communicate effectively. |
| Resource Investigator (RI) | Extroverted, enthusiastic, curious, communicative. Ability to respond to challenge. | Liable to lose interest once initial fascination has passed. |
| Monitor Evaluator (ME) | Serious, strategic and discerning, showing sensitive understanding. Sees all options. Judges accurately. | Lacks drive and ability to inspire others. Can be overly critical. |
| Team Worker (TW) | Co-operative, mild mannered, perceptive and diplomatic. Listens, builds, averts friction, calms the waters. | Indecisive in crunch situations. Can be easily influenced. |
| Completer Finisher (CF) | Painstaking, conscientious, anxious. Searches out errors and omissions. Delivers on time. | Inclined to worry unduly. Reluctant to delegate. Can be a nitpicker. |

Which is your preferred role(s)? Which is your least preferred role? What about your team and/or colleagues? Why not discuss this with them?

*'When a team of dedicated individuals makes a commitment to act as one, the sky is the limit. Together they can reach the heights of excellence and perform the extraordinary.'*

## Allowable Weaknesses

Each team role has a number of helpful behaviours typically associated with it. It also has a flip side or allowable weakness. This is the price paid for the strength of a particular team role. For example:

- *A monitor evaluator* with a capacity for careful analysis and objectivity may not be the best person to inspire others as enthusiasm interferes with assessment.

- *A completer-finisher* with the need to make sure things are done properly is often poor at delegating.

Attempting to correct allowable weaknesses may undermine the strength of that team role. However, it is important to manage the weakness to prevent unacceptable behaviour. For example:

- *A resource investigator* may lose enthusiasm once the initial excitement has passed, but it is not acceptable to let clients down by neglecting to make follow-up arrangements.

- *A shaper* may be prone to frustration and irritation, but this becomes unacceptable when they are unable to recover a situation with good humour or an apology.

## Successful Teams

Belbin identified certain critical factors in determining the success or failure of a team:

- A similarity in the personal qualities of the person leading the team and the typical characteristics within the co-ordinator team role

- The presence of one strong *plant*

- A reasonable spread of mental abilities

- Wide coverage of all team roles

- A good match between functional role and team role characteristics

- Awareness by team members of the various team roles

## Ideal Team Size

Although there are nine team roles, a team of this size can be difficult to manage – a better size for a team is six. This means that some team members take on more than one team role, but it is still big enough for the key roles of plant and co-ordinator to be the main focus of two of the team members.

With people who have clearly developed team role profiles and can comfortably take on more than one role, a team of four can cover all team roles. This, however, means that team members who take on plant or co-ordinator roles can't concentrate on just doing this, which can weaken their contribution.

Teams of three can function effectively if those involved are of high mental ability, have strong implementing skills, and act in unison. Inevitably, personalities will have a much bigger impact on decisions.

## Understanding Team Role Profiles

Certain team role combinations can work well for individuals, for example:

- *Shaper/implementers* combine drive with practical ability

- *Plant/monitor evaluators* combine creativity and the capacity for good decision making

More unusual combinations might also offer opportunities, but present problems when they conflict.

## Managing Yourself

Belbin's research suggests that it is important to play to team role preferences rather than trying to develop all roles equally.

The development of a computer-based assessment programme has identified distinct groups of profiles:

- The *coherent profile* – the individual's self-perception matches with others' perception of their role.

- The *discordant profile* – where the individual's self-perception conflicts with the view of others.

- The *confused profile* – where the individual does not have a strong preference for any particular team role. This situation is more common amongst young or inexperienced people/managers.

Once team roles are identified, individuals can begin to focus on their strengths. Where the profile is less clear, individuals can work to develop team roles. Effective self-management of team roles means:

- Establish which team role preferences you have which fit with other people's perceptions of you, and signal these to the team

- Identify those roles you have an average preference for, and work to develop them

- Actively avoid taking on team roles that are foreign to you, and look to others in the team to fill these gaps

## Relationships at Work

Belbin suggests that interpersonal tensions at work fall into three main categories:

- Avoidance of building a relationship because it is difficult to see how it would work

- Where there is an existing difficult relationship

- Where people experience success at one level, such as achieving the task, but they don't like working together

There are a number of ways of dealing with difficult team relationships:

- *Identify hidden strengths*: sometimes a weakness may indicate a possible strength. For example, a prospective Monitor Evaluator may appear unduly cynical, but these qualities can sometimes be very valuable within the team.

- *Define your role:* clarifying your team role preference can generate understanding and acceptance, and encourage others to do the same.

- *Sacrifice your team role*: if others are unlikely to change, you may have to make an adjustment. Although it is important to play to your strengths, it may be necessary for you to move to a manageable second in the interest of team harmony.

- *Use of a third party:* some difficult relationships can benefit from the presence of a third party. For example a *Team Worker* can facilitate a relationship between a Shaper and a Plant.

- *Contracting out:* sometimes the best thing to do is to delegate a particular team role by either:
  - Assigning responsibility for a piece of work for which a particular team role is needed
  - Stating that there is a team role void and asking for volunteers.

## Characteristics of the Development of a Team/Group

Tuckman some years ago studied teams and group dynamics, and suggested four major stages of development that a team passes through before becoming a cohesive unit. They are:

**FORMING**

This happens when a team or group of unknown people initially come together.

**STORMING**

Sometimes this stage does not happen, but often one or two individuals will want to dominate the group, and will make their mark, perhaps by being aggressive, being a know-it-all, or trying controlling tactics.

**NORMING**

This process is reached when members of the group have settled down with each other, and must occur before the next (and most productive) phase begins.

**PERFORMING**

This is the ultimate purpose of the formation of any group or team.

**(RE-FORMING)**

When a person leaves a group or team, and a new person joins, there is a change in group dynamics, and therefore the process is repeated from the first phase of forming

**(ADJOURNING)**

This is the other possible fifth stage when the team completes the project and dissolves.

When a team works well together members concentrate on getting the job done. In contrast, when a team fails to build relationships between its members it wastes valuable time on struggles for control.

## Stage 1: Forming

The task objective of this stage is to clarify goals. The process objective is to make the transition from a group of individuals to becoming members of a team. The desired outcome for the first stage is commitment to the task and acceptance of team membership.

Group members:
- Have generally positive expectations about outcomes
- Show some anxiety and concern about why they are there, what the purpose of the group means for them, what they will do, what the leader will do, where they fit
- Have some anxiety about other members – who they are, what they are like
- Are dependent on authority.

Group work on tasks:
- Is low to moderate task accomplishment
- Is energy focused on defining the goals, how to approach the task, and what skills are needed?

The length of this stage depends on how clearly the task is defined, and how easy it is to achieve. With simple, easily defined tasks the forming stage will be relatively short requiring perhaps only 5–10% of the time available. In groups with complex goals and tasks this stage may extend to over 30–60% of the team's life.

The leader's behaviour that is most important during this stage is to help the group with the task. This includes:

➤ Facilitating and offering reassurance
➤ Providing a route map for discussion
➤ Leading the discussion
➤ Setting realistic goals
➤ Establishing communication and decision-making procedures

## Stage 2: Storming

The task objective of the Storming stage is to acknowledge and face conflict openly. The process objective is to ensure that individual members listen actively and attentively to all viewpoints. The diversity of opinions shared at this stage provides the team with a vital source of group energy.

Group members:
- Experience some discrepancy between initial hopes and expectations, and the reality of the situation
- Become dissatisfied with dependence on authority
- Often experience feelings of frustration or anger about goals and tasks
- May have negative reactions to the formal leader or other members
- Sometimes experience feelings of incompetence or confusion

Group work on tasks:
- May be disrupted by negative feelings
- Reflects slowly increasing task accomplishment and skill development

The length of this stage is difficult to predict, but generally constitutes a relatively small amount of the group's life. Some groups, however, become stuck in this stage, and continue to be demoralised and relatively unproductive.

For the leader Storming is a particularly difficult time. There are disagreements about authority and influence in the team, and members seek clarification of roles and procedures. The temptation for the leader during this stage is to control it by becoming very directive. However, this only exacerbates the problem, and often unresolved issues will resurface later on. The appropriate leadership style involves a balance between being directive and supportive, a kind of mentoring style. This includes:

➢ Redefining and clarifying goals and expectations
➢ Managing conflict
➢ Encouraging differences of opinion
➢ Focusing the team's energy on problem solving

## Stage 3: Norming
This stage has the task objective of encouraging sharing of information and opinions. The process objective is to increase group cohesion. The overall theme is one of co-operation.

Group members:
- Become less dissatisfied as team roles and responsibilities become clearer
- Develop a new ability to express criticism constructively

- Are more friendly, confide in each other, discuss the team dynamics
- Develop a sense of team cohesion, a common spirit, and goals

Group work on tasks:
- Slowly increases as skills and understanding develop
- Is enhanced by positive feelings among members

The length of this stage depends on the ability of the group to develop norms and processes that enhance their ability to work together. Since the feeling of group cohesiveness is new and fragile, members may tend to avoid conflict or differences for fear of losing the positive climate. This can slow the group's development.

The leader's behaviour most appropriate for this stage includes:

- ➤ Encouraging members to take more responsibility for task and process
- ➤ Establishing and maintaining team ground rules and boundaries (the 'norms')
- ➤ Making sure necessary resources are available
- ➤ Inviting experimentation with working methods
- ➤ Encouraging the team to work through conflict

## Stage 4: Performing
The task objective of performing is to focus energy on productivity and solving problems creatively. The process objective is to promote the independent working of the team.

Group members:
- Have positive feelings about being part of the team
- Feel confident about outcomes
- Recognise, support, and challenge each other's competence and accomplishments
- Communicate openly and freely without fear of rejection or conflict
- Focus their energy on task accomplishment

Group work on tasks:
- Is enhanced by pride in a job well done
- Is easier, more efficient, and satisfying with a continuing increase in skills, knowledge and confidence

The time it takes to arrive at this stage depends on the successful resolution of dissatisfaction, and the complexity of the task and its definition.

For the leader this can be a difficult stage as the team becomes more self-reliant, and less reliant on the leader. However, there is still a role for the leader in celebrating successes and guarding against complacency. Appropriate behaviour may include:

> Celebrating successes
> Encouraging team to review, monitor and evaluate their progress
> Making sure the resources needed are available

## Stage 5: Adjournment

With ongoing work teams, this stage is not usually reached unless there is some drastic reorganisation. However, it is a natural progression for ad hoc groups or project teams. The task objective of this stage is to complete the task. The process objective is to encourage, appreciate and reward team performance.

Group members:
- Begin to be concerned about impending dissolution
- Often experience a sense of loss or sadness about ending the task
- Sometimes deny feelings by joking, missing meetings, or expressing dissatisfaction
- Often have strong positive feelings about accomplishment

Group work on tasks:
- Generally decreases, but in some cases there may be increased work activity to meet deadlines or overcome loss

The appropriate leader behaviour at this stage includes:

> Accepting one's own feelings of loss
> Acknowledging the feelings of others
> Recognising and rewarding the work done

The other element of stage 5 could be the re-forming when a team member(s) leaves and the team process starts again. What stage is the team(s), you either lead or work within, at? Is it Forming, Storming, Norming or even Performing? Why not get together with the team and discuss where you are in this process, and what needs to happen to take the team closer to becoming a high-performing team?

A successful sports coach when asked about his success formula commented, 'There are just three things I would tell the team:

If anything goes wrong *I* did it.

If anything goes semi-good *we* did it.

If anything goes good, then *you* did it.'

Think of a Formula One motor racing team – the ideal example of team working. For months before the race the team works hard on the car to get it ready for the driver on the day. During practice sessions and during the race itself all team members have their roles to play.

When the driver comes in for a pit stop, every second counts! Each team member performs their task as quickly as possible with perfect timing, working in harmony with the rest of the team. How does the Formula One team do this so effectively? Through training, understanding what the driver needs, and lots of practice.

It is worth applying the principles of the Formula One pit team to your own life, career or job.  Work with your colleagues to understand exactly how to deliver excellence. Practise your processes and procedures so that when the customer turns up, your team can perform to perfection. Perfect your team-working to win!

## Forming Powerful Partnerships

Meeting with like-minded people and discussing the challenges and triumphs of mastering your life, achieving your vision, and accomplishing your goals has real power.

Have you ever thought of joining or forming a support group of like-minded people who are moving in a similar direction to you? To attend regular meetings where victories and success are shared and celebrated, problems solved and overcome, and new ideas generated. These meetings can be unparalleled in their ability to produce on-going results and in achieving a positive atmosphere where everyone has an opportunity to grow as a person, and feel supported in going beyond their current reality. If you have joined our team of associates you will have experienced this. Powerful indeed!

Professional life-coaches, counsellors, advisors and consultants cost money, but the insight and wisdom they can impart in a brief session may be priceless. It is thought that in the future people will not ask, 'If you have a life-coach,' but 'Who is your life-coach?'

Books, tapes, CDs and courses can also put you in touch with some of the finest minds on our planet. Be the beneficiary of their knowledge and experience, and when you experience positive changes in your life as a result, be sure to tell them. The most rewarding aspect of my work is when someone tells me something like this – it's something money cannot buy!

### Developing your Human Relations Plan

## Objectives

One reason we don't see improvement as a result of reading a book or by doing a course is that we don't apply what we have learned. It's important at this stage not to let what we have learnt in the last three chapters evaporate, so you need to set objectives/goals in three areas; *work/career, home life,* and *social* life to effect real change in your behaviour.

Before completing this plan you may want to have a brief look over the last three chapters and to any notes you have made or at anything you need to improve upon. Each week, after putting into practice your proposed steps for each section of the plan, make careful notes to record how well you have done. Evaluate your progress – was it unsatisfactory, satisfactory or exemplary? Make notes of how you felt you got on, and what you can do next.

## My human relations plan at work/in business

## My number one challenge/problem is?

Chapter and page numbers where there is information to help:

What have other people done to overcome similar?

The steps I will put into practice immediately are:

1.

2.

3.

4.

5.

**My second challenge/problem is:**

Chapter and page numbers where there is information to help:

What have other people done to overcome similar?

The steps I will put into practice immediately are:

1.

2.

3.

4.

5.

**My third challenge/problem is:**

Chapter and page numbers where there is information to help:

What have other people done to overcome similar?

The steps I will put into practice immediately are:

1.

2.

3.

4.

5.

## My human relations plan at home

### My number one challenge/problem is:

Chapter and page numbers where there is information to help:

What have other people done to overcome similar?

The steps I will put into practice immediately are:

1.

2.

3.

4.

5.

### My second challenge/problem is:

Chapter and page numbers where there is information to help:

What have other people done to overcome similar?

The steps I will put into practice immediately are:

1.

2.

3.

4.

5.

**My third challenge/problem is:**

Chapter and page numbers where there is information to help:

What have other people done to overcome similar?

The steps I will put into practice immediately are:

1.

2.

3.

4.

5.

## My human relations plan in my social life

### My number one challenge/problem is:

Chapter and page numbers where there is information to help:

What have other people done to overcome similar?

The steps I will put into practice immediately are:

1.

2.

3.

4.

5.

**My second challenge/problem is:**

Chapter and page numbers where there is information to help:

What have other people done to overcome similar?

The steps I will put into practice immediately are:

1.

2.

3.

4.

5.

**My third challenge/problem is:**

Chapter and page numbers where there is information to help:

What have other people done to overcome similar?

The steps I will put into practice immediately are:

1.

2.

3.

4.

5.

I urge you to take action with these action plans. You will make a positive difference to your life and to the lives of those around you. And once you have started implementing your action plans, celebrate your success – you deserve it!

The enormous benefits of being open to how other people choose to live their lives, especially when working as a team is now apparent. Use the knowledge well, and above all enjoy the journey! When you are ready, move on to **Action 9** where you will discover ways to develop and invest in yourself and put into practice everything you have learned so far.

# Action 9

## Value Your Most Important Asset

*'Fortunate, indeed, is the man who takes exactly the right measure of himself, and holds a balance between what he can acquire and what he can use, be it great or be it small!'*
Peter Latham 1789–1875

Positive people are healthier. That's because our cells are constantly eavesdropping on our thoughts and being changed by them. A bout of depression can wreak havoc with your immune system and falling in love can boost it.

Despair and helplessness raise the risk of heart attacks and cancer, whilst joy and fulfilment help keep you healthy and extend life. This means that the line between biology and psychology can't be drawn with any certainty. A remembered stress, which is only a wisp of thought, releases the same flood of destructive hormones as the stress itself.

This Action is the one that people neglect most through lack of time, yet your greatest asset is you! I particularly remember a conversation with a friend who had formerly been fit and positive with everything to live for. However, after the trauma of a divorce, subsequent depression, and redundancy from his life-long employment, he severely neglected his physical and mental health. His words to me were, 'Bernard, I have lots of money due to my redundancy, but I realise I have misjudged my priorities. Happiness and health are the most important things for me *now*.'

Over recent years we have seen an explosion of both diet and fitness products, and at the same time a growth of ill-health due to sedentary life styles and unhealthy eating habits. What is the missing link? Is it a lack of willpower, a lack of planning or commitment, or the inability to keep life in balance?

# The Importance of Balance

You may have noticed some apparent contradictions in the previous chapters – should we go for an exciting action plan or spend time reflecting and accepting? Should we be flexible or firm, assertive or accepting, giving or receiving? The answer is it's all a matter of balance.

We all know what the opposite of balance is, and many of us have one or more addictions. In addition to the well known ones such as drugs, alcohol, smoking, food, and gambling, there are many others including work, religion, shopping, and other people (sex, romance, dependency). Almost anything can become an addiction. There is a difference between total commitment and addiction. If *it* runs you, it's an addiction. If you can stop *it* for an indefinite period of time, it's a preference, or commitment.

One of the most successful programmes for overcoming addiction, and achieving balance, is the 12 step programme originally created to help alcoholics.

1. We admitted we were powerless over our addiction – that our lives had become unmanageable.

2. Came to believe that a power greater than ourselves could restore us to sanity.

3. Made a decision to turn our will and our lives over to the care of this higher power.

4. Made a moral searching and fearless moral inventory of ourselves.

5. Admitted to our higher power, to ourselves, and to another human being the exact nature of our wrongs.

6. Were entirely ready to have our higher power remove all these defects of character.

7. Humbly asked our higher power to remove our shortcomings.

8. Made a list of all persons we had harmed, and became willing to make amends to them.

9. Made direct amends to such people wherever possible, except when to do so would injure them or others.

10. Continued to take personal inventory and when we were wrong, promptly admitted it.

11. Sought, through prayer and meditation, to improve our conscious contact with our higher power, praying for knowledge of our higher power's will for us and the power to carry that out.

12. Having a spiritual awakening as the result of these steps, we tried to carry this message to others and practise these principles in all our affairs.

The above may appear somewhat evangelical, but I have included the 12 steps because of their success with so many thousands of individuals over many years. Take from it whatever you can.

Once you overcome your addiction, you can overcome anything. This is where the impossible becomes possible, the unimaginable imaginable, the unmanageable manageable. The single most important investment you can make in life is in yourself. You are the instrument of your own effectiveness and performance, and you need to recognise the importance of investing in yourself in these four key areas; physical, creative, educational and social wellbeing.

## Physical Wellbeing

### Diet and nutrition
This involves caring for your physical body. Let's look firstly at what you eat. Why eat healthily? A good diet is necessary for good nutrition, increased energy, and physical endurance and strength. We are currently experiencing an epidemic in the West of obesity and the related illnesses such as diabetes due to bad diet.

**You are what you eat!**

Ask ten people and you will get twenty suggestions of good diets and what worked for them. A doctor once said, 'Eat breakfast like a king, lunch like a prince, and evening meal like a pauper.' What was his message? Give your body a chance to burn off the calories you take in. The less food the body has to process at night, the healthier it will be. Another view is to eat food which is as natural and unprocessed as possible – a policy I adopted some 12 years ago. Now, although I am over the age of 40, I am the same weight as I was at 16, and I haven't needed to visit a doctor in those 12 years. In addition I have more energy than at any other time in my life and I enjoy a productive, varied, and full life.

Developing a more healthy diet is a habit that is relatively easy to adopt and its rewards, although not immediate can, in the long term, be the difference between longevity or premature death.

*'One should eat to live, and not live to eat.'*
Molière (Jean-Baptiste Poquelin) 1622–73

There is a growing concern over the number of people diagnosed as obese. In the last 20 years the number has tripled and, if this trend continues, over a quarter of adults in England will be obese by 2010. A recent National Audit Office report outlined the significant cost of obesity in 1998 as follows:

- 18 million days of sickness absence
- 40,000 lost years of working life
- 30,000 deaths – of which 9,000 related to obesity before state retirement age
- £0.5 billion cost to the National Health Service (NHS)
- £2 billion indirect costs to the economy

One choice we can take on the path to a healthier lifestyle is organic food. Organic food is better for the planet, better for the farmer, better for his livestock, and better for you. By choosing organic food you get the extra benefit of avoiding the added colourings, flavourings, preservatives, emulsifiers, stabilizers and artificial sweeteners found in processed foods, as well as the residues of pesticides, hormones, and antibiotics. The nutritional content is usually higher as well.

Food grown in rich, naturally fertilized soil will offer higher levels of vitamins, minerals, trace elements, and beneficial phytonutrients (plant nutrients) that can help protect you against two of the biggest killers, heart disease and cancer.

Foods such as fruit and vegetables with high vitamin and mineral content help build healthier bodies and immune systems. There is considerable concern however that our consumption of antibiotics consumed through the animal products we eat, may lead to resistant strains of bacteria in people and consequently reduce the effectiveness of our immune systems.

There are over 3,000 chemicals approved for food by government agencies, but they may also cause allergies such as asthma and eczema as well as behaviour disorders such as attention deficit disorder.

A study in Britain in 2000 also provided evidence of the biodiversity benefits of organic production. Organic farm fields contain five times as many wild plants, 57% more species of wildlife, 25% more birds around the edges of fields, 44% more birds in the fields during autumn and winter, three times as many butterflies, and over twice the number of small insects.

There is also a rising concern about the unacceptable way intensively farmed animals are kept, and scares such as BSE, foot and mouth disease, salmonella and listeria and their link to intensive farming methods have encouraged more people to look to organic and more natural options.

Eating the recommended five portions of fruit and vegetables (1 portion = a heaped handful) could reduce the risk of death from chronic diseases such as heart disease, stroke and cancer by 20% (Department of Health 2000 The NHS plan, London). It is estimated that diet may contribute to the development of at least one third of all cancers, and that increasing fruit and vegetable consumption is on a par with stopping smoking in cancer prevention. Yet still only 13% of men and 15% of women eat the recommended five portions (British Heart Foundation).

A study in late 2005 showed that each increase of one portion of fruit and vegetables a day lowered the risk of coronary heart disease by 4% and the risk of stroke by 6%. Evidence also suggests an increase in fruit and vegetable intake helps lower blood pressure. Other health benefits include delaying the development of cataracts, reducing asthma symptoms, improving bowel function, and helping to manage diabetes.

Be aware also of being lured into low-calorie diets – they are a common cause of nutritional deficiency if maintained for a long time. It is difficult for a woman to consume enough food on 1,500 calories (2,000 for a man) to provide the full spectrum of vitamins, minerals, trace elements and phytonutrients necessary for healthy living.

## A Healthy Diet
One third of your food should be fresh (preferably organic) fruits, salads or vegetables (raw or cooked). We need five portions a day (about one and a half pounds in weight) for a good daily intake of vitamins, minerals and dietary fibre as well as heart disease and cancer fighting phytonutrients.

Another third of your diet should be potatoes, whole grain bread or pasta, whole grains (rice or oats), beans, lentils and other legumes for slow-release carbohydrates, fibre, B vitamins, and minerals, again offering protection from heart disease.

If you are a meat eater, get most of your protein from fish, seafood, poultry or game, but limit your red meat and egg intake. Dairy products are a major source of calcium, but need to be used with common sense. Choose low fat options and eat no more than two or three portions a day.

Avoid expensive processed foods and use home-made soups, vegetable casseroles, and beans as alternatives to meat. Limit all meat, especially processed meat products such as sausages, hot dogs, burgers, and luncheon meats which contain huge amounts of hidden fats.

Boost your immune system with some pumpkin seeds or shellfish for zinc, and Brazil nuts for selenium. Beta-carotene and vitamin C and E are essential antioxidants and defend cells in the body from attack, so eat plenty of fruit, salads, and dark green, yellow and orange produce, as well as avocados, cold-pressed olive oil, and nut oils.

Below is a list of good foods and then below that some guidance for wise choices from this list depending on our age.

- Dates – high potassium
- Eggs – protein, iron, zinc, vitamins A, D, E, B6 & B12 & calcium
- Lentils – protein
- Oatmeal – iron, zinc, calcium and B vitamins
- Oranges – vitamin C
- Parsley – beta-carotene, vitamin C and iron
- Pumpkin/sesame seeds – B vitamins, iron, zinc, magnesium, protein, calcium, potassium and unsaturated fatty acids
- Spinach – high in beta-carotene (powerful antioxidant), potassium, calcium and folic acid
- Avocados – rich in vitamin E
- Bananas – vitamin B6 & potassium (good for Pre Menstrual Syndrome – PMS) & fibre (good for digestion)
- Carrots (1 a day supplies the entire day's requirement of beta-carotene)
- Cauliflower – silicone (for strong bones, healthy hair and good skin)
- Potatoes – vitamin C, slow release carbohydrate, fibre, folic acid and minerals

- Sunflower seeds – B vitamins, vitamin E, minerals, unsaturated fats, protein
- Thyme – antibacterial properties that help fight acne
- Apricots – beta carotene
- Blackcurrants – beta carotene, vitamin C
- Citrus Fruit – beta carotene, soluble fibre
- Broccoli – beta carotene
- Peppers – beta carotene, vitamin C
- Yoghurt – B vitamins, calcium
- Oats – B vitamins, protein, soluble fibre, vitamin E, magnesium, potassium & Zinc
- Wheat Germ – B vitamins & Zinc
- Almond – Protein, unsaturated fats, Zinc, Magnesium, potassium, iron and some B vitamins, Vitamin E, calcium,
- Game – B vitamins & Zinc
- Green leafy vegetables – high in fibre, calcium
- Onions – fibre
- Cheese – protein, calcium, phosphorous, Vitamins A, B, D & E
- Feta, Cottage & Curd cheese – low in fat
- Grapes – natural sugar, vitamin E, antioxidants
- Sage – healing & antiseptic
- Sprouts – protein, B vitamins & minerals
- Melon – vitamin C, vitamin A, Phosphorous, Potasium, Zinc
- Chickpeas – zinc, magnesium, calcium, protein, vitamin B, iron, potassium, phosphorus
- Kidney beans – zinc, magnesium
- Liver – zinc, magnesium
- Shellfish – zinc, magnesium
- Mackerel – zinc, magnesium
- Turnips – calcium
- Dried fruit – calcium
- Seeds –calcium, vitamin E
- Nuts – calcium, vitamin E, calcium, magnesium, iron, zinc
- Brown rice – calcium
- Herring – calcium
- Sardines – calcium
- Tuna – calcium
- Skimmed milk – calcium
- Apples – soluble fibre
- Beans – soluble fibre
- Pears – soluble fibre

- Root vegetables – soluble fibre
- Kiwi fruit – vitamin C
- Garlic – good for reducing cholesterol
- Soya bean – fibre, protein, phyto-estrogens
- Spring greens – potassium, calcium, iron, beta-carotene, vitamin C, folic acid

Foods rich in vitamin B include; whole grains (wheat, oats), fish/seafood, poultry, eggs, dairy products/milk/yoghurt, leafy green vegetables, beans, peas, citrus fruits such as oranges

Foods rich in vitamin C include; citrus fruits, strawberries, tomatoes, broccoli, cabbage

Foods rich in vitamin D include; milk/dairy products, fish, egg yolks

Foods rich in vitamin E include; whole grains (wheat/oats), wheat germ, leafy green vegetables, sardines, egg yolks, nuts

Foods rich in vitamin k include; leafy green vegetables, liver, pork, dairy products

Foods with high protein content include; beef, poultry, fish, eggs, dairy products, nuts, seeds, legumes like black-beans

Foods with high potassium content include; apricots, artichokes, avocados, bananas, cantaloupe, cod, dates, dry beans, watermelons, figs, greens, honeydew melons, kiwi fruit, lentils, nuts, oranges, peaches, potatoes, prunes, pumpkins, raisins, salmon, sardines, tomatoes

Foods with moderate potassium content include; apples, broccoli, Brussel sprouts, carrots, celery, cherries, mango, mushrooms, pears, plums, peppers

Iron rich foods include; liver, lean red meats, seafood, beans such as kidney & lentils, whole grains, cereals, bread, rice, pasta, greens, spinach, turnip, greens, tofu

Non-dairy foods containing calcium include; salmon, sardines, spinach, tofu, rhubarb, collard greens, turnip, okra, white beans, greens, baked beans, broccoli, peas, Brussel sprouts, sesame seeds, almonds

Common foods containing fibre; apples, banana, bran flakes, broccoli, cooked butternut squash, corn, corn flakes, English muffin, high fibre bran, kidney beans, oats & porridge, orange, peanut butter, pear, baked potato (with skin), beans, spaghetti, spinach, strawberries, rice, whole wheat bread

Good foods for childhood and adolescence include dates, eggs, lentils, oatmeal, oranges, parsley, pumpkin seeds, and spinach.

Teenagers should drink fresh juice rather than carbonated beverages, and plenty of citrus fruits and fruit salads.

As we enter our twenties we need food to protect us from the stress of everyday living, including the partying! Skin problems such as acne are devastating, so one day a week eat nothing but fruit and vegetables, and drink plenty of water and herbal teas to cleanse the system. Good foods for the twenties include avocados, bananas, carrots, cauliflower, potatoes, sunflower seeds, and thyme.

In work environments, there is a worry over conditions such as *sick office syndrome* due to ozone emissions from office equipment, pollution from paints, and infections spread by air conditioning. To combat this you need foods high in carotenoids such as beta-carotene in carrots. In addition to carrots try to eat at least two of the following each day; apricots (fresh or dried), blackberries, blueberries, broccoli, lettuce (dark green or red), peppers (yellow or red), prunes, spinach, sweet potatoes, spring greens, strawberries, tomatoes or watercress.

When we enter our thirties and forties we are in the prime of our life with more natural energy, but still need a healthy diet to boost our resistance to infection and disease. To help maintain our immune system we need a good supply of beta-carotene, vitamin C, B vitamins and zinc. Apricots, blackcurrants, citrus fruit, broccoli, peppers, sprouts, yoghurt, oats, wheat germ, almonds, eggs, game and oily fish will help with all these key areas.

High fibre foods are good for our heart, and we should eat plenty of green leafy vegetables, onions and garlic. Use cold-pressed olive oil on salads, and cut down on animal fats, salt and refined carbohydrates. And drink alcohol in moderation!

Other foods good for these prime years include almonds, celery, cheese, Feta, cottage and curd cheese, grapes, sage, sprouts, melon, dried fruit, almonds, whole-grain cereals, bananas, pumpkin seeds, chickpeas, kidney beans, liver, shellfish, mackerel, cabbage, celery, spinach, turnips, dried fruits, seeds, nuts, brown rice, chickpeas, herring, sardines, tuna, eggs, low-fat cheese, yoghurt and skimmed milk.

On entering our fifties, the different physiologies of men and women mean we have different nutritional needs. Good nutrition for older men is even more crucial as they are twice as likely to have a heart attack or stroke as a woman between the ages of 55 – 74. Once a woman reaches the menopause, however, she is also at a greater risk of suffering a stroke or heart attack.

Increase the amount of fibre, particularly soluble fibre from oats, beans, apples and bananas – citrus fruits, pears and root vegetables are also a good starting point. Vitamin C, which reduces the risk of blood clots comes from red, green and yellow peppers, oranges, kiwis and black currants. Garlic is good for reducing cholesterol while fresh fruit, carrots and dark green leafy vegetables help prevent heart disease. Salt is the silent killer, so cut down on all foods containing salt to help reduce blood pressure.

For men in their fifties good foods include artichokes (two a week for the liver and gall bladder – good for men with a history of alcohol consumption), brazil nuts (heart health & prostate cancer prevention), garlic, salmon, shellfish, watercress (vital for smokers or ex-smokers as it helps inhibit the proliferation of lung cancer cells), and yoghurt for digestion.

Good foods for the menopausal woman include chickpeas, almond and hazel nuts, oats, peppers, sesame & pumpkin seeds, sunflower seeds, soya beans, spring greens, and vegetable oils (wheat germ oil & other types of oils for vitamin E & unsaturated fatty acids).

In our sixties and beyond we can expect the brain to lose some of its cells, muscles to lose some strength, joints some flexibility, digestion, eyes and ears some sharpness, but with a positive attitude to life and attention to your diet, your age will not stop you doing what you want to do. This is the time for getting maximum nutrition in a digestible form. Liver, chicken and sardines provide high doses of B vitamins necessary for releasing the energy from the food you eat, and for the proper functioning of the nervous system including the brain.

A steady blood sugar level is important, so eat meals at regular intervals with enough carbohydrate-rich foods to supply starches and natural sugars. Dried fruits such as dates, figs and apricots every day is another way of keeping blood sugars in balance.

To keep rheumatism at bay, add turnips and their leafy tops to the diet. Along with celery and parsley they eliminate uric acid which aggravates joint problems. Strawberries are also good for the joints.

Protein can come from chicken, sardines, mackerel, salmon and trout to keep muscle strength. Lentils are another good source of protein if you are a vegetarian.

Chicory or artichokes will stimulate your liver. Whole-grain breads and cereals, dried fruits, greens and plenty of fresh fruit will help with constipation. Raw garlic is a natural antibiotic and helps keep the bowels regular. As with all ages restrict the intake of fatty foods and eat beef, pork and lamb infrequently. Foods with plenty of soluble fibre such as oats, root vegetables, citrus fruits, bananas, apples and baked beans are good as they help reduce the cholesterol in the blood. Garlic and olive oil do the same. All these foods along with reducing salt and caffeine will help reduce blood pressure.

## Water intake

Above all, don't neglect your water intake. Drink eight glasses of water or two litres every day spread as evenly as possible throughout your day. As well as eliminating toxins, water helps regulate body temperature, carries nutrients and oxygen to cells, and helps digestion. Do not, however, confuse water intake with tea, coffee, and alcohol, as they are diuretics and our liver has difficulty processing these toxins into something the body can use.

In summary, no amount of beauty treatment can make up for a poor diet and an unhealthy life-style – the most important ingredient for good skin and hair is good food. Beauty starts from within.

## Exercise

As well as giving you great skin and a fit body, physical exercise releases endorphins which act as a natural anti-depressant and stress reliever.

1 in 5 people in the UK take no exercise at all.
16% exercise every day.
23% exercise 3 – 4 times a week.

Yet regular moderate physical activity like swimming, a brisk walk or cycling will reduce your risk of coronary heart disease and other chronic diseases by almost *50%* through helping you maintain a healthy weight and reducing blood pressure and cholesterol levels. Physical activity can also reduce the risk of premature death by 20%–30%, reduce the risk of obesity, encourage healthy growth in young people and through creating healthy lifestyles can significantly reduce the cost of healthcare and workplace absence. Absent staff cost UK businesses over £11 billion each year. The annual cost of physical *inactivity* in England is estimated at £8.2 billion. A further estimate of £2.5 billion costs is attributed to obesity.

If you say that you do not have enough time for exercise, I suggest that you do not have time not to exercise. You do not need any special equipment to take exercise. Going to the gym or participating in a team sport is good for both exercise and expanding your social circle however, but a good exercise programme can be developed from home and should include endurance, flexibility and strength exercises.

Endurance exercises include walking, jogging, swimming and cycling all exercise the most important muscle of all, your heart muscle.

Flexibility can be achieved through stretching. It is recommended you do stretching exercises before and after any endurance exercise. Before the exercise it loosens, warms and helps prevent any muscle injury during the exercise. Afterwards it dissipates the lactic acid that gives you stiff muscles after exercise.

You can improve your strength by doing muscle resistant exercises. At home you can do press-ups, sit-ups, or work with some weights. You will be amazed at the general feel-good factor of having a fitness programme and the long-term effects are enormous.

It has been reported that physical exercise at work can dramatically reduce absenteeism for employers. The British Heart Foundation (BHF) has produced the Workplace Health Activity Toolkit (WHAT), which provides information, practical ideas and materials for employers to increase the activity levels of their staff. To order a copy of WHAT go to: www.bhf.org.uk

The BHF emphasises the point that regular exercise is not only good for the heart but also helps reduce the risk of strokes, diabetes and problems associated with stress and obesity. According to the BHF, just thirty minutes of regular, moderately intense activity accumulated over a day is enough to help prevent serious illnesses such as strokes and coronary heart disease. Regular exercise can also make a big difference to energy levels and working efficiency. Are you ready to make that commitment of 15 – 45 minutes a day?

## Sleep

The next important area for physical health is sleep. Half the world's population regularly experience sleep deprivation. Research suggests that in the short-term poor sleep reduces our performance and levels of concentration, and drivers with less than 6 hours sleep each night put themselves and others at serious risk. The longer term effects of bad sleep, such as stress and illness, can lead people to physical and mental burn-out by the time they are in their thirties.

Sleep disturbances can have a serious effect on health, doubling the risk of death in older people who are otherwise healthy. About 1 in 10 in Britain suffers from seriously interrupted sleep, so it is a big problem. Many people are wandering around with low levels of energy and concentration, and can be irritable and even angry due to lack of sleep.

Quality sleep is essential for our physical as well as our mental well-being. The primary function of sleep is to restore and revitalise our bodies. It also improves our mood, increases mental alertness, and boosts our immune system.

Factors that cause poor sleep include stress/anxiety, adverse noise levels, environmental changes, incorrect room temperature, shift work/jet lag, medication side effects, depression/worry, bad bed position, and inferior bedding or mattress.

What can you do to sleep better? It may seem a strange question to ask, but what do you do in bed? Sleep, read, watch TV, eat food, catch up on e-mails on the lap-top, argue or make love with your partner? Watching TV or working on your laptop sends messages to your brain to be active in bed, not restful, so reserve your bed for sleeping. A heavy meal before bed, caffeine, alcohol and nicotine do not help. Exercise a few hours before going to bed, and get into a bedtime routine by having a bath, reading, or whatever relaxes you. Ensure your bedclothes and mattress encourages sleep rather than inhibit it. If you still experience problems, consult your doctor or other health professional.

## Our Creative Wellbeing and Development

The creative and spiritual part of you is at the core of your life. This private element of yourself is a vitally important one, but one that is easily neglected in our rapid paced society.

When you connect with this creative side you will be inspired and uplifted, although how we do this varies from person to person – what works for me may not work for you. Here are few ideas to help inspire creativity for you.

I find the beauty and peacefulness of nature allows me to connect with my creative side. It gives me an opportunity for deep reflection that in turn helps me resolve some of the challenges I face, so that I come back refreshed, invigorated and inspired.

### Meditation
Meditation is one of the most ancient human activities. In a state of meditation you focus your concentration on a single object which calms your mind and increases your awareness.

The experience that underlines meditation is familiar to all of us; the mother and her baby united in a gentle rhythm as she rocks and sings; on holiday lying on the beach, giving ourselves over quietly to the sun and the air, engulfed by the lulling rhythms of the sea; on the top of the mountain we can breathe in the silence above the earth, and can be shaken by the immensity so that our mind becomes still. If you have ever experienced something similar, you have in fact experienced a spontaneous meditative mood described by Abraham Maslow as *peak experiences.*

Perhaps meditation can be seen as this spontaneous process developed into a formal practice, and there are literally hundreds of ingenious ways of intentionally evoking this process handed down over generations. All these practices develop the ability to bring about a special kind of free-floating attention where rational thought is bypassed. It is a characteristic of this state that the person is completely absorbed by his or her particular object of meditation.

Meditation is not, however, emptying the mind or making the mind go blank; its goal is to attune the mind to a single focus. Meditation can attune our mind to our vision, mission or a chosen ideal such as oneness with spirit, love, tranquillity, peace, harmony, success, or happiness. Meditation is a willingness to listen to the reverberations of your vision and to bring the mind back to your vision every time it strays to other thoughts.

The paradox of meditation is that although you do very little, a lot actually happens. Your body slows down, breathing becomes more regular, heart rate and blood pressure decrease, and there is a general relaxing effect. In fact research suggests that meditation can be up to 100% effective in reducing stress as your subconscious mind also relaxes. In the conscious mind one thought can trigger several more; during meditation the reverse is true.

For many people the meditative practice can be a spiritual experience. With the body and subconscious relaxed, the effect of our vision increases as our imagination encapsulates more of its meaning. This can be deep, inspirational and meaningful.

When your mind and body are relaxed, your mind opens up to new and creative ideas, and this is how meditation can help your creative or spiritual side.

**Meditation is not absolutely nothing!**

*'All of humanity's problems stem from*
*man's inability to sit quietly in a room alone.'*
Pascal

## Yoga

Yoga is another effective relaxation method. Used for centuries to clear the mind, it is easy and simple to do, and is suitable for all ages and fitness levels. Its benefits are both physical and emotional. Physically it strengthens the muscles and spine, increasing flexibility; emotionally it helps balance body-mind-spirit connection, giving you a feeling of peace.

Yoga is practised by engaging in a series of stretches, both gentle and challenging, focussing on the neck, back, hips, legs and spine. After just a few minutes people report that they feel more alive, peaceful, relaxed and their minds are clear.

## Great Literature, music or the arts

Immersing oneself in great literature, inspirational music, or the arts can also lift your spirit. I can testify to this as I previously said, the impact of Nelson Mandela's book *Long walk to freedom* had an enormous impact on me both personally and professionally. Immersing oneself in literature like this can have a positive influence upon us, inspire us toward greatness, and give us faith to be creative for our future achievements.

When was the last time you read any great literature, listened to classical or other inspirational music, admired the wonderful works in an art gallery or museum, or experienced the stimulus of opera or the theatre? Try it! It could renew and refresh you.

## Reflecting on your vision/mission

Consider finding a peaceful place and reflect on the statement for your future vision/mission that you wrote as part of **Action 3**? This will help give you a deep understanding of your centre and your purpose, and give you an opportunity to recommit.

## Visualisation

On a daily basis you may want to visualise the day's events before they happen. Some believe that the greatest battles of life are fought out daily within the realms of inner silence. Quell any inner conflict, develop a sense of peace by visualising the day ahead. It is in this time of silence that people sometimes experience a life-changing thunderbolt that communicates a sense of destiny, empowering them to make the world a better place or touch the lives of many people in a positive way.

Do not rely upon the power of visualisation alone, but express your intentions with an All Out Massive Action (AOMO)! The key to successful visualisation is a mental process of acting as if you are seeing it – the key to manifesting it is to act as though it is real.

## Positive suggestion and self-hypnosis

Powerful *suggestion* and self-hypnosis can also be a source of inspiration. Hypnosis has been used successfully for eliminating pain in place of analgesia in procedures such as amputations, major surgery, and caesarean deliveries. Being able to do such amazing things reveals the power of our mind. However, it can make hypnosis look like something mysterious and magical, when actually hypnosis is based around three ordinary processes – relaxation, suggestion, and imagery. Hypnosis is simply a way to communicate with your subconscious mind, and operates through suggestion and imagery. When the subconscious mind is relaxed it can be reached directly. Thus, relaxation is the first stage.

You actually experience a form of hypnosis every night when you go to sleep as the senses shut down and the conscious mind switches off, external stimuli fade away and your own thoughts become your reality. It is then that the subconscious mind becomes the dominant force, and this is a perfect time to make a suggestion to your subconscious mind, planting the seeds of thought for your vision, ideal or perfect life. This process can become a major tool in using your deeper mind to bring your vision to life and the achievement of your goals.

Just as someone continually suggesting you are inadequate can lead you to believe it, so positive suggestion can have beneficial effects. Positive suggestions have been used to help heal the incurable as well as aid people to do the un-doable. Continually repeating 'I am capable of doing anything I wish' or 'I am unstoppable in the pursuit of my dreams' can help create the desired effect.

Suggestion is particularly potent when you are already motivated toward a particular goal, and are taking action to reach it: success then becomes almost inevitable. This can happen in exam situations, in therapy, and for addictions (I used it to give up smoking). Unlike the conscious mind, the subconscious responds to suggestions. Here's an example. Let me suggest that this book is as light as a feather. What happened? You probably checked the weight, and evaluated the suggestion. The conscious mind tends to evaluate, then agree or disagree, checking for logic and consistency compared to past experiences.

Now *pretend* that the book is as light as a feather. *Pretend* that it is so light that it simply rests in your relaxed hands and arms. How does this feel? Does the book feel light? Yes? To achieve this you simply focussed your mind on some things and ignored others. For example you may have focussed on how relaxed your hands and arms were, or how weightless the book felt in your hands. When pretending the subconscious mind does not respond in the same way, but accepts the statement as true and acts accordingly, ignoring contrary data.

The subconscious mind will automatically accept suggestions as affirmations, and does not understand the meaning of negative suggestions such as *no* or *not*. In 'Do not think about the tail of a horse,' your subconscious mind drops the word *not* and the phrase 'tail of a horse' is immovably implanted in your subconscious.

The subconscious mind must be redirected to look at or think of something else, supplanting the negative with a positive alternative such as, 'If you think about the tail of a horse, you will immediately think about your ideal future.' Suggestions must always be phrased as positive affirmations. Ask yourself now what it is you want your subconscious mind to believe, to do, to experience?

A great suggestion for a positive affirmation is to make your **vision** or **ideal** a fact rather than a desire or wish. Feel it and let your imagination grow it by repeating it from time to time and you will experience how suggestion can operate through affirmation and give you the groundbreaking results you deserve.

Once you are relaxed and ready for suggestion, mentally repeat to yourself your vision or ideal and allow it to create in you the feelings that it suggests. Then allow those feelings to develop into images. Let yourself have a daydream based on your vision.

The next step could be to use this hypnotic daydream experience to help you imagine how an ideal attitude might help you respond differently to a particular situation. Allow yourself to get into the feeling of your vision and then view your current situation. Daydream about this situation in the mood of your vision/ideal, and you may even find a novel solution for your situation. Imaginative forces operate within patterns set by an *ideal*.

To yield constructive results, evoke your own imaginary scene as a powerful tool for further work with the use of imagination for inspiration and creative problem solving – it could be an image of you sitting on a beach in the sun or looking out from your mountain top retreat – whatever image inspires you.

### Inspirational people

People can obviously be a source of deep inspiration. Find someone who has done something interesting or exciting. Seek them out, talk to them, benefit from their inspiration, learn about them and what compelled them to do what they do. You will, without doubt, come away uplifted, inspired and perhaps even a changed person.

Now make some notes about what you are going to do to tap into your creative side.

## Your Educational Wellbeing and Development

### Television

Most of our mental development comes through our formal education, but once that is complete few of us continue that mental stimulus, often opting instead for many wasted hours in front of the television. If you watch television, be selective, choose inspiring, informative and educational programmes that fit comfortably with your values and will help take you towards your vision or purpose.

Used in a positive way, TV can enrich our life and, as a servant rather than a master, it is a tool of immense value. However, if we don't master it, television can numb our mind and influence us in a negative way. In **Action 4** we learnt about self-management, and this is an area in our life where we need to manage ourselves with self-discipline, and self-awareness.

## Courses

Continual education has become a lot easier in the last few years and in addition to classroom based learning there are many other methods including correspondence courses and e-learning. The continual exercising, expanding, and testing of your mind is something that will increase your opportunities in life. Courses give us rich opportunities to improve our employment chances through gaining new knowledge or skills, and they help improve our relationships and happiness in life. The very fact that you are reading this book shows you are a person who is open to learning, and willing to expand your mind.

There are also many great minds available to us through reading good literature to help us expand our knowledge. It has been said, 'The person who does not read is no better off then the person who can't read.'

## Writing

Writing is another way to broaden your horizons. I mentioned the merits of keeping a journal – writing about your thoughts, experiences and insights gives mental clarity, and helps put things into perspective and context. When writing, we communicate at much deeper levels of thought, feelings, ideas and other softer emotions. *The Magic of Writing Things Down* is a book by inspirational writer, Sallyann Sheridan which reveals tips and techniques on how to use writing in this way. The book, which is deliberately concise for busy people, shows methods which, quite literally, have helped thousands of people change their lives for the better.

## Inspirational people

Once again other people can be a vast help in the educational dimension, offering a rich source of educational, cultural content, and exposing us to diverse and challenging views.

In 1989 I attended the 100th birthday celebrations of one of the most interesting men I have ever met. As we talked of his earlier life and involvement in World War One, I was immensely moved by his informative, inspired and touching stories of courage, valour, friendship, compassion and dignity. I learned more in those few hours than from countless television programmes, convincing me that conversation, particularly with elderly people, is something to be deeply valued and something we do not search out enough.

## Planning, organising, setting goals & practising *Action 4.*

Another form of educational expansion and regeneration is to practise organising and planning. When you exercise your imagination, visualisation skills and become more creative you expand your mind. It is said that business success is created in the boardroom with the creation of a successful strategy; that wars are won in the Field Marshall's tent, and individual success is created by mentally designing our future, rather than just letting our future happen.

With regard to the three areas we have looked at so far – the physical, creative/spiritual, and mental/educational – you may wonder where you will get the time to do all this. Because these areas are truly vital for your future growth, it is worth making sacrifices to develop them.

Doing this will have a massive impact on every area of your life – on the decisions you take, the problems you encounter, the challenges you face, and the balance in your life. It will make you more effective as a person, help build your long-term physical, creative and mental strength, and give you a real winner's edge in life.

Before we move on, spend 15 – 30 minutes thinking about the key areas we have discussed so far in this Action. What will you change physically by means of your diet and exercise programme? How will you improve your rest, relaxation and sleep?

What will you do to exercise your creative and spiritual side? Will you spend time reflecting or meditating? Will you tap into the beauty of nature, perhaps going to your own sanctuary of peace? Will you use the inspiration of music, visual media, great literature, or the arts? Or will you engage in conversations with inspirational people?

What will you do to exercise your educational and mental side? Will you sign up to that course you've been thinking about doing? Will you start seeking out a more educational content to your daily routine, and reduce the amount of time devoted to less important material? Or will you seek out the education other people can give? Will you read one book a month? Or start writing that journal or those letters in a deep and meaningful way? Will you commit to regular planning, prioritising and organising in your life and strive toward your destiny and purpose? Remember what we said in **Action 4** – if you fail to plan, you plan to fail!

Now write down an action plan of what you are going to bring into your life, what you are going to give up (to give yourself a better life), and when in your daily routine you will incorporate this. You may find you can join some areas up. For example, whilst preparing a healthy meal, or taking exercise you could also spend that time visualising your future or in deep reflective thought.

## My Social Wellbeing & Development

The social element is more about making a commitment to practise some of the sound interpersonal principles we have learned so far in our everyday interaction with people.

> *'Treat a person as he is, and he will remain as he is.*
> *Treat him as he could be, and he will become what he should be.'*
>
> Jimmy Johnson

By affirming and believing in other people you uplift them (which uplift's you). You make a difference in their life (and make a difference in yours). You inspire them (and inspire yourself). You encourage them to achieve their dreams (and are encouraged to achieve your own dreams).

So what can you do to exercise the social ingredient in your life? Firstly, think about those that are nearest and dearest to you and those with whom you work. What can you do either to improve those relationships or to help the other person in some way in their life? Write down your ideas for future reference.

You could decide to join a social group to interact with different people. Or enrol on a course where you can stimulate your creative and educational development as well as practise your social component.

Social activities include community groups, sports, dancing, walking, hobby clubs, and educational courses. There are 60 million people in the United Kingdom alone, so you can be sure to find some who have a similar outlook or interest to yourself – it's a matter of going out there and finding them!

If you have difficulty finding something you want, start a group. By this point you are someone who has the confidence, initiative, determination and social skills to make a success of initiating such a group.

There is always the pub to meet people socially, or going out for a meal with friends, an ideal opportunity to practise your new listening skills. Families also used to meet more regularly before business and our jobs ate up our time. I have never heard of anyone on their deathbed wishing they had worked longer hours. Deep, meaningful relationships with close family members and friends are something to be treasured.

We also now live in a multi-cultural society. This gives another opportunity to expand both our social activity and cultural understanding by seeking out people from different cultures to gain a greater understanding of them and their culture. By opening our minds, we expand our education of culture as well as exercising our social, listening and understanding skills.

Robert Putnam describes social well-being and social capital as 'features of social organisation, such as networks, norms and social trust that facilitate co-ordination and co-operation for mutual benefit.' The major components of social capital are trust, norms, reciprocity, networks and connections. Social capital has been shown to have both positive economic effects, and important effects on health and well-being. We are social animals: for example, one extraordinary statistic shows that if you presently do not belong to any group, joining a club or society of some kind halves the risk that you will die in the next year.

Corey Keyes defines social well-being as 'the appraisal of one's circumstance and functioning in society.' The concept includes how people feel about the society in which they live, and their sense of belonging, as well as how much they contribute to society.

Now write down what commitment you will make to enhance your social element.

## Balance and How these Elements Impact Organisations as well as Individuals

Balance is the key to becoming truly effective. Balance applies to organisations as well as individuals: if an organisation neglects its finances (physical resources), has no purpose, mission, integrity (creative/spiritual dimension), has little or no recognition and development of the personnel (mental/educational dimension) or mistreats its customers, staff, suppliers and human relations generally (social element) it will not survive over the long-term.

The reason for balance is very important: your physical health affects your mental health, and things you do to enhance your social side will also enhance your creative side. As you improve in any one of these areas, you will improve in the others. Practise these four elements on a daily basis and you will grow and change in a positive way.

You may now want to revaluate your vision and mission statement and see if you have included the four key elements.

# Put Aside Time to Celebrate

Life is an evolving process rather than a series of destinations. And in the process some doors close and others open. In this, and the previous eight Actions, you have been given the information and challenges to make major change to your life. Now would be a good time to step back and see how the pieces of all of these Actions come together to impact your life as a whole.

This book and the accompanying training programme is designed to be kept by you as a living document that you return to regularly to measure your progress. You are not competing with or comparing yourself with anyone else – the real test is your progress from when you started. Whether you have grown one centimetre or 100 metres, take some time out to celebrate your achievements and the brand new you.

Look back now and judge for yourself on how you have done. What has worked well for you? What has not worked so well? Where will you go from here? And how you are going to change over the next year? Write down how you will review and celebrate your success.

Becoming an influential figure and a person who transmits positive energy will transform many lives. This change comes from within, from your core. How are you going to be an influential and transformational figure?

That which you persist in doing will get easier, because your ability will increase. Keep a balance between doing and increasing your ability to do, as this empowers you to create a purposeful, fulfilled, enlightened, useful, peaceful life.

In this Action you discovered the importance of your greatest asset – you! You are the one thing which supports every other investment you make. Without you, you have no other assets or investments.

Enjoy your journey.

# Action 10

## Make a Difference

*'You do not have to be a fantastic hero to do certain things, to compete. You can be just an ordinary chap, sufficiently motivated to reach challenging goals.'*
Sir Edmund Hillary

### Going from success to significance!

When involved in one-on-one coaching sessions with people I have often found a real desire within them to leave this world a better place, although they may not have the courage or knowledge to explore this further. In this chapter I suggest some ideas and causes that may inspire you to make a difference. 'Think big – big ideas have a far greater chance of success,' is a familiar proverb, and some people say that raising £1 million for a cause is far easier than a few hundred pounds. However bigness for bigness sake can be both dangerous and contrary to the initial inspiration as an ancient Chinese proverb warns: 'In shallow waters dragons become the sport of shrimps.' To succeed, big ideas need to be practical, inspirational or exceptional. The key is, of course, excellence.

In December 2004, a TV documentary told the story of 9-year-old Kirsty Howard who, in spite of her inoperable heart condition, is raising £3 million for the Francis House Childrens' Hospice in Manchester where she regularly stays. Kirsty is making a difference in the lives of many people.

Are there things we can do together to help our communities? Can we commit to positive action?

### What Will Matter
by Michael Josephson

Ready or not, some day it will all come to an end.
There will be no more sunrises, no minutes, hours or days.
All the things you collected, whether treasured or forgotten will
pass to someone else.

Your wealth, fame and temporal power will shrivel to
   irrelevance.
It will not matter what you owned or what you were owed.
Your grudges, resentments, frustrations and jealousies will
   finally disappear.
So too, your hopes, ambitions, plans and to do lists will expire.
The wins and losses that once seemed so important will fade
   away.
It won't matter where you came from or what side of the tracks
   you lived on at the end.
It won't matter whether you were beautiful or brilliant.
Even your gender and skin colour will be irrelevant.

So what will matter? How will the value of your days be
   measured?
What will matter is not what you bought but what you built, not
   what you got but what you gave.
What will matter is not your success but your significance.
What will matter is not what you learned but what you taught.
What will matter is every act of integrity, compassion, courage
   or sacrifice that enriched, empowered or encouraged
   others to emulate your example.
What will matter is not your competence but your character.
What will matter is not how many people you knew, but how
   many will feel a lasting loss when you're gone.
What will matter is not your memories but the memories that
   live in those who loved you.
What will matter is how long you will be remembered, by
   whom and for what.

Living a life that matters doesn't happen by accident.
It's not a matter of circumstance but of choice.
Choose to live a life that matters.


Practising random anonymous acts of kindness without expecting
anything in return is an effective way to get in touch with the joy of
giving. A while ago someone in a queue of cars passing over a toll
bridge paid for the car immediately behind them, and inspired a
chain reaction of generosity in other drivers as each followed suit.
Often a single act of kindness sets a series of kind acts in motion.

## Being service orientated

You could even make service an integral part of your life. Asking the question, 'How can I be of service?' each day will reveal endless opportunities. You can work for the good of your community, contribute to a worthy cause, volunteer to spend time helping needy people, clear an area of litter, or even go to www.join-me.co.uk to meet like-minded randomly kind people. We looked at the concept of Win/Win in **Action 6** and such service is a perfect example – it is fun, personally rewarding, sets a good example, and helps others – a win for all. If everyone did this, imagine what kind of world we would live in.

If you are troubled by conscious or subconscious expectations of something in return, 'I did the vacuuming, so you should do the dusting,' gently dismiss them. Just do it and your positive feelings will quickly return. Just as physical exercise releases feel good endorphins, acts of kindness do the emotional equivalent. Think now of something really thoughtful you can do for someone else, write it down, and commit to doing it.

*'We must be the change we wish to see in the world.'*
Gandhi

Mother Teresa once said, 'We cannot do great things on this earth. We can only do little things with great love.' Don't find yourself saying, 'I want to help make a difference and I will when I am really successful.' Spending an hour with someone who is lonely now can mean more than a large donation by a big corporation for whom it is merely a drop in the ocean.

Deep within us all is a longing to know that our lives were important, that our being here on planet earth mattered. As Ernest Becker once said, 'What we fear is not so much extinction, but extinction with insignificance.'

What is your ambition? What is the legacy you would like to leave?

*'Let us endeavour so to live that when we come to die even the undertaker will be sorry.'*
Mark Twain

The subject of death is often taboo, but if we are not prepared to consider death, we are not fully prepared to consider life.

**What do you see? Do you blank out things? Are you going to limit your significance to the UK?**

*'We do not know whether it is good to live or die. Therefore, we should not take delight in living nor should we tremble at the thought of death. We should be equiminded towards both. This is the ideal.'*

Gandhi

As you don't have a never-ending life, now is the time to fulfil your legacy. If you generate an attitude of living what you believe so fully that your life (however long or short) becomes fulfilled, you are on the right track to making a difference. If you are not actively living your belief, it's just a wish! Perhaps, at the moment, you really believe something else, but are afraid to admit that to yourself!

To really go after our dream, you must let go of things that are not really important. If you place your hand in water it leaves no impression when you remove it because the water is not attached to your hand. But, on the contrary, when your hand is in the water, it is surrounded, engulfed and embraced by it. Can you allow yourself to experience life as fully as water experiences your hand, then let go as completely as water?

There will be a little water left on your departing hand, just as you leave a bit of yourself with the people you meet and the things you come into contact with, but when the time comes to go, let go. When bringing up your children, hold them close, nurture and support them, and then let them go. You may also be overly attached to material things, but on your deathbed will you wish you had more possessions, or that you had done more toward fulfilling your dreams?

## Creative Power

I mentioned earlier about the creative power within us that gives us the courage, motivation and commitment to make a difference, but we must also always be aware of its destructive potential. History is full of people who misused their power to create evil, and gain domination over others. The names of Mussolini, Hitler, and Stalin are associated with the misery they brought to humanity.

*'All that is necessary for evil to triumph*
*is for good men to do nothing.'*
Edmund Burke

Ask yourself, 'Am I making the right use of the immense creative power within me?' Am I using it to bring harm or peace to others? Am I ready for the opportunities and experiences I will attract? '

We all have this power within us. It is ours to use or misuse, to do with it what we will. The creative power within us directed in the right direction can bring humanity the peace, happiness and universal brotherhood we have sought for so long. What you believe and what I believe, and what the people of the world believe will make the world of tomorrow. The power of these beliefs could rock the world.

*'Never doubt that a small group of thoughtful, committed people can*
*change the world. Indeed, it is the only thing that ever has.'*

A nucleus of interest in the common good, worthy projects making a positive difference established in communities all around the country, indeed all around the world, with large numbers of men, women and children studying and applying the power of right thinking, will produce great changes.

> *'The future is an extension of time and causation*
> *beyond the reach of the physical senses.'*

When I first read the above statement, it struck a chord, as I realised that the forces I set in motion today by my thinking will produce the results in my world tomorrow, a true cause and effect! The only permanence is change, and it is up to us to ensure this change is positive and for the good, the common good of all humanity.

What could a change in thinking do for humanity? Could it liberate the entire human race from all sorts of bondage – war, internment, poverty and suffering? Promote true understanding and tolerance of others with everyone working for each other, and living within moderate means, so there is enough to go around for everyone? Build a peaceful, secure and sustainable future for us, our children, grandchildren and descendants hereafter?

We are not in this world alone – we are here to help others, as we will be helped. What we do is important. The work of each and every one of us counts. No good or grand effort will be ever lost.

Every day, do the best you can; improve the conditions for you and everyone else, as well as improving yourself. You need not necessarily worry about national and international events and situations that seem beyond your circle of control, but perhaps exercise your influence in your local community. By doing your bit and inspiring others to do theirs, you might somewhere along the line spark the fire of something massively life-changing.

## Finding an opportunity through a crisis

Even a crisis can present itself as an opportunity for humanity. In the Chinese language, the symbol for crisis is the combination of both *danger* and *opportunity*. One crisis that became an opportunity was the terrible famine in Ethiopia that inspired rock star Bob Geldof to make a difference to literally millions of lives. He raised more than £80 million on July the 13th 1985 at Wembley, London, UK through Live Aid, a monumental effort to help the starving of Africa.

It was a spectacular musical event, but to Bob Geldof the music came second to raising money in the face of real human tragedy. He targeted the biggest stars of the day, in many cases begging or even swearing at them to perform, as he also swore at the audience when he pleaded, 'Don't go to the pub. Please stay in and give us your money. There are people dying now.' The response was massive. Men, women and children in Africa are alive today because of one man's vision, foresight and sheer determination. It was a day that was historic in British culture and history, and even world culture and history.

## Areas Where we can Make a Difference

Areas where we can also make a positive difference in the world are all around us – below are some causes for consideration.

### Climate change

The latest climate models suggest that global temperatures will rise by an average of between 1.4 and 5.8 degrees C by 2100. A warming of just 2 to 3 degrees C in the next 100 years will put at least 3 billion people at risk from water shortage, cause an extra 300 million to face malaria, and put 100 million more in danger of coastal flooding.

To reduce our climatic impact for life after 2050 we need to act now. Two of the main ways to reduce emissions are via transport and power usage, and the good news is that it can also save us money.

Road transport is responsible for over 20% of the UK's total carbon dioxide emissions. Two options that will considerably reduce this are:

- Smaller more fuel-efficient vehicles
- Cleaner vehicles that run on greener fuels such as:

  - LPG — Particularly good for smaller vehicles with high mileage (cars & light vans)
  - Natural Gas — For heavy goods vehicles with depot based refuelling sites.
  - Electric vehicles — Good for urban driving.
  - Electric hybrids — Available as passenger cars at present
  - Bio diesel — Can be used in existing diesel engines without modification
  - Fuel cells — Also known as *zero emission* vehicles. Not yet commercially available.

Grants are available (check current legislation) for buying the new vehicle types and for converting existing vehicles to cleaner fuels. For further details go to: www.transportenergy.co.uk

Many of us could easily cut heating, lighting and power bills by up to 20% by:

- Switching off lights in empty rooms
- Not heating unused spaces
- Using daylight – it's free. Keeping windows and skylights clean.
- Cleaning light fittings so more light can get through
- Not using brighter bulbs than necessary. Using energy-saving bulbs
- Keeping windows closed in cold weather. If it gets too hot turn the heating down.
- Try setting the thermostat at 19 degrees – costs rise by 8% for every 1 degree increase
- Not blocking radiators with furniture to improve efficiency and output
- Turning off electrical equipment when not in use

Advice is available from:

> www.cibse.org,
> www.envirowise.gov.uk,
> www.saveenergy.co.uk,
> www.greenenergycentre.org.uk,
> www.ukcip.org.uk,

We are already seeing catastrophic climate changes such as flash floods, hurricanes, and droughts. This blue and green planet of ours is a delightful environment – its life is our life, its future is our future. In the face of such global problems as the greenhouse effect and depletion of the ozone layer, a solution can be found by everyone working together.

*'My work will be finished if I succeed in carrying the conviction that every person is the guardian of his or her self-respect and liberty.'*
Mahatma Gandhi

## Poverty and Inequality

In 1960, the top 20% of the worlds richest countries had 30 times the income of the poorest 20%, by 1995 this had increased to over 80 times. The 20% of us who live in the highest income countries consume over 85% of the world resources.

Just over 200 of the world's richest people have a combined wealth of over £1 million, million. Just 5% of this – around £35 billion – is enough for basic education, healthcare, adequate food, water and sanitation for all the people in the world! We already have enough wealth to look after everyone.

More than 1,300 million people still live in poverty – that equates to at least one in six of the world's population, with worse conditions for women than men, and for black people than white. Children are forced into compulsory recruitment into armed conflict or trafficking or production of drugs, while in South Asia between 25 and 45 million children are sold into slave labour to pay off debts. It is estimated that over 250 million children between the ages of 5 and 14 work in developing countries, and up to 60 million work in hazardous circumstances including many between the ages of 5 – 11.

In the UK since 1979 the richest 10% have seen their income rise by 65% in real terms, whilst the income of the poorest 10% has actually dropped by 13%. High-income families also eat healthier foods, and live longer, whereas lower-income families have a higher chance of premature death due to diet related illnesses such as stroke and heart disease.

The global economy is increasingly widening the gap between rich and poor countries and people. Some facts:

- 1 in 9 people live in poverty in Australia (ACOSS).
- In real terms the rich countries give nothing to the poor ones – the poor give to the rich in debt repayments.
- Only a few years ago it was reported that 35.5 million people (1 in 4 children) live below the poverty line in the USA.
- Hundreds of thousands of rural people in Pakistan, Papua New Guinea, Peru and even Australia have no guaranteed water supply.
- The World Bank has stated 'A substantial increase in the resources for fighting poverty in the poorest countries appears entirely affordable. It's a matter of political will.'
- Every 3.6 seconds somebody starves to death.

- In Brazil over 10 million people have been pushed into poverty by having their land confiscated to make way for western demands upon their resources.
- Nadine Gordimer (winner of the 1991 Nobel prize for literature) stated towards the end of the last century 'The new century is not going to be new at all if we offer only charity, that palliative to satisfy the conscience and keep the same old system of haves and have-nots quietly contained.' Concerned charities today aim to help build infrastructure with their money.
- People are made poor when they are exploited for cheap labour. On the sugar plantations in the Philippines people earn around 60p a day.
- People are made poor when they have little access to education. In Bangladesh over 50% of men and 80% of women have had no education (UNICEF).
- People are made poor when terms of trade allow exploitation by big western businesses. In 1965, about 20 tonnes of raw sugar sold on the world market would buy a tractor, in 1979 about 60 tonnes was needed, in 1990 about 85 tonnes, and it is still increasing.
- People are made poor when countries must repay huge debts to richer countries. Brazil owes more than US $120 billion to first world countries, enough for Britain to build more than two Channel Tunnels every year.
- People become poorer in war torn countries. In places like Sudan and Mozambique food is expensive and healthcare and education virtually non-existent.
- Too often help goes to the bigger farmers, and smaller farmers are ignored, getting into debt which forces them to move from the land to the cities searching for work.
- Over 1.3 billion people live in absolute poverty, over 100 million are homeless, 14 million go hungry every day, over 15 million children under 5 die each year, and over 900 million are without education.

Useful fact sheets are available from; Church Action on Poverty, Central Building, Oldham Street, Manchester M1 1JT

Oxfam believe aid should be used to create a fairer world because not only is it morally right, but also many problems that affect us all such as war, terrorism, illegal drugs and environmental destruction have their roots in poverty. Helping those in poorer countries will benefit all of us.

Aid set up in the right way can have a far reaching impact, such as when Oxfam set up water systems for more than 1 million people fleeing conflict in central Africa. Unfortunately many aid agencies cannot finance large scale projects such as transport networks and building of infrastructure. These major projects tend to be funded by official aid either as bilateral grants or loans paid from one government to another paid back with interest, or multilateral grants or loans made by an international institution such as the World Bank, European Union, or the World Health Organisation.

Each year developing countries pay the West nine or ten times more in debt repayments than they receive in grants. Each person in the Third World owes much more than their year's wage; that's for those that have a wage. Africa spends about four times as much on debt repayment as it does on healthcare. It is estimated that Latin America owes over 30% of what it produces and Sub-Saharan Africa over 80% of its Gross Domestic Product (GDP) to Western creditors. These enormous debts mean ordinary people suffer.

There is an opportunity in all this for richer nations to pay the % of GDP in aid as agreed by the United Nations, an opportunity to ensure aid promotes self-sufficiency and long-term development, an opportunity to write off outstanding debt to give these countries a chance, and an opportunity to involve the beneficiaries in the planning and undertaking of the work.

We live in the richest fifth of the world's population and we receive over 80% of the total world income, so we can afford it. The poorest fifth receive less than 2%. If our government paid what the United Nations has agreed, it would be equal to something like £70 per person from our taxes – we currently pay less than half of this. Ending extreme poverty is within our reach. Good health, adequate nutrition, literacy and employment must be treated as essential human rights. Find out more on The United Nations website; www.un.org/publications.

Quotes from poor people taken from the World Bank website: www.worldbank.org:

*'My children were hungry and I told them the rice is cooking,*
until they fell asleep from hunger.'

An older man, Egypt

*'Each day there is a funeral in a nearby village*
*because of the distance to the hospital.'*

Musanya, Zambia

*'Poor people cannot improve their status because they live day to day, and if they get sick then they are in trouble because they have to borrow money and pay interest.'*
Tra Vinh, Vietnam

Helpful organisations include:

- Catholic Fund for Overseas Development (CAFOD) aims to put their faith into action and promote human development and social justice, working alongside the poor regardless of race or religion, forming global partnerships for change, and campaigning for a fairer world. They publish useful fact and information sheets. www.cafod.org.uk

- Joseph Rowntree Foundation is an independent, non-political body which funds programmes of research and innovative development in the fields of housing, social care and social policy. www.jrf.org.uk

- Oxfam work tirelessly to help the poorer nations, and also produce a wide range of publications, and have an excellent informative website www.oxfam.org.uk

- The Institute for Fiscal Studies is an independent research institute. www.ifs.org.uk

- UNICEF promotes children's rights world-wide through building awareness, implementing programmes, and raising funds. They aim to reduce childhood deaths and illnesses, and protect children in the midst of war and natural disaster including those affected by AIDS. www.unicef.org.uk

- World Vision works to provide the people of the UK with the most effective ways to help the world's poor build a better future for themselves and their children. www.worldvision.org.uk

- www.ecologyfund.com

- www.amnesty.org

- www.kidscanmakeadifference.org

A programme screened on UK TV in January 2005 used a telephone survey to ask the UK's population whether the government should fulfil its obligation of overseas aid even if it diverted taxes away from UK services. A staggering 99% of voters said 'Yes.'

## Other worthwhile causes and charities include:

**YMCA.** Hundreds of unique projects working with and for young people in more than 250 communities throughout the UK.
www.ymca.org.uk

**CARE International.** An independent humanitarian organisation working to end world poverty touching the lives of over 30 million of the world's poorest people.
www.careinternational.org.uk
e-mail: info@ciuk.org

**Care For The Wild International.** Dedicated to promoting the conservation and welfare of wildlife in Britain and abroad.
www.careforthewild.com
e-mail: info@careforthewild.com

**Help The Hospices.** The national charity for the hospice movement offers support through funding, training, advice and information.
www.helpthehospices.org.uk
e-mail: info@helpthehospices.org.uk

**RTCW (Round Table Children's Wish Ltd).** A children's charity with the mission of 'making wishes come true for children with life threatening illnesses'.
www.rtcw.org
e-mail: info@rtcw.org

**Rainbow Trust Children's Charity.** Offers practical and emotional support to families who have a child with a life threatening or terminal illness.
www.rainbowtrust.org.uk
e-mail: enquiries@rainbowtrust.org.uk

**Action For Blind People.** Creates opportunities and choice through work, housing, leisure and support to enable blind and partially sighted people to transform their lives.
www.afbp.org

**The Arthritis Research Campaign (arc).** The fourth largest medical research charity in the UK advances the understanding, prevention and treatment of arthritis and related conditions by funding research and providing comprehensive information.
www.arc.org.uk
e-mail: info@arc.org.uk

**British Organ Donor Society – BODY.** Gives support to involved families and supplies information for the public and educationalists.
www.argonet.co.uk/body
e-mail: body@argonet.co.uk

**Childline.** The UK's free 24-hour helpline for children in distress or danger including valuable outreach services to schools.
www.childline.org.uk
e-mail: supporterservices@childline.org.uk

**Crimestoppers Trust (Charity).** A crime hotline 0800 555 111 where anyone with crime information can phone anonymously without fear of reprisals to themselves or their family.
www.crimestoppers-uk.org
e-mail: fundraising@crimestoppers-uk.org.

**The Fire Services National Benevolent Fund.** Supports serving and retired Fire Service personnel and their dependents by providing vital services including rehabilitation, recuperation, sheltered accommodation, and financial assistance.
www.fsnbf.org.uk

**Children 1st** Provides a safe and secure childhood for Scotland's children.
www.children1st.org.uk

**The Variety Club Children's Charity.** Changes the lives of sick, disabled and disadvantaged children throughout the UK, providing Sunshine Coaches, wheelchairs, medical equipment and much more.
www.varietyclub.org.uk

**The British Vascular Foundation (BVF).** Raises public awareness, provides patient information, and funds research to find cures and better treatment for vascular (circulatory) disease.
www.bvf.org.uk
e-mail: bvf@care4free.net

**Afasic.** A UK charity supporting 1 million children, young people and their families affected by the hidden disability of speech and language impairments.
www.afasic.org.uk
e-mail: info@afasic.org.uk

**Support Dogs.** Trains dogs to alert people with epilepsy before they have a seizure, and dogs to help people with disabilities by performing tasks in and out of the home.
www.support-dogs.org.uk
e-mail: supportdogs@btconnect.com

**Plantlife – The Wild Plant Conservation Charity.** Works to protect endangered wild plants and their habitats across the UK through research and practical conservation.
www.plantlife.org.uk
e-mail: enquiries@plantlife.org.uk

**International Myeloma Foundation (UK).** Informs and supports people affected by myeloma, improving treatment and standards of care through research and education.
www.myeloma.org.uk

**Breast Cancer Campaign.** Specialises in funding independent breast cancer research throughout the UK.
www.breastcancercampaign.org
e-mail: info@bcc-uk.org

**The British Red Cross.** As part of the world's largest independent humanitarian network, the charity provides essential care and support to people in crisis in the UK and across the globe.
www.redcross.org.uk
e-mail: esonsino@redcross.org.uk

**Street Child Africa.** Gives African street children love and protection, education, medical care, baby care, counselling, skills and vocational training, employment and a chance to leave the streets.
www.streetchildafrica.org.uk
e-mail: info@streetchildafrica.org.uk

**FARM Africa.** A specialist organisation working with very poor families in rural Africa to improve agricultural production and reduce poverty through innovative and sustainable approaches.
www.farmafrica.org.uk
e-mail: farmafrica@farmafrica.org.uk

**War Child UK.** An international relief and development agency dedicated to providing effective and sustainable aid to vulnerable children caught up in conflict around the world.
www.warchild.org.uk
e-mail: info@warchild.org.uk

**Association for International Cancer Research (AICR).** Funds and supports worldwide research into the causes of cancer.
www.aicr.org.uk

**Battersea Dogs Home.** A well loved charity that welcomes support.
www.dogshome.org
e-mail: fundraising@dogshome.org

**Action Against Hunger.** One of the leading international organisations in the fight against hunger and malnutrition, helping over 5 million people worldwide.
www.aahuk.org

**Habitat for Humanity.** Helping provide homes for people who live in poverty in all parts of the world.
www.habitatforhumanity.org.uk

**Tackle Africa.** A football charity helping tackle AIDS in Africa through footballing trips in Africa.
www.tackleafrica.org

**The 'Can Do Exchange'.** A unique kind of market to help people buy, sell, barter, hire or use community currencies to exchange all kinds of resources including transport, information sheets, office equipment, meeting rooms, and people skills.
Tel: 0870 4207976 or www.candoexchange.org

## You Can Make a Difference

How many Third World lives have died for you today?
How many children went hungry to subsidise your pay?
Look in your food cupboard and count them all up?
How much work did it take to fill your coffee cup?
You can make a difference if you only stop to think
You can make a difference caring about what you eat and drink
You can make a difference with everything you do
You can make a difference to the world around you
See the glossy adverts on the television screen
Where everyone's so happy, everything's so new and clean
If you buy their product then you'll never be sad
If you believe a word of that then you've been had
You can make a difference if you only stop to think
You can make a difference caring about what you eat and drink
You can make a difference with everything you do
You can make a difference to the world around you
Search out the alternatives to corporation greed

Instead of feeding their profits, feed someone's need
Their prices have been bought by blood and by guns
Don't support their exploitation, don't let them have won
You can make a difference if you only stop to think
You can make a difference caring about what you eat and drink
You can make a difference with everything you do
You can make a difference to the world around you

**©1997 Dave Floyd**

## How You Can Make a Difference

There are many little things we can all do to make a difference – try some of the suggestions below.

- Smile when you meet someone – it makes you and them feel good.
- Be an encourager.
- Fit energy saving light bulbs – they can save over £50 in their lifetime. www.est.org.uk
- Recycle plastic bags or use a shopping bag. Over 1 billion plastic bags are used annually throughout the country, taking over 100 years to decompose in landfill sites. www.recoup.org/business/default.asp
- Take a couple of hours and learn to save a life. www.sja.org.uk, www.redcross.org.uk
- Use public transport wherever possible – a double-decker bus carries as many people as 40 cars. www.pti.org.uk, www.liftshare.com
- Read a child (or adult) a story – can you remember the joy of being read to? www.readtogether.co.uk
- Buy and consume only what you need – live the simple life for a while.
- Turn your thermostat down by one degree and save over £20 a year. www.nef.org.uk
- Use a shower instead of a bath – if you've only got a bath, have fun sharing with your partner.
- Make everything you can. A homemade card, for example, with a heart-felt message, or a cake – be imaginative. And remember the greatest gift – love – doesn't cost anything at all.

- Finish uncompleted jobs.
- Compete with yourself, rather than other people. Co-operate with them instead, it feels much better.
- Keep to the speed limit – not only will you save fuel, it's also safer. www.thinkroadsafety.gov.uk
- Accept and give compliments.
- Talk to someone either much older or much younger than you. www.ageconcern.org.uk, www.contact-the-elderly.org.uk
- Put loose change in a charity tin – if you put in just 1p per week and everyone else did the same, it would be worth well over £300 million a year!
- Walk or cycle instead of using the car to save fuel, help the environment and improve your physical health. At work, choose the stairs instead of the lift. www.whi.org.uk, www.walktoschool.org.uk
- Turn off electrical appliances at night: a TV on standby uses half the amount of electricity as when it is turned on. www.greenenergy.org.uk
- Start growing your own produce – it's good for you, inexpensive, productive and pleasurable.
- Do something to restore our countryside. www.bbc.co.uk/nature
- Recycle your mobile phone, or keep the one you have. We replace over 15 million in the UK each year, or 1500 tonnes of landfill space. www.fonebak.org has more details.
- Give blood, it could save someone's life. www.blood.co.uk .
- Become an organ donor. You can register at: www.uktransplant.org.uk
- Check out your investments to see if the company invests ethically. www.eiris.org
- Watch less TV. Instead, go for a walk, swim, or do something creative. www.whitedot.org
- Change the environment around you: use fresh flowers, new photos for your desk at work, change the configuration of the furniture in your house, put up uplifting poems or quotes.
- Tell a good joke – remember, laughter is the best medicine. www.lotsajokes.com, www.ahajokes.com

- If you are going abroad, or have foreign language speaking people in your community, learn some friendly phrases and use them. www.bbc.co.uk/languages
- Support local charities with your time, expertise, money and enthusiasm.
- Use cutlery instead of plastic replacements – we use over 3 billion plastic cups from vending machines each year. www.wasteonline.org.uk
- Turn off any lights not being used, at work as well as at home. www.saveenergy.co.uk www.dark-skies.org.uk
- Have more meals together as a family – make family time. www.parenthood.com
- Just face the music and dance (to your own tune). As Spuk Tiding once said, *'If you are not afraid to face the music, you may someday lead the band.'*
- Buy more in charity shops and pay full price for it or more! www.charityshops.org.uk
- Become waste aware, reuse, recycle & reduce.
- Develop your own *Health Farm* and invite your friends. Set the scene with natural beauty products, relaxing music, aromatherapy oils, and perhaps even invite a reflexologist or massage therapist. This pampering will make you all feel refreshed and invigorated.
- Adopt a child or pet in need!
- Praise a child or young person.
- Don't leave the tap running whilst brushing your teeth – it can use 9 litres of water a minute.
- Recycle your unwanted computer and other electronic equipment – young children in the third world will see it as something fantastic. www.computer-aid.org
- Begin each day with a smile; it will lift your mood.
- Send someone a handwritten letter. www.bbc.co.uk/dna/getwriting
- Have a goal to make a difference either in the world at large, to other people, your local community etc.
- Recycle your books. Give them to a charity shop, or a book club. www.oxfam.org.uk www.bookcrossing.com

- Eliminate stress in your life, and help others overcome their stress.
- Make a commitment to make a difference in the life of someone tomorrow, perhaps through a compliment or a small gift.
- How much can you afford to give away each month? Set up a standing order with the charity of your choice.
- On every car journey, make a point of letting at least one person pull out in front of you. Over 80% of us in the UK have been victims of road rage.
- Love your enemies as well as your friends.
- Buy fairly traded products to give the people who grow them a fair deal. www.fairtrade.org.uk www.marketradefair.com
- Take charge of your life, your health, your finances, your future, your career – once you can control your life, you can reach out to others.
- Carry with you uplifting quotes, or word cards with single words such as inspiration, compassion, faith, freedom, hope etc, and choose one to focus on each day.
- Take the time to really listen to people. www.mind.org.uk
- Join a club.
- Don't overfill your kettle – if everyone did this we would save enough electricity to run the street lighting in the whole country!
- Recycle your spectacles: over 200 million people in the world need them, but can't afford them. www.vao.org.uk www.ukorbis.org/bins/index.asp
- Write some poetry and give it to someone – as a present it will be difficult to surpass.
- Shop locally, keep money in your local economy and eat fresher food. www.regionalfoodanddrink.co.uk, www.farmersmarket.net
- Hug someone, especially someone in your family – children in particular thrive on affection.
- Ask yourself (again!) 'What is my life purpose?'
- Stay young – relive some childhood experiences.
- Get to know your neighbours.

- Raise your own energy and that of others by using uplifting words.
- Believe that you and others deserve the best.
- Grow or make something with your loved ones, especially children. www.bbc.co.uk/gardening, www.bbc.co.uk/children, www.wigglywigglers.co.uk
- Take total responsibility for your life. Be imaginative, purposeful and focused on making a difference.
- Be prepared to say 'No!'
- Let go of blame.
- Emulate the great qualities of someone admirable (Mother Teresa, Nelson Mandela, Gandhi), whilst at the same time remember Sir Edmund Hillary's words at the beginning of this Action in praise of the *ordinary chap.*'
- Accentuate positive thoughts and eliminate negative ones. Make a list of things that energise and uplift you such as going for a walk, art, music, a poem, cooking, dancing, swimming, singing.
- Improve your diet by eating only locally grown less processed food and ensuring you eat the recommended five portions of fruit and vegetables a day.
- Use both sides of the paper.
- Appreciate this precious moment in your life.
- Identify what people and feelings are important to you. Take time to treasure and appreciate them.
- Buy a *good gift* from the Good Gifts catalogue produced by Charities Advisory Trust. They include a hive of bees for poor landless people (£20), a weekly supply of milk for a low income family (£20) and a whole meadow of flowers (£20). Every charity promises to use the money for the reason stated. Call 020 7794 8000 or visit www.goodgifts.org
- Pick up rubbish in the street, or if it's too big, phone the council to pick it up.
- Replace *should* with *could*. Make a list of all your *shoulds* and rephrase each one starting with 'If I really want to I could…'
- Plant a tree. www.sustainableharvest.org, www.treesforhelath.org www.treecouncil.org.uk, www.treeforall.org.uk, www.moortrees.org
- Make your next day, next week, next month and next year your best ever – decide now!

- The next time you feel low, make a success list; a list of all the things you have been successful at and all the things you will be successful at.
- Make your next holiday more natural, holistic or simple such as, walking, connecting with nature, or going to a rural retreat.
- Learn a traditional craft.
- Check whether the technology you use could be harmful to your health, the environment or even your relationships.
- Treat yourself to something completely different such as a foot-spa, Yoga or meditation session.
- You are not immortal! Imagine you have four weeks left on this planet, what would you do? What would you say to the people you care for? Live this day as if it were your last.

*'Look well to this day, for it is life, the very life of life!*
*For yesterday is but a dream and tomorrow is only a vision.*
*But today well liven, makes every yesterday a dream of*
*happiness, and every tomorrow a vision of hope,*
*look well therefore to this day.'*

Anon

- Never give up.
- Share the above ideas with friends and family.

## What Qualities do you Need to Make a Difference?

**Commitment and determination:** These qualities are essential to make a difference over the long term in the area you choose.

**Genuine desire** will motivate you to make a difference.

**Teamwork:** Rarely can you do it alone – a team can achieve so much more.

**Cultural interaction:** For anyone working in a different country, the ability to interact with people from different cultures and nationalities is essential.

**Stress:** The ability to cope with stress is fundamental as many charity projects work with local people suffering from either conflict or natural disasters. Even in relatively peaceful areas heavy workloads may also increase stress levels.

**Adaptability:** Again, particularly for charity work, you must be able to adapt quickly to conditions that may change rapidly.

**Responsibility:** Everyone involved in this sort of work must be prepared to make responsible decisions and take responsibility for their actions, especially if human lives are at stake.

**Creative and lateral thinking.** Could you approach your Member of Parliament (MP) or Euro MP about your cause? Find out who your MP is by visiting;www/locata.co.uk/comons/ Ask for their suggestions on the next step for you and your cause, and whether they can help. Be polite, persistent and ensure you have your facts straight. Follow up your visit with a letter, and keep them in touch.

**Language skills:** Language skills are essential if you embark on an overseas project.

**Compassion, forgiveness, caring for others, and respect** are important qualities when serving others.

## Success

Before concluding this final Action, I want to return to a topic we looked at in the First Action – success and becoming a Success Giant.

Success is one of those words that we all understand, or do we? Most of us equate success with money, but if you've been around a few years you know that although money can make your life easier, it cannot buy happiness. True success is a state of being in which we feel a sense of joy, fulfilment, and achievement.

Forget what the media proclaims. Ignore what friends and family consider a success. Focus instead on what success means to you. If you feel good about the person you are, then you are successful. If you feel fulfilment doing what you do, this is your soul shouting encouragement at being the real you. This is success.

### Success is about self-belief

You must believe in what you do, be willing to share your knowledge and expertise with others, and acknowledge that others have the same rights to success.

- o If you can laugh at your own mistakes, and find the strength to get back up when you fail, then you are on the road to success.
- o If an elderly person holds your respect, and a child makes you believe in life itself, then you are successful.
- o If you shake the hand of an individual down on his luck as warmly as you do that of a statesman, then you are successful.

# How to Identify Successful people

*Genuinely* successful people share the following traits:

- They have the sound of success, not in their actual words, but the way they talk and react.

- They do not put on an act – they are just themselves.

- They are happy and content on the inside as well as the outside.

- They have accomplished what they have set out to do.

Successful people are men and women in every walk of life – different ages, nationalities, and colour. These people face problems and look for solutions, and each morning brings them fresh opportunities.

You are successful if you feel successful in the small achievements as well as the larger ones. You are successful if you have all that you need, and know the difference between want and need. Share what you have and see how it multiplies in return.

You are successful, in your own way; you just need to realise it from within.

I remember the catastrophic earthquake in Asia on Boxing Day 2004, resulting in tragedy and suffering, but also stories of immense human courage, and survival against the odds. The mass outpouring of grief, compassion, and financial generosity from all around the planet in response to such disasters tells me that the time has never been more right for us to consider how we can make a difference, no matter how small.

The 1st January 2005 edition of *The Times* supplement magazine was devoted to *The A – Z of how to be good in 2005* and a recap of the points made will help us make that difference.

**A** is for **Architecture** and aiming for energy-efficient living as in the visionary eco-friendly development BedZED in Beddington, Sutton in London that uses car pools, collects rainwater and heats houses from the sun's energy. The report also warns that we are consuming the planet's resources faster than its ability to regenerate them. If everyone in the world consumed like the Americans we would need an extra 5 planets to have enough resources for all, like the UK an extra 3, and like Mozambique, just .25 of one.

**B** is for **Bono**, the lead singer of rock band U2, whose vision is to rid the world of poverty and injustice. He urges that '...we finally say no to extreme, stupid poverty, the kind that sees children dying of hunger in a world of plenty, of illnesses that could be prevented with a 20p jab. The question isn't 'Can we?' It is 'Will we?'

**B** is also for **Bee-keeping**; about four fifths of the world's plants rely on pollination, mostly by bees, to survive. Humans have used bees for centuries, and our love of them is well founded. If bees died out, the planet would follow.

**C** unsurprisingly is for **charity**. One UK company that enthusiastically promotes community volunteering (over 12,000 staff took part in 2003) reports increased job satisfaction and teamwork as a result, as well as knock-on benefits to recruitment and staff retention. The article also mentioned becoming a mentor, for example with Nacro, the national crime-reduction charity, helping steer vulnerable young people away from crime and rehabilitating former criminals. One volunteer said, 'I find it rewarding and satisfying because it makes a difference to people.' The article also reported how homelessness has more than doubled since 1997, and more than a million children in the UK live in bad housing. Are these areas where we could make a difference?

**D** is for **dinner parties** and the importance of buying locally and seasonally to cut down on food miles. Choose an organic main course, and include super foods such as blueberries, broccoli and pumpkin that help prevent diseases such as diabetes, hypertension, Alzheimer's and some cancers, and finish dinner with an easy conscience artisanal cheese. We should also support fair prices and working practices by opting for Fairtrade produce wherever possible.

**E** is for **eating out** and looking for places that supply organic, free-range, seasonal, humane, vegetarian and non-GM products.

**F** is for **fashion**, and beautiful eco-wear includes tartans, knits and silk in soft, earthy shades.

**G** is for **gardening** and this article explained that horticulture and urban living need not be mutually exclusive with the exciting possibility of bringing a slice of Scandinavian or Scottish hilltop to the inner city lowlands of London, perhaps through creating turf roofing.

**H** is for **hobbies**, and the article asked why so few of us have hobbies in these time-deficient days when hobbies are such rich sources of contentment?

**I** is for **investment** and ensuring our money does the right thing through investing in socially screened funds. These vary from *light green* screening (avoidance of arms concerns, for example), to *dark green* screening (actively seeking out responsible operators).

**J** is for **jewellery** and this article talked about crystals and precious stones with innate energy including: *Amethyst:* strengthens the immune system, and is an energiser with protective qualities. *Aquamarine:* calms nerves, clears the mind, help's banish fears and phobias. *Gold.* Improves circulation, balances hemispheres of the brain and attracts positive energy. *Jade:* emotional balancer, radiates divine unconditional love, dispels negativity.

**K** is for **kids.** There are 50,000 children in foster care in the UK, but a shortfall of 10,000 foster carers. This article focussed on the major contribution of caring foster parents such as Vali Bugden who has shared her home with nearly 200 children. 'It was amazing to be loved by someone... and not to be beaten every day,' said one girl who lived with Vali for 5 years, 'We went on trips, we had fun, she was my mum. I hate to think what would have happened if I hadn't come here.'

**L** is for **love**, and this article explained that '...we never give up the search for love.' As 16th-century lovers wrote sonnets, and 19th-century lovers penned letters, so 21st-century lovers post their details into cyberspace.

**M** is for **mothers**. 'Of course they always know best – but we don't always listen.' One daughter took cooking lessons from her mother and gained enough expertise to host her own dinner parties. Why not learn from our mother (or father)? They're a fund of information.

**N** is for **Nothingness.** This article shows that the threat to the world's unspoilt places affects our own health and happiness. Only 2% of the UK's ancient woodlands survive, yet we seem intent on cutting down yet more. As Zac Goldsmith put it, 'We're busy dismantling nature's building bricks – an unprecedented arrogance.' Poets, ecologists, philosophers, and even successful businessmen believe that we thrive on contact with nature. Some of Britain's wildest places can be explored via The Wilderness Foundation UK (tel: 01245 443073 or www.wildernessfoundation.org.uk.)

**O** is for **order**, and Aggie Mackenzie who made the TV programme *How clean is your house?* emphasises the terrible impact a messy home can have on people's happiness. A tidy home is a happy home is a healthy home. Order gives us the space to think.

**P** is for **pleasure**, and this article talked about people's desire to get high from being in love, looking at a wonderful view, or the buzz gained from coffee, alcohol, tranquillisers or illegal drugs. Natural highs, however, enhance, rather than detract from, our general well-being.

**Q** is for **quality.** Serious quality always lasts and a thing of beauty is a joy forever unlike ephemeral fashion trends. Sieff, an antique shop in Tetbury, Gloucestershire chose to exhibit a few carefully chosen pieces in a clean white room, showing how one fine piece could add drama to any interior.

**R** unsurprisingly is for **recycling**, and this article talks about how DEFRA, the Department for Environment, Food and Rural Affairs, wants councils to recycle 25% of household waste. Why not compost your vegetable waste? For options go to www.naturemill.com or www.wigglywigglers.co.uk. Much of the public, however, has yet to grasp that the triple command *Reduce, Re-use, Recycle* means in that order.

**S** is for **space**, and this article talked about how we all want more space, but at what cost? The article suggests we run our lifestyle through Global Action Plan's carbon calculator to see how much we contribute to climate change and how to cut back. www.globalactionplan.org.uk

**T** is for ethical **tourism**. Look for companies that support sustainable tourism with the emphasis on commitment to local communities and conservation including Oxford based ATG walking holidays (www.atg-oxford.co.uk), eco-friendly holiday online agency Responsible Travel www.responsibletravel.com and *The Good Alternative Holiday Guide* (£12.99) available from www.tourismconcern.org.uk.

Conservation Corporation Africa (CC Africa) is one remarkable model of communities, conservation, and tourism working harmoniously side by side. Working with the philosophy, 'Care of the land, care of the wildlife, care of the people.' CC Africa's 'Seven Worlds of Wonder' in Zululand not only conserves richly diverse habitats ranging from wetlands to sand forests, but has also established schools, a clinic, clean water, jobs, training, and even bursaries to Universities through its charitable foundation. As Nelson Mandela said: 'What these people understand is that conservation is about people.' www.ccafrica.com

**U** is for **utopia**, and this article talks about our universal dream of discovering the good life – whether it's a complete life change or just a place to escape the workday.

**V** is for **vanity**. We can look after ourselves by using more natural and organic products, drinking more water (for the skin), and even dispense with synthetic cosmetics altogether.

**W** is for **water**. 'Maybe this is what the future will look like: depleted water supplies will have changed everything. Fresh clean water will be so rare it will be guarded by armies...' Anita Roddick – Founder, The Body Shop. Water covers 70% of the planet, 97% is sea-water, 2% is locked in the polar ice caps leaving 1% for human use. More than half of that is polluted. One billion people do not have water within a 15-minute walk of their homes. The average African family use 23 litres of water a day, the average American family uses more than 946 litres. Every 8 seconds a child dies from contaminated water. A leaky tap that loses a drop per second loses 16 bathtubs full a month, and 10,000 litres a year.

**X** is for **voting** -something we seem to be lethargic about. If democracy is the rational way to manage social conflict, we have to make collective choices, no matter how awkward. Voting is our social duty.

**Y** is for **Yes** you can do it. If we think our cause is worth it, no sacrifice is too great – the key to us finding the inner strength to make headway in life.

**Z** is for **Zen** the Japanese word for meditation. It goes something like this: eyes closed, spine straight, legs tucked back and apart, breathing going deeper and deeper into the body, down and out through the diaphragm and shoulders and into the limbs, which sounds strange but it works. Research indicates that meditation is often 100% effective against stress.

We've reached the end of these **10 Actions**® and our journey together, and I thank you for your attention and contribution. Now go out and achieve your dream. Make a positive, inspirational and influential difference.

Finally, let me share with you this favourite piece of inspirational writing that has brought peace and tranquillity to my life, inspired, uplifted and centred me.

## DESIDERATA

*Go placidly amid the noise and the haste, and remember what peace there may be in silence. As far as possible, without surrender, be on good terms with all persons. Speak your truth quietly and clearly; and listen to others, even to the dull and the ignorant; they too have their story. Avoid loud and aggressive persons; they are vexations to the spirit. If you compare yourself with others, you may become vain or bitter, for always there will be greater and lesser persons than yourself. Enjoy your achievements as well as your plans.*
*Keep interested in your own career, however humble; it is a real possession in the changing fortunes of time. Exercise caution in your business affairs, for the world is full of trickery. But let this not blind you to what virtue there is; many persons strive for high ideals, and everywhere life is full of heroism. Be yourself. Especially do not feign affection. Neither be cynical about love; for in the face of all aridity and disenchantment it is as perennial as the grass. Take kindly to the counsel of the years, gracefully surrendering the things of youth. Nurture strength of spirit to shield you in sudden misfortune. But do not distress yourself with dark imaginings. Many fears are born of fatigue and loneliness. Beyond a wholesome discipline, be gentle with yourself. You are a child of the universe no less than the trees and the stars; you have a right to be here. And whether or not it is clear to you, no doubt the universe is unfolding as it should. Therefore be at peace with god, whatever you conceive him to be. And whatever your labours and aspirations, in the noisy confusion of life, keep peace in your soul. With all its sham, drudgery and broken dreams, it is still a beautiful world. Strive to be happy.*

Max Ehrmann

*'You can make a difference. We can all make a difference.'*
Bernard Genge